外研社·英语

主编 鲁子问

高中英语
文化意识教育
实践路径

鲁子问 陈晓云 ● 著

外语教学与研究出版社
FOREIGN LANGUAGE TEACHING AND RESEARCH PRESS
北京 BEIJING

图书在版编目（CIP）数据

高中英语文化意识教育实践路径／鲁子问，陈晓云著 . -- 北京：外语教学与研究出版社，2019.1

（外研社·英语学科核心素养理论与实践系列／鲁子问主编）

ISBN 978-7-5213-0759-7

Ⅰ.①高… Ⅱ.①鲁… ②陈… Ⅲ.①英语课-教学研究-高中 Ⅳ.①G633.412

中国版本图书馆 CIP 数据核字 (2019) 第 038554 号

出 版 人　徐建忠
项目策划　范海祥
责任编辑　黄江岩
责任校对　杜晓沫
封面设计　水长流文化
出版发行　外语教学与研究出版社
社　　址　北京市西三环北路 19 号（100089）
网　　址　http://www.fltrp.com
印　　刷　三河市北燕印装有限公司
开　　本　650×980　1/16
印　　张　15
版　　次　2019 年 3 月第 1 版 2019 年 3 月第 1 次印刷
书　　号　ISBN 978-7-5213-0759-7
定　　价　42.00 元

基础教育出版分社：

地　　址：北京市西三环北路 19 号 外研社大厦 基础教育出版分社 (100089)
咨询电话：(010)88819117/88819688
传　　真：(010)88819422
网　　址：http://www.unischool.cn
电子信箱：beed@fltrp.com

购书咨询：(010) 88819926　电子邮箱：club@fltrp.com
外研书店：https://waiyants.tmall.com
凡印刷、装订质量问题，请联系我社印制部
联系电话：(010) 61207896　电子邮箱：zhijian@fltrp.com
凡侵权、盗版书籍线索，请联系我社法律事务部
举报电话：(010) 88817519　电子邮箱：banquan@fltrp.com
物料号：307590001

外研社·英语学科核心素养理论与实践系列

专家委员会

顾　问：文秋芳

前　言

中国教育已经进入核心素养时代，英语教育亦然。《普通高中英语课程标准（2017 年版）》的颁布，明确了英语学科的核心素养的内涵，文化意识即为其中之一。发展英语学科核心素养，需要英语教育实践，发展学生的文化意识这一核心素养亦不例外。为了探讨高中英语文化意识的教育实践的可能路径，我们基于跨文化教育与品格教育的理论和自己多年在英语学科教学中实施跨文化教育的实践与反思编写了本书，以作为高中英语文化意识教育实践的参考。

英语教育本质上是文化教育，正因为此，《普通高中英语课程标准（2017 年版)》将高中英语课程性质确定为"基础文化课程"。本书作者之一鲁子问自 1996 年开始系统探讨英语学科的跨文化教育，还以此作为选题完成博士论文，20 多年来，以著作、教材、课堂教学、讲座等形式，进行了较多的理论思考及较为广泛的教育实践。本书另一作者陈晓云自开始从事高中教学之时就在高中英语课堂教学实践中努力实践跨文化教育，并在班主任工作与英语学科教学中实践品格教育，形成了非常积极的影响。本书既有二位作者的思考与实践，也有反思与分析，尤其是对跨文化理解等的深入讨论，更是基于二位作者对在国外学习和工作中跨文化交往的困顿的反思和总结。同时，本书也参考了国内外跨文化教育、品格教育的相关理论和实践，尤其是借鉴了美国品格教育运动的诸多成果。除特别注明之外，本书的案例均来自二位作者在国内外的实践，案例设计的材料来自教材或者网络。由于教材可能出现各种变化，本书没有呈现教材内容，也没有标注教材名称，只是作为案例参考。特此致谢！

本书第一章、第二章由鲁子问（教授，博士，博士生导师，兴义民族师范学院中国民族师范教育研究中心主任，教育部教师教育资源委员会专家，《义务教育英语课程标准（2011 年版）》研制组成员）完成，第三章、第四章、第五章、第六章由陈晓云（广州大学附属中学教师、国培项目专家）完成。

本书是基于作者个人理论研究与教育实践的探讨，必然存在诸多疏漏与不足，特请读者指出，以便我们修正。特此致谢！

鲁子问　陈晓云

2018 年 10 月

目　录

第一章 高中英语文化意识教育的基本概念

第一节 高中英语教育的文化意识内涵

一、英语学科核心素养

人类社会必须改变生存与发展方式，因为人类进入工业文明时代以来消耗了大量的自然资源，已经对人类赖以生存的地球带来诸多严重的破坏，导致人类面临严重的生态危机。人类必须改变对自然资源的过度消耗，转而更多地开发人类自身的资源——人类自身的人力资源(human resources，本义为人的资源)，将人类自身的人力资源转化为人力资本(human capital，本义为人的资本)，促进人类社会朝着良性的方向发展，转向人与自然和谐存在的生态文明时代。这一转变已经成为人类共识，这一转变也是人类社会发展历史上的一次革命，一次从工业文明转为生态文明的革命性转向。而这一转向对教育提出了根本性转向的要求，要求教育不能只关注发展学生运用自然资源的能力，还要专注于发展学生更加充分与合理地开发和运用人类自身资源的能力。基于这一转向，世界各国普遍将教育目标调整到关键能力上，我国也制定了中国学生发展核心素养体系。

我国学生的发展核心素养由能够适应终身发展和社会发展的必备品格和关键能力组成，英语学科核心素养主要包括语言能力、文化意识、思维品质、学习能力。

随着人类社会从工业文明转向生态文明，人的语言能力越来越重要，因为语言既可以促进人类交往，也可以促进人类认知，从而促进人类更加有效地建设生态文明。而外语也更加重要，因为外语能力能促进人类更广泛、更深入地交往，进一步发展认知的广度与深度。

英语是当今世界广泛使用的语言，是国际交流与合作的重要沟通工具，是思想与文化的重要载体。学习和使用英语对汲取人类优秀文明成果、借鉴外国先进科学技术、传播中华文化、增进中国与其他国家的相互理解与交流具有重要的意义和作用，也能促进人类命运共同体的生态文明的建设，而这对于来自与英语世界有着较大文化差异的中国的学生来说更加重要。基于此重要性，《普通高中英语课程标准（2017 年版）》（以下简称"2017 高中英语课标"）为普通高中英语课程规定了明确的任务，即：与义务教育阶段的课程相衔接，旨在为学生继续学习英语和终身发展打下良好基础。普通高中英语课程强调对学生语言能力、文化意识、思维品质和学习能力的综合培养，具有工具性和人文性融合统一的特点。普通高中英语课程应在义务教育的基础上，帮助学生进一步学习和运用英语基础知识和基本技能，发展跨文化交流能力，为他们学习其他学科知识、汲取世界文化精华、传播中华文化创造良好的条件，也为他们未来继续学习英语或选择就业提供更多机会；普通高中英语课程同时还应帮助学生树立人类命运共同体意识和多元文化意识，形成开放包容的态度，发展健康的审美情趣和良好的鉴赏能力，加深对祖国文化的理解，增强爱国情怀，坚定文化自信，树立正确的世界观、人生观和价值观，为学生未来参与知识创新和科技创新，更好地适应世界多极化、经济全球化和社会信息化奠定基础。

基于这一任务，2017 高中英语课标提出了英语学科的核心素养。英语学科核心素养是学生通过学科学习而逐步形成正确的价值观念、必备品格和关键能力。英语学科核心素养主要包括语言能力、文化意识、思维品质和学习能力。每一项素养都是正确的价值观念、必备品格和关键能力的体现。不过语言能力、学习能力更多指向关键能力，文化意识、思维品质更多指向正确的价值观念、必备品格。就其关系而言，语言能力是基础要素，文化意识是价值取向，思维品质是心智表征，学习能力是发展条件。

英语学科核心素养涵盖了知识、能力和态度，四大核心素养相互渗透，融合互动，协调发展，是所有学生应具有的、学以致用的基础性综合素养，具有个人价值和社会价值，是英语课程的育人指引，也是学业质量的评价标准。从 2017 高中英语课标对四项素养的界定可知，四项核心素养都与文化意识密不可分。

2017 高中英语课标对四项核心素养进行了专门界定，指出：语言能力指在社会情境中，以听、说、读、看、写等方式理解和表达意义的能力，以及在学习和使用语言的过程中形成的语言意识和语感。英语语言能力是构成英语学科核心素养的基础要素。英语语言能力的提高包含文化意识、思维品质和学习能力的提升，有助于学生拓展国际视野和思维方式，开展跨文化交流。文化意识指对中外文化的理解和对优秀文化的认同，是学生在全球化背景下表现出的跨文化认知、态度和行为取向。文化意识体现英语学科核心素养的价值取向。文化意识的培育有助于学生增强国家认同和家国情怀，坚定文化自信，树立人类命运共同体意识，学会做人做事，成长为有文明素养和社会责任感的人。思维品质指思维在逻辑性、批判性、创新性等方面所表现的能力和水平。思维品质体现英语学科核心素养的心智特征。思维品质的发展有助于提升学生分析和解决问题的能力，使他们能够从跨文化视角观察和认识世界，对事物作出正确的价值判断。学习能力指学生积极运用和主动调适英语学习策略、拓宽英语学习渠道、努力提升英语学习效率的意识和能力。学习能力构成英语学科核心素养的发展条件。学习能力的培养有助于学生进行英语学习的自我管理，养成良好的学习习惯，多渠道获取学习资源，自主、高效地展开学习。

随后，对每一素养的目标也做了总体规定。语言能力总体目标是具有一定的语言意识和英语语感，在常见的具体语境中整合性地运用已有语言知识，理解口头和书面语篇所表达的意义，识别其恰当表意所采用的手段，有效地使用口语和书面语表达意义和进行人际交流。文化意识总体目标是获得文化知识，理解文化内涵，比较文化异同，汲取文化精华，形成正确的价值观，坚定文化自信，形成自尊、自信、自强的良好品格，具备一定的跨文化沟通和传播中华文化的能力。思维品质总体目标是能辨析语言和文化中的具体现象，梳理、概括信息，建构新概念，分析、推断信息的逻辑关系，正确评判各种思想观点，创造性地表达自己的观点，具备多元思维的意识和创新思维的能力。学习能力总体目标是树立正确的英语学习观，保持对英语学习的兴趣，具有明确的学习目标，能够多渠道获取英语学习资源，有效规划学习时间和学习任务，选择恰当的策略与方法，监控、评价、反思和调整自己的学习内容和进程，逐步提高使用英语学习其他学科知识的意识和能力。（下文中以表格形式给出了每一项素养的三级目标，作为总体目标的说明，也作为素养和学业水平测评的依据）

二、文化意识的内涵

2017 高中英语课标确定普通高中英语课程的性质是基础文化课程，基础是其阶段性质，文化则是其内容性质。由此可见，文化是高中英语课程的基本性质，所以英语学科核心素养规定了文化意识这一素养维度，而且其他素养中也包含了文化内容。

2017 高中英语课标在其基本理念第一条、第三条都明确了文化意识教育的基本地位。第一条基本理念为"发展英语学科核心素养，落实立德树人根本任务"，内容为：普通高中英语课程具有重要的育人功能，旨在发展学生的语言能力、文化意识、思维品质和学习能力等英语学科核心素养，落实立德树人根本任务。实施普通高中英语课程应以德育为魂、能力为重、基础为先、创新为上，注重在发展学生英语语言运用能力的过程中，帮助他们学习、理解和鉴赏中外优秀文化，培育中国情怀，坚定文化自信，拓展国际视野，增进国际理解，逐步提升跨文化沟通能力、思辨能力、学习能力和创新能力，形成正确的世界观、人生观和价值观。基本理念第三条为"实践英语学习活动观，着力提高学生学用能力"，内容为：普通高中英语课程倡导指向学科核心素养发展的英语学习活动观和自主学习、合作学习、探究学习等学习方式。教师应设计具有综合性、关联性和实践性特点的英语学习活动，使学生通过学习理解、应用实践、迁移创新等一系列融语言、文化、思维为一体的活动，获取、阐释和评判语篇意义，表达个人观点、意图和情感态度，分析中外文化异同，发展多元思维和批判性思维，提高英语学习能力和运用能力。

2017 高中英语课标所规定的英语课程的总目标，也明确指出文化意识的重要内涵，即：全面贯彻党的教育方针，培育和践行社会主义核心价值观，落实立德树人根本任务，在义务教育的基础上，进一步促进学生英语学科核心素养的发展，培养具有中国情怀、国际视野和跨文化沟通能力的社会主义事业建设者和接班人。同时也规定了核心素养的目标。

为了促进高中英语课程中的文化意识教育，2017 高中英语课标对文化素养的内容作出了具体规定。

表 1-1 2017 高中英语课标所规定的文化意识素养具体内容（按级别）（序号为本书作者所加，以使其更加清晰）

素养级别	素养 2：文化意识
一级	1. 能够在明确的情境中根据直接提示找出文化信息； 2. 有兴趣和意愿了解并比较具有文化多样性的活动和事物； 3. 感知中外文化的差异，初步形成跨文化意识，通过中外文化对比，加深对中国文化的理解，坚定文化自信； 4. 了解中外优秀文化，形成正确的价值观； 5. 感知所学内容的语言美和意蕴美； 6. 能够用所学的英语简单介绍中外文化现象。
二级	1. 能够选择合适的方式方法在课堂等现实情境中获取文化信息； 2. 具有足够的文化知识为中外文化的异同提供可能的解释，并结合实际情况进行分析和比较； 3. 提高跨文化意识，在进行跨文化交流时，能够注意到彼此之间的文化差异，运用基本的跨文化交际策略； 4. 尊重和理解文化的多样性，具有国际视野，进一步坚定文化自信； 5. 感悟中外优秀文化的精神内涵，树立正确的价值观； 6. 理解和欣赏所学内容的语言美和意蕴美； 7. 有传播中国特色社会文化的意识，能够用所学的英语描述、比较中外文化现象。

（续表）

素养级别	素养 2：文化意识
三级	1. 能够运用多种方式方法在真实生活情境中获取文化信息； 2. 基于对中外文化差异和融通的理解与思考，探究产生异同的历史文化原因； 3. 具有跨文化意识，能够以尊重文化多样性的方式调适交际策略； 4. 领悟世界文化的多样性和丰富性，具有人类命运共同体的意识； 5. 分析、鉴别文化现象所反映的价值取向，坚定文化自信； 6. 汲取优秀文化，具有正确的价值观、健康的审美情趣和道德情感； 6. 能够用所学的英语讲述中国故事，描述、阐释中外文化现象。

对于以上内容，我们可以从中外文化理解、中外文化传播、价值观建构、品格教育四个维度进行分析，其内涵如下。

表 1-2　2017 高中英语课标所规定的文化意识素养具体内容（以上表三级目标为基础合并整理并结合三级目标的要求而形成）

中外文化理解与传播能力发展	1. 文化认知：能够运用多种方式方法在真实生活情境中获取文化信息； 2. 文化理解：有兴趣和意愿了解并比较具有文化多样性的活动和事物，能够注意到彼此之间的文化差异，领悟世界文化的多样性和丰富性。具有足够的文化知识为中外文化的异同提供可能的解释，结合实际情况进行分析和比较，感知中外文化的差异。基于对中外文化差异和融通的理解和思考，探究产生异同的历史文化原因； 3. 文化自信：通过中外文化对比，加深对中国文化的理解，坚定文化自信； 4. 文化表达：能够运用所学的英语介绍、比较中外文化现象，有传播中国特色社会主义文化的意识。能够用所学的英语讲述中国故事，描述、阐释中外文化现象。

价值观念与必备品格养成	1. 世界意识：尊重和理解文化的多样性，能够以尊重文化多样性的方式调适交际策略。逐步提高和形成跨文化意识，具有国际视野，具有人类命运共同体意识； 2. 文化价值：分析、鉴别文化现象所反映的价值取向。了解中外优秀文化，感悟中外优秀文化的精神内涵，汲取优秀文化。具有正确的价值观和道德情感； 3. 文化审美：理解和欣赏所学内容的语言美和意蕴美，具有健康的审美情趣。

　　显然，英语课程的品格内涵都是基于其文化内涵的。中外文化理解与传播能力是品格的基础，这些品格内涵均需基于中外文化理解而养成。

　　文化意识之外的其他英语学科核心素养也有一些内容与文化意识相关，在开展文化意识教育时，应进行整合。其中，语言能力目标要求学生能深刻认识英语和英语学习与个人发展、国家发展和社会进步的密切关系，深刻认识语言与世界、语言与文化和思维之间的紧密联系，能在英语理解活动中，推断作者的意图、情感、态度和价值取向，能在英语表达活动中表达个人观点和情感，体现意图、态度和价值取向，等等（以三级目标为例，下同）；在思维品质目标中，要求学生能正确观察语言和文化的各种现象，能通过辨析、判断各种观点和思想的价值，作出正确的评价，等等；在学习能力目标中，要求学生能全面和正确认识英语学习的重要意义，对英语学习抱有浓厚的兴趣和强烈的愿望，勇于面对学习困难并加以解决，对英语学习有很强的自信心和成就感，等等。这些都是价值观念、必备品格在其他素养中的体现。

　　文化知识是文化意识教育的基础性内容。2017高中英语课标对文化知识内容作出了较为具体的规定。这些内容对高中英语文化意识具有一定的规定性，当然教师也可以根据学生、教材等而作出相应的调整。

表 1-3　2017 高中英语课标规定的文化知识内容

课程类别	文化知识内容要求
必修	1. 了解英美等国家的主要传统节日及其历史与现实意义；比较中外传统节日的异同，探讨中外传统节日对文化认同、文化传承的价值和意义； 2. 了解英美等国家的主要习俗；对比中国主要习俗，尊重和包容文化的多样性； 3. 了解英美等国家主流体育运动，感悟中外体育精神的共同诉求； 4. 了解英美等国家主要的文学家、艺术家、科学家、政治家及其成就、贡献等，学习和借鉴人类文明的优秀成果； 5. 发现并理解语篇中包含的不同文化元素，理解其中的寓意； 6. 理解常用英语成语和俗语的文化内涵；对比英汉语中常用成语和俗语的表达方式，感悟语言和文化的密切关系； 7. 在学习活动中初步感知和体验英语语言的美； 8. 了解英美等国家人们在行为举止和待人接物等方面与中国人的异同，得体处理差异，自信大方，实现有效沟通； 9. 学习并初步运用英语介绍中国传统节日和中国优秀传统文化（如京剧、文学、绘画、园林、武术、饮食文化等），具有传播中华优秀传统文化的意识。
选择性必修	1. 了解英美等国家地理概况、旅游资源（自然及人文景观、代表性动植物、世界文化遗产等），加深对人与自然的关系的理解； 2. 了解英美等国家政治和经济等方面情况的基本知识；比较中外差异，认同人类共同发展的理念； 3. 理解常用英语典故和传说；比较汉语中相似的典故与传说，分析异同，理解不同的表达方式所代表的文化内涵； 4. 了解常用英语词汇表达方式的文化背景；对比汉语词汇相似的表达方式，丰富历史文化知识，从跨文化角度认识词语的深层含义； 5. 在学习活动中理解和欣赏英语语言表达形式（如韵律等）的美；

（续表）

课程类别	文化知识内容要求
选择性必修	6. 理解和欣赏部分英语优秀文学作品（戏剧、诗歌、小说等）；从作品的意蕴美中获得积极的人生态度和价值观念启示； 7. 通过比较、分析、思考，区分和鉴别语篇包含或反映的社会文化现象，并作出正确的价值判断； 8. 了解英美等国家主要大众传播媒体，分析辨别其价值取向； 9. 了解中外文化的差异与融通，在跨文化交际中初步体现交际的得体性和有效性； 10. 使用英语简述中华文化基本知识，包括中华传统节日、中华传统文化的表现形式（如京剧、文学、绘画、园林、武术、饮食文化等）及其内涵，主动传播和弘扬中华优秀传统文化。
选修（提高类）	1. 了解英美等国家的主要文化特色，吸收国外的优秀文化成果； 2. 了解世界重要历史文化现象的渊源，认识人类发展的相互依赖性和共同价值，树立人类命运共同体意识； 3. 了解英美等国家对外关系特别是对华关系的历史和现状，加深对祖国的热爱，捍卫国家尊严和利益； 4. 理解和欣赏经典演讲、文学名著、名人传记等，感悟其精神内涵，反思自己的人生成长； 5. 在学习活动中观察和赏析语篇包含的审美元素（形式、意蕴等），获得审美体验，形成对语言和事物的审美感知能力； 6. 运用中外典故和有代表性的文化标志表达意义和态度，有效进行跨文化沟通； 7. 了解中国对外经济、政治、文化的积极影响，感悟中华文明在世界历史中的重要地位，树立中华文化自觉，坚定文化自信。

从以上内容可以看出，其实这些列在"文化知识"名目下的内容，有一些不是文化知识，而是价值观念和必备品格层面的内容，这说明这

9

里的文化知识本身包括了价值观念和必备品格的内容。

2017高中英语课标对文化意识的教学提出了一些建议，并分享了一些案例。这些建议和案例具有一定的指导性和代表性，但也因为各种原因，会存在一定的局限性。教师需要了解、分析、学习这些建议与案例，但也不能拘于这些建议与案例。除了2017高中英语课标中的"实施建议"以外，学校和教师还可以通过开设校本课程，进行文化专题教育。

总之，教师要树立语言教学与文化学习相互促进、相互渗透的意识，引导学生通过探索、体验、比较、对比等多种方式学习中外文化基础知识，实现将文化知识转化为内在的具有正确价值取向的认知、行为和品格。要关注中外文化的差异与融通，正确认识和对待他国文化，吸收中外文化精华，积极发展跨文化沟通策略和能力，并树立国家认同感，自觉传播和弘扬中华优秀文化，坚定文化自信。

第二节 英语教育与文化教育

英语教育是语言教育，也是文化教育。

英语是一种语言，英语教育自然是基于和关于这一语言的教育。语言教育通常应以培养学生运用语言的能力为目的，即使是学习古汉语、古希腊语等当代已经不再在日常生活中广泛运用的语言，也是为了发展对古汉语、古希腊语的理解性的运用能力，以及极少部分人的表达性的运用能力，如当代中国仍然有少部分人会运用古汉语进行古体诗词创作，撰写介绍地方、景点与机构的各种"赋"体文等等，甚至完成一篇高考作文。

对于中国中小学生来说，英语是一种外国语，英语教育是外语教育。从人类外语教育的历史看，对于已经基本完全形成母语运用能力的中小学生来说，外语教育离不开外语知识教育，以外语知识为基础的外语教育有利于高效地培养运用外语的能力。

因此，对于中国中小学生来说，英语语言教育是以英语知识教育为基础的培养运用英语的能力的活动，其目的是培养运用英语的能力，英语知识教育只是为培养运用英语的能力这一目的而提供基础。因此，从本质上说，中小学的英语教育应该是能力教育，而不是知识教育。

那么，英语教育作为语言教育，其本质应该是培养学生运用英语的能力。

英语不仅仅是一种语言，也是以英语为母语、国语和工作语言的人类群体的文化的重要内容，还是这些文化的载体，甚至是世界文化的重要载体（因为当前人类很多群体使用英语表达自己的文化，而且很多国际组织也使用英语记载人类文化）。因此英语教育也是文化教育，甚至可以说，更是文化教育。

对于中国中小学生来说，英语国家文化是不同于中华文化的外在的文化，因此，英语教育作为文化教育对于中国中小学生应该是一种跨文化的教育。跨文化教育的目的是通过认知和理解外在文化，建立起开放合理的认知、理解、选择和吸取外在文化的跨文化心态、价值取向和行为模式。英语教育作为文化教育，其本质应该是通过让学生认知英语国家的文化，建立其认知、理解、选择和吸取英语国家文化的开放合理的跨文化心态、价值取向和行为模式。

因此，我国中小学英语教育的总体目标应是：通过英语语言知识、语言技能和文化知识教育，培养学生运用英语进行交际和自我表达的基本能力，并促使学生形成开放、合理的跨文化意识与相关情感态度及价值观，同时促进学生思维能力、创新精神、终身学习能力等的发展，即语言能力、文化意识、思维品质、学习能力等英语学科核心素养的发展（鲁子问等，2010）。

在当今语言世界，文化作为一个语词，含义复杂，而且大相径庭，千差万别。这也使把握或者规范文化这个语词的语义成为当今一大学术难题，且众说纷纭，学者们已经为"文化"一词厘定出数以百计的定义。

在古代汉语中，"文"与"化"最早是两个单字，二字连用较早出现于汉代，刘向的《说苑·指武》中已有"圣人之治天下也，先文德而后武力。凡武之兴，为不服也，文化不改，然后加诛"的文句，其语义为"以文德教化天下"。在现代汉语中，"文化"二字已成为一个固定词语，而且是一个多义词，基本语义是：人类在社会历史发展过程中所创造的物质财富和精神财富的总和，特指精神财富，如文学、艺术、教育、科学等。

英语中的 culture 一词，源于拉丁语，其古典语义为"耕种，驯化，培育"等，基本语义是 a set of ideas, beliefs, and ways of behaving of a particular organization or group of people（一个特定的组织或人类群体的观念、信仰、行为方式体系）。

1982 年，联合国教科文组织在墨西哥城召开了"世界文化政策大会"，会议讨论并提出了文化定义，这被认为是"国际上的看法"（赵中建，1999：497），是 126 个国家、94 个组织的 960 多名与会代表对文化的视点的综合（UNESCO，1982）。会议发表的《墨西哥城文化政策宣言》对文化作了这样的界定（UNESCO，1982；1989）：

> "会议表达了人类各种文化和精神目标的最终会聚的希望，并承认：
>
> 从最广泛的意义讲，文化现在可以看成是由一个社会或社会集团的精神、物质、理智和情感等方面的显著特点构成的综合的整体，它不仅包括艺术和文学，也包括生活方式、人类的基本权利、价值体系、传统和信仰。"
>
> "文化赋予人类对自己进行思考的能力。文化使我们真正成为有理性的，有批判精神的，有道德的人。通过文化，我们认清了价值的意义，并进行抉择。"
>
> "他们（会议的参加者们——引者注）并不忽视知识和艺术活动中所表现出的创造性的重要性，但他们认为应该扩大文化的概念，使其包括行为模式和个人对他或她自己、对社会和对外界的看法。由此出发，社会的文化生活可以看作是通过它的生活和生存的方式，通过感觉和自身感觉、行为形式、价值系统和信仰而表现出来的。"

由此可知，文化是一个社会或社会集团的精神、物质、理智和情感等方面的显著特点构成的综合的整体，包括艺术、文学、生活方式、人类的基本权利、价值体系、传统和信仰。

文化教育则是以文化为内容，而且为目的的教育实践，其意义在于使我们真正成为有理性的、有批判精神的、有道德的人，使我们认清了价值的意义，并进行抉择。

正如本节一开始所言，英语教育既是语言教育，也是文化教育。文化教育是英语教育不可或缺的基本内容，也是英语教育的基本目的，而且文化教育的目的本身也是英语教育的目的。

中国学生英语教育中的文化教育的特征是跨文化教育，不仅包括英语国家的文化的教育，也包括基于英语的世界文化的教育，以及从跨文化视角促进中华文化发展的教育。基于此，我们可以理解在中国基础教育阶段，英语教育的文化教育，是对英语国家，乃至用英语呈现的其他国家的文学、艺术、生活方式、价值体系、传统和信仰的跨文化理解教育，通过跨文化理解教育使我们真正成为有理性的、有批判精神的、有道德的人，使我们认清所理解文化的价值的意义，并进行跨文化判断与选择。

第三节　英语教育与品格教育

如前所述，核心素养包含正确价值观念、必备品格和关键能力，而英语教育的文化意识内涵和其他素养的内容既包括了关键能力，也包括了正确价值观念、必备品格，亦即：英语教育包含品格教育，而且在文化意识维度的核心素养中必然包含品格教育。

基础教育是终生教育的基础，其所教授的知识可能无法影响一个人的一生，因为这些知识在20年后就会进行更新，但基础教育所塑造的品格则会影响人的一生，因为品格一旦形成，往往具有长期的稳定性。英语作为基础教育的主要学科，英语教育必然具有所有学科教育的共同责任：品格教育。

英语的"character"一词来源于古希腊语"karacter,"原意是烙印（impression），指在硬币上刻下标记或印盖的封印等，当代语义是"the mental and moral qualities distinctive to an individual"（可理解为个人的道德品质和心理品质的总和）。现代汉语中，品格的内涵是品质性格，有关道德的行为。从学术的视角看，品格具有哲学、心理学和教育学的含义。从伦理哲学角度看，品格是指一个人在生活实践中因一定的生活习惯或方式养成的稳定的个性品质。从心理学角度看，品格可视为性格，一般指人对现实的态度和行为方式中的比较稳定的、具有核心意义的个性心理特征。但从道德心理学的视角来看，品格主要是指人的个性心理中那些积极健康的特征，是道德认知、情感、动机、行为等多种道德心理成分在个体身上的稳定表现，是人格的道德维度，是道德教育要着力培养的一个重要方面。从教育学角度看，品格是指体现了一定道德规范（如核心价值和美德），内在于个体的，包含了认知、情感和意志成分的道德习惯（蔡春，2010）。

品格教育就是培养品格的教育实践，由于教育的规定性，品格教育以培养人的优良品格为目标。美国品格教育联盟提出，品格教育是一项培养青少年良好品格的长期过程。良好的品格应该包括理解、互助、公平、诚信、同情心、责任感、尊重自己和他人等核心价值观念。学校、家庭、社区三者需要帮助青少年形成良好的品格（苏蓉，2012）。

品格教育具有悠久历史，孔子、苏格拉底等人类早期教育家都有大量的品格教育实践。根据道德上的普遍主义和方法上的实质主义，品格教育有广义和狭义之分，源自亚里士多德的教育传统，一切以培养美德或品格为目的、不拘泥于传统德育模式的主张都可视为狭义的品格教育，而基于公民教育、宗教教育、自由主义等立场的品格教育可称为广义的品格教育（蔡春，2010）。

基础教育阶段英语学科的品格教育是基础教育品格教育的组成部分，具有跨文化特性。

首先，英语课程教学内容中有不少其他学科教学内容不涉及的，或者英语课程更有特色的品格教育内容，这些是英语教育的品格教育的优势内容，如记忆单词所需要的意志力和克服困难的品格。

其次，英语国家的品格教育中有不少值得我国的品格教育学习的内容，这些内容应该成为英语教育的品格教育的内容，如英国学生的绅士与淑女品格教育。

最后，品格分析发现，我国学生的品格取向和英语国家的品格取向有着不少差异（Park, N. 等，2006），这些差异可能制约跨文化交往，造成跨文化交往中的误解。英语教育的品格教育应让我国学生充分了解英语国家学生的品格取向，以在跨文化交往中能准确理解对方的品格取向。如（见表1-4）：

表 1-4　品格分析

Table II. Strengths profiles.

	Weighted						
Nation	US	US	UK	CA	AU	NZ	NL
N	83576	83576	11125	9504	5977	1491	1481
ρ with weighted US profile	–	0.94	0.84	0.91	0.86	0.84	0.81
ρ with US profile	0.94	–	0.94	0.99	0.97	0.96	0.92
kindness	1 (3.99)	5 (3.96)	5 (3.82)	5 (3.97)	5 (3.93)	5 (3.90)	6 (3.74)
fairness	2 (3.98)	1 (4.00)	2 (3.92)	1 (4.03)	1 (4.03)	3 (3.98)	3 (3.84)
honesty	3 (3.98)	4 (3.97)	6 (3.77)	4 (3.98)	6 (3.91)	6 (3.90)	5 (3.77)
gratitude	4 (3.94)	6 (3.96)	14 (3.59)	7 (3.89)	8 (3.81)	10 (3.77)	14 (3.50)
judgment	5 (3.91)	2 (3.99)	1 (3.94)	2 (4.01)	2 (4.03)	2 (4.00)	2 (3.88)
love	6 (3.87)	7 (3.91)	7 (3.71)	8 (3.86)	7 (3.83)	7 (3.82)	6 (3.74)
humor	7 (3.87)	9 (3.82)	11 (3.64)	12 (3.79)	14 (3.71)	14 (3.68)	12 (3.60)
curiosity	8 (3.86)	3 (3.99)	3 (3.90)	3 (3.99)	3 (4.03)	1 (4.01)	1 (3.92)
beauty	9 (3.76)	10 (3.82)	9 (3.67)	9 (3.85)	9 (3.81)	8 (3.81)	10 (3.65)
creativity	10 (3.75)	11 (3.77)	8 (3.69)	11 (3.80)	10 (3.79)	9 (3.78)	8 (3.70)
perspective	11 (3.74)	12 (3.77)	13 (3.61)	10 (3.81)	12 (3.76)	11 (3.73)	11 (3.63)
social intelligence	12 (3.74)	13 (3.75)	12 (3.63)	14 (3.76)	13 (3.73)	13 (3.70)	9 (3.66)
leadership	13 (3.71)	14 (3.74)	10 (3.65)	13 (3.78)	11 (3.78)	12 (3.72)	15 (3.50)
teamwork	14 (3.68)	15 (3.66)	17 (3.51)	15 (3.68)	16 (3.65)	17 (3.62)	18 (3.43)
learning	15 (3.67)	8 (3.89)	4 (3.87)	6 (3.92)	4 (3.94)	4 (3.92)	4 (3.82)
bravery	16 (3.67)	16 (3.65)	15 (3.54)	16 (3.68)	17 (3.65)	15 (3.66)	13 (3.58)
forgive	17 (3.65)	17 (3.65)	16 (3.54)	17 (3.67)	15 (3.69)	16 (3.65)	16 (3.49)
hope	18 (3.61)	19 (3.60)	20 (3.33)	20 (3.58)	19 (3.55)	19 (3.56)	20 (3.38)
industry	19 (3.59)	18 (3.62)	18 (3.41)	18 (3.61)	18 (3.59)	20 (3.56)	17 (3.49)
religiousness	20 (3.55)	21 (3.53)	24 (2.87)	23 (3.36)	24 (3.25)	24 (3.23)	24 (3.01)
zest	21 (3.48)	20 (3.57)	19 (3.37)	19 (3.59)	20 (3.55)	18 (3.57)	19 (3.43)
prudence	22 (3.47)	22 (3.50)	21 (3.30)	21 (3.52)	21 (3.45)	21 (3.41)	21 (3.32)
modesty	23 (3.46)	23 (3.40)	22 (3.30)	22 (3.41)	22 (3.35)	22 (3.32)	23 (3.18)
self-regulation	24 (3.27)	24 (3.27)	21 (3.17)	24 (3.32)	23 (3.30)	23 (3.30)	22 (3.24)
Nation	IE	DE	ZA	ES	BE	SG	SE
N	515	490	323	261	190	172	170
ρ with weighted US profile	0.85	0.80	0.93	0.83	0.81	0.68	0.79
ρ with US profile	0.95	0.91	0.92	0.94	0.92	0.79	0.90
kindness	5 (3.83)	7 (3.75)	3 (4.05)	5 (3.91)	5 (3.80)	8 (3.79)	5 (3.79)
fairness	2 (3.91)	4 (3.80)	1 (4.06)	3 (3.98)	3 (3.86)	3 (3.87)	1 (3.91)
honesty	6 (3.81)	6 (3.77)	2 (4.06)	6 (3.85)	6 (3.79)	4 (3.86)	7 (3.76)
gratitude	11 (3.66)	14 (3.53)	6 (4.02)	9 (3.75)	14 (3.58)	12 (3.68)	16 (3.53)
judgment	1 (3.93)	2 (3.94)	4 (4.03)	4 (3.98)	1 (3.94)	1 (3.98)	2 (3.86)
love	8 (3.68)	9 (3.65)	7 (3.99)	8 (3.77)	8 (3.74)	9 (3.73)	6 (3.78)
humor	9 (3.68)	10 (3.61)	12 (3.84)	10 (3.75)	11 (3.62)	15 (3.65)	11 (3.70)
curiosity	4 (3.84)	1 (3.96)	5 (4.02)	2 (3.99)	4 (3.85)	7 (3.79)	3 (3.85)
beauty	7 (3.71)	5 (3.80)	9 (3.93)	7 (3.83)	7 (3.77)	6 (3.83)	13 (3.62)
creativity	10 (3.68)	8 (3.72)	8 (3.94)	11 (3.73)	9 (3.66)	10 (3.72)	8 (3.74)
perspective	12 (3.66)	12 (3.59)	10 (3.91)	13 (3.68)	12 (3.62)	11 (3.70)	9 (3.74)
social intelligence	13 (3.66)	11 (3.60)	11 (3.85)	15 (3.65)	10 (3.63)	16 (3.64)	10 (3.71)
leadership	14 (3.66)	13 (3.54)	16 (3.80)	12 (3.69)	15 (3.58)	13 (3.68)	14 (3.62)
teamwork	17 (3.53)	16 (3.48)	21 (3.65)	14 (3.67)	16 (3.51)	14 (3.66)	17 (3.53)
learning	3 (3.85)	3 (3.90)	13 (3.83)	1 (4.00)	2 (3.89)	5 (3.84)	4 (3.83)
bravery	16 (3.59)	15 (3.53)	14 (3.83)	17 (3.57)	13 (3.59)	17 (3.60)	12 (3.66)
forgive	15 (3.67)	17 (3.45)	19 (3.73)	16 (3.61)	19 (3.45)	18 (3.56)	15 (3.57)
hope	19 (3.38)	20 (3.39)	17 (3.78)	18 (3.50)	20 (3.37)	19 (3.52)	20 (3.43)
industry	18 (3.42)	19 (3.40)	18 (3.75)	21 (3.45)	17 (3.48)	20 (3.50)	18 (3.48)
religiousness	24 (3.12)	24 (3.08)	15 (3.82)	24 (3.15)	24 (3.01)	23 (3.38)	24 (3.08)
zest	20 (3.37)	18 (3.42)	20 (3.67)	20 (3.49)	18 (3.47)	2 (3.91)	19 (3.47)
prudence	21 (3.34)	21 (3.32)	23 (3.50)	19 (3.50)	21 (3.36)	21 (3.48)	22 (3.28)
modesty	22 (3.30)	23 (3.13)	22 (3.53)	23 (3.37)	22 (3.22)	22 (3.41)	23 (3.15)
self-regulation	23 (3.22)	22 (3.25)	24 (3.42)	22 (3.39)	23 (3.21)	24 (3.30)	21 (3.30)

(continued)

（续表）

Table II. Continued.

Nation	Weighted						
	FR	IN	FI	HK	CH	AT	IT
N	156	135	132	115	110	107	100
ρ with weighted US profile	0.79	0.76	0.79	0.86	0.81	0.81	0.77
ρ with US profile	0.90	0.84	0.90	0.90	0.92	0.93	0.90
kindness	5 (3.88)	8 (3.97)	5 (3.79)	7 (3.75)	6 (3.83)	6 (3.92)	6 (3.87)
fairness	3 (3.94)	1 (4.11)	1 (3.91)	5 (3.78)	2 (4.01)	1 (4.10)	2 (4.04)
honesty	8 (3.76)	2 (4.06)	7 (3.76)	2 (3.81)	4 (3.90)	5 (3.97)	8 (3.82)
gratitude	11 (3.68)	6 (4.03)	16 (3.53)	10 (3.66)	7 (3.83)	14 (3.70)	10 (3.76)
judgment	6 (3.86)	4 (4.04)	2 (3.86)	1 (3.84)	3 (3.94)	4 (4.02)	4 (3.98)
love	9 (3.75)	14 (3.86)	6 (3.78)	6 (3.76)	5 (3.88)	7 (3.85)	11 (3.72)
humor	13 (3.57)	16 (3.79)	11 (3.70)	13 (3.61)	12 (3.75)	13 (3.73)	13 (3.65)
curiosity	2 (4.05)	3 (4.04)	3 (3.85)	3 (3.80)	1 (4.11)	3 (4.04)	3 (4.02)
beauty	4 (3.90)	7 (4.00)	13 (3.62)	8 (3.68)	15 (3.73)	8 (3.84)	5 (3.94)
creativity	7 (3.78)	11 (3.96)	8 (3.74)	16 (3.54)	11 (3.77)	10 (3.82)	7 (3.84)
perspective	15 (3.54)	9 (3.97)	9 (3.74)	9 (3.67)	13 (3.74)	11 (3.82)	12 (3.66)
social intelligence	12 (3.65)	17 (3.77)	10 (3.71)	11 (3.61)	10 (3.78)	12 (3.75)	16 (3.55)
leadership	10 (3.70)	12 (3.93)	14 (3.62)	12 (3.59)	8 (3.80)	9 (3.83)	9 (3.77)
teamwork	17 (3.47)	15 (3.85)	17 (3.53)	15 (3.56)	19 (3.60)	16 (3.67)	14 (3.65)
learning	1 (4.06)	5 (4.03)	4 (3.83)	4 (3.80)	3 (4.01)	2 (4.06)	1 (4.11)
bravery	14 (3.55)	18 (3.76)	12 (3.66)	14 (3.57)	16 (3.67)	17 (3.64)	17 (3.53)
forgive	16 (3.48)	21 (3.70)	15 (3.57)	17 (3.46)	14 (3.74)	15 (3.67)	15 (3.59)
hope	20 (3.29)	13 (3.87)	20 (3.43)	18 (3.45)	17 (3.67)	19 (3.56)	21 (3.35)
industry	19 (3.38)	19 (3.72)	18 (3.48)	19 (3.45)	20 (3.58)	18 (3.60)	20 (3.39)
religiousness	24 (2.84)	10 (3.97)	24 (3.08)	20 (3.38)	24 (3.23)	24 (3.19)	24 (3.20)
zest	18 (3.42)	22 (3.70)	19 (3.47)	22 (3.36)	18 (3.63)	20 (3.56)	18 (3.49)
prudence	21 (3.28)	20 (3.72)	22 (3.28)	21 (3.37)	21 (3.47)	21 (3.50)	19 (3.45)
modesty	22 (3.25)	23 (3.64)	23 (3.15)	24 (3.33)	23 (3.34)	23 (3.28)	22 (3.30)
self-regulation	23 (3.24)	14 (3.50)	21 (3.30)	23 (3.33)	22 (3.44)	22 (3.43)	23 (3.25)

Nation	HU	AR	MX	JP	NO	UY	CV
N	98	91	88	79	77	74	66
ρ with weighted US profile	0.77	0.80	0.79	0.79	0.71	0.83	0.86
ρ with US profile	0.86	0.92	0.88	0.92	0.84	0.95	0.95
kindness	7 (3.60)	8 (3.87)	8 (3.87)	7 (3.75)	9 (3.71)	6 (3.80)	4 (3.94)
fairness	2 (3.73)	3 (4.01)	1 (4.12)	3 (3.86)	4 (3.90)	4 (3.85)	1 (4.11)
honesty	8 (3.60)	7 (3.88)	5 (3.95)	5 (3.79)	6 (3.80)	5 (3.85)	5 (3.91)
gratitude	14 (3.33)	5 (3.91)	7 (3.94)	9 (3.74)	18 (3.53)	8 (3.72)	9 (3.83)
judgment	1 (3.94)	4 (4.01)	3 (4.06)	4 (3.85)	2 (3.94)	1 (3.95)	2 (4.05)
love	11 (3.47)	9 (3.87)	4 (3.97)	6 (3.76)	8 (3.78)	9 (3.69)	7 (3.87)
humor	9 (3.58)	16 (3.66)	22 (3.62)	14 (3.63)	11 (3.70)	14 (3.59)	12 (3.79)
curiosity	4 (3.71)	1 (4.13)	2 (4.09)	1 (4.01)	1 (4.02)	2 (3.91)	6 (3.88)
beauty	6 (3.67)	6 (3.90)	10 (3.84)	10 (3.74)	14 (3.57)	7 (3.77)	10 (3.82)
creativity	3 (3.72)	10 (3.82)	14 (3.79)	8 (3.75)	5 (3.82)	10 (3.67)	14 (3.76)
perspective	10 (3.53)	12 (3.76)	13 (3.80)	11 (3.73)	7 (3.80)	12 (3.64)	8 (3.85)
social intelligence	15 (3.33)	14 (3.70)	12 (3.81)	12 (3.64)	10 (3.71)	13 (3.61)	16 (3.71)
leadership	17 (3.32)	13 (3.74)	9 (3.85)	13 (3.63)	12 (3.64)	11 (3.66)	11 (3.81)
teamwork	16 (3.33)	11 (3.77)	11 (3.83)	20 (3.44)	16 (3.54)	17 (3.53)	13 (3.78)
learning	5 (3.70)	2 (4.07)	6 (3.95)	2 (3.90)	3 (3.92)	3 (3.89)	3 (3.95)
bravery	13 (3.35)	15 (3.69)	17 (3.75)	18 (3.48)	13 (3.61)	15 (3.55)	17 (3.69)
forgive	12 (3.41)	20 (3.61)	16 (3.76)	19 (3.46)	15 (3.55)	18 (3.43)	15 (3.72)
hope	20 (3.18)	18 (3.63)	15 (3.79)	15 (3.57)	19 (3.51)	21 (3.36)	19 (3.56)
industry	22 (3.10)	19 (3.62)	19 (3.72)	16 (3.55)	20 (3.49)	16 (3.54)	18 (3.59)
religiousness	24 (2.93)	21 (3.48)	18 (3.75)	24 (3.15)	23 (3.03)	24 (3.04)	24 (3.25)
zest	19 (3.20)	17 (3.64)	20 (3.65)	21 (3.41)	17 (3.54)	20 (3.40)	21 (3.48)
prudence	18 (3.29)	24 (3.34)	21 (3.63)	17 (3.49)	22 (3.36)	19 (3.42)	20 (3.50)
modesty	21 (3.11)	23 (3.39)	23 (3.53)	22 (3.38)	24 (2.98)	22 (3.35)	22 (3.45)
self-regulation	23 (3.01)	22 (3.42)	24 (3.45)	23 (3.32)	21 (3.41)	23 (3.31)	23 (3.28)

（续表）

Table II. Continued.

	Weighted						
Nation	IL	KY	HR	PH	GR	DK	MY
N	60	57	56	55	53	52	49
ρ with weighted US profile	0.80	0.80	0.76	0.71	0.87	0.69	0.73
ρ with US profile	0.93	0.92	0.87	0.84	0.93	0.82	0.84
kindness	7 (3.86)	5 (4.00)	6 (3.86)	14 (3.85)	3 (3.90)	9 (3.79)	8 (3.68)
fairness	2 (3.96)	4 (4.00)	4 (3.90)	2 (4.09)	1 (3.99)	6 (3.81)	1 (3.92)
honesty	9 (3.79)	7 (3.93)	8 (3.77)	7 (3.95)	8 (3.82)	7 (3.81)	4 (3.86)
gratitude	10 (3.75)	8 (3.90)	15 (3.59)	5 (4.02)	9 (3.81)	12 (3.72)	9 (3.68)
judgment	4 (3.95)	2 (4.06)	2 (3.97)	1 (4.10)	2 (3.91)	4 (3.94)	2 (3.90)
love	5 (3.95)	10 (3.82)	13 (3.64)	8 (3.92)	7 (3.86)	5 (3.87)	12 (3.59)
humor	14 (3.66)	14 (3.75)	11 (3.69)	17 (3.75)	10 (3.68)	13 (3.71)	14 (3.54)
curiosity	1 (4.04)	1 (4.07)	3 (3.97)	4 (4.06)	6 (3.86)	1 (4.16)	5 (3.80)
beauty	8 (3.82)	9 (3.88)	7 (3.85)	6 (4.01)	4 (3.89)	14 (3.70)	7 (3.69)
creativity	6 (3.88)	6 (3.95)	5 (3.88)	12 (3.88)	11 (3.67)	2 (4.04)	6 (3.72)
perspective	11 (3.79)	11 (3.79)	9 (3.75)	9 (3.92)	14 (3.60)	8 (3.80)	13 (3.58)
social intelligence	13 (3.68)	17 (3.62)	12 (3.65)	16 (3.77)	12 (3.63)	11 (3.75)	20 (3.47)
leadership	12 (3.69)	12 (3.76)	10 (3.74)	10 (3.92)	13 (3.61)	18 (3.55)	10 (3.62)
teamwork	16 (3.62)	19 (3.61)	16 (3.56)	11 (3.89)	18 (3.51)	20 (3.45)	11 (3.60)
learning	3 (3.96)	3 (4.02)	1 (4.01)	3 (4.08)	5 (3.86)	3 (4.00)	3 (3.88)
bravery	17 (3.62)	13 (3.76)	14 (3.62)	19 (3.74)	19 (3.49)	15 (3.64)	23 (3.41)
forgive	15 (3.66)	16 (3.65)	17 (3.52)	18 (3.75)	20 (3.47)	16 (3.64)	21 (3.45)
hope	19 (3.59)	20 (3.55)	19 (3.49)	15 (3.85)	16 (3.52)	17 (3.61)	15 (3.53)
industry	20 (3.47)	15 (3.66)	18 (3.51)	22 (3.59)	17 (3.52)	19 (3.45)	19 (3.48)
religiousness	22 (3.34)	23 (3.30)	23 (3.33)	13 (3.86)	23 (3.21)	23 (3.11)	17 (3.50)
zest	18 (3.60)	18 (3.62)	21 (3.47)	20 (3.64)	15 (3.55)	10 (3.76)	22 (3.44)
prudence	21 (3.44)	21 (3.52)	20 (3.49)	23 (3.52)	21 (3.41)	22 (3.25)	16 (3.53)
modesty	24 (3.14)	22 (3.41)	22 (3.35)	21 (3.61)	22 (3.35)	24 (3.04)	18 (3.49)
self-regulation	23 (3.31)	24 (3.27)	24 (3.27)	24 (3.45)	24 (3.17)	21 (3.26)	24 (3.23)
Nation	VE	UZ	AZ	BR	AE	CN	BS
N	47	46	44	41	39	36	34
ρ with weighted US profile	0.79	0.69	0.82	0.66	0.71	0.72	0.84
ρ with US profile	0.90	0.79	0.93	0.94	0.84	0.78	0.94
kindness	8 (3.87)	6 (3.83)	5 (3.94)	11 (3.80)	8 (3.89)	14 (3.64)	5 (3.94)
fairness	1 (4.12)	4 (3.90)	1 (4.08)	4 (4.01)	5 (3.95)	2 (3.86)	6 (3.90)
honesty	5 (3.99)	10 (3.73)	6 (3.88)	9 (3.81)	7 (3.92)	9 (3.77)	8 (3.83)
gratitude	7 (3.90)	17 (3.51)	10 (3.79)	7 (3.88)	3 (4.03)	8 (3.78)	4 (3.95)
judgment	2 (4.08)	1 (4.02)	4 (3.98)	5 (4.01)	2 (4.03)	1 (3.94)	1 (3.99)
love	9 (3.84)	13 (3.68)	7 (3.85)	12 (3.75)	11 (3.77)	4 (3.83)	9 (3.80)
humor	17 (3.69)	12 (3.69)	12 (3.71)	17 (3.63)	20 (3.51)	16 (3.61)	11 (3.79)
curiosity	4 (4.02)	3 (3.93)	2 (4.06)	3 (4.07)	4 (4.02)	12 (3.70)	2 (3.98)
beauty	10 (3.80)	9 (3.76)	9 (3.79)	6 (3.95)	6 (3.95)	3 (3.86)	7 (3.87)
creativity	6 (3.92)	7 (3.79)	8 (3.82)	2 (4.10)	9 (3.87)	10 (3.71)	10 (3.80)
perspective	11 (3.80)	11 (3.71)	14 (3.68)	10 (3.81)	10 (3.81)	5 (3.82)	14 (3.74)
social intelligence	15 (3.73)	8 (3.79)	15 (3.66)	14 (3.68)	18 (3.54)	6 (3.81)	16 (3.63)
leadership	18 (3.64)	15 (3.67)	16 (3.65)	13 (3.69)	12 (3.73)	13 (3.65)	12 (3.78)
teamwork	12 (3.78)	18 (3.47)	17 (3.63)	15 (3.66)	19 (3.52)	17 (3.58)	13 (3.75)
learning	3 (4.07)	2 (3.98)	3 (4.03)	1 (4.11)	1 (4.13)	7 (3.80)	3 (3.95)
bravery	13 (3.78)	14 (3.67)	13 (3.70)	8 (3.82)	13 (3.71)	19 (3.51)	18 (3.55)
forgive	20 (3.61)	5 (3.90)	11 (3.75)	20 (3.59)	17 (3.55)	15 (3.61)	15 (3.71)
hope	16 (3.75)	21 (3.29)	20 (3.54)	18 (3.63)	14 (3.69)	11 (3.71)	17 (3.59)
industry	14 (3.78)	16 (3.54)	19 (3.54)	19 (3.63)	16 (3.60)	22 (3.44)	21 (3.37)
religiousness	22 (3.57)	24 (3.07)	24 (3.20)	21 (3.47)	22 (3.46)	20 (3.48)	24 (3.26)
zest	19 (3.63)	19 (3.38)	18 (3.63)	22 (3.44)	15 (3.68)	21 (3.46)	19 (3.48)
prudence	21 (3.59)	20 (3.34)	21 (3.37)	16 (3.64)	21 (3.46)	18 (3.55)	20 (3.45)
modesty	24 (3.27)	23 (3.25)	23 (3.21)	24 (3.12)	23 (3.37)	23 (3.44)	23 (3.28)
self-regulation	23 (3.37)	22 (3.28)	22 (3.24)	23 (3.33)	24 (3.28)	24 (3.39)	22 (3.29)

(continued)

（续表）

Table II. Continued.

Nation	Weighted						
	CF	TR	CL	TW	IS	NG	VU
N	32	27	25	24	24	24	23
ρ with weighted US profile	0.85	0.70	0.72	0.72	0.83	0.80	0.65
ρ with US profile	0.93	0.80	0.83	0.84	0.88	0.81	0.73
kindness	7 (3.82)	4 (3.97)	9 (3.96)	9 (3.50)	6 (3.82)	4 (4.01)	12 (3.64)
fairness	2 (4.01)	8 (3.90)	3 (4.15)	7 (3.58)	1 (4.03)	1 (4.15)	11 (3.65)
honesty	5 (3.88)	2 (4.02)	4 (4.06)	8 (3.54)	5 (3.84)	2 (4.09)	3 (3.82)
gratitude	9 (3.78)	14 (3.79)	11 (3.89)	5 (3.62)	4 (3.84)	14 (3.73)	14 (3.61)
judgment	1 (4.06)	3 (4.00)	1 (4.21)	4 (3.69)	3 (3.90)	3 (4.03)	6 (3.71)
love	8 (3.81)	7 (3.92)	16 (3.83)	6 (3.59)	2 (4.03)	6 (3.94)	8 (3.67)
humor	11 (3.74)	16 (3.70)	14 (3.86)	12 (3.40)	15 (3.52)	20 (3.62)	15 (3.61)
curiosity	3 (3.97)	5 (3.94)	5 (4.06)	3 (3.73)	8 (3.80)	8 (3.87)	2 (3.83)
beauty	15 (3.66)	11 (3.83)	7 (3.98)	2 (3.78)	7 (3.81)	7 (3.87)	7 (3.69)
creativity	5 (3.88)	6 (3.93)	6 (4.02)	11 (3.45)	19 (3.40)	10 (3.87)	1 (3.89)
perspective	10 (3.76)	9 (3.86)	10 (3.95)	10 (3.48)	13 (3.63)	9 (3.87)	9 (3.67)
social intelligence	12 (3.72)	13 (3.81)	15 (3.84)	14 (3.36)	14 (3.54)	11 (3.85)	10 (3.67)
leadership	13 (3.71)	15 (3.71)	12 (3.88)	23 (3.15)	11 (3.65)	12 (3.84)	13 (3.61)
teamwork	17 (3.61)	18 (3.59)	17 (3.80)	18 (3.32)	12 (3.64)	16 (3.75)	16 (3.54)
learning	6 (3.86)	1 (4.10)	2 (4.20)	1 (3.85)	9 (3.78)	13 (3.79)	5 (3.72)
bravery	14 (3.68)	10 (3.85)	8 (3.97)	13 (3.38)	16 (3.51)	5 (3.95)	4 (3.79)
forgive	16 (3.65)	22 (3.33)	22 (3.57)	16 (3.36)	10 (3.73)	15 (3.78)	22 (3.19)
hope	19 (3.51)	19 (3.41)	18 (3.77)	15 (3.36)	23 (3.30)	18 (3.65)	20 (3.30)
industry	22 (3.40)	17 (3.68)	13 (3.87)	21 (3.23)	18 (3.47)	19 (3.64)	17 (3.53)
religiousness	23 (3.21)	24 (3.19)	21 (3.63)	22 (3.20)	24 (2.95)	21 (3.56)	21 (3.25)
zest	21 (3.41)	12 (3.83)	20 (3.66)	19 (3.29)	20 (3.38)	17 (3.65)	18 (3.44)
prudence	18 (3.59)	23 (3.31)	19 (3.69)	20 (3.26)	17 (3.50)	24 (3.42)	24 (3.19)
modesty	20 (3.43)	20 (3.41)	24 (3.46)	24 (3.11)	21 (3.37)	22 (3.48)	19 (3.38)
self-regulation	24 (3.19)	21 (3.41)	23 (3.52)	17 (3.33)	22 (3.32)	23 (3.45)	23 (3.19)

Nation	BH	CZ	NI	PL	ZW	PT
N	21	21	21	21	21	20
ρ with weighted US profile	0.68	0.71	0.74	0.64	0.78	0.81
ρ with US profile	0.83	0.82	0.85	0.75	0.90	0.88
kindness	8 (3.89)	7 (3.74)	6 (3.88)	6 (3.79)	7 (3.62)	5 (3.98)
fairness	4 (3.99)	4 (3.83)	1 (4.03)	4 (3.96)	4 (3.71)	1 (4.10)
honesty	5 (3.93)	12 (3.61)	4 (3.96)	16 (3.46)	5 (3.68)	4 (3.98)
gratitude	9 (3.81)	15 (3.57)	16 (3.63)	8 (3.73)	8 (3.60)	11 (3.81)
judgment	1 (4.06)	5 (3.83)	2 (4.00)	1 (4.09)	1 (3.82)	3 (3.98)
love	6 (3.91)	8 (3.73)	8 (3.77)	17 (3.42)	11 (3.49)	15 (3.77)
humor	16 (3.58)	11 (3.63)	17 (3.59)	14 (3.50)	16 (3.40)	10 (3.82)
curiosity	3 (4.01)	1 (3.98)	5 (3.94)	5 (3.90)	2 (3.82)	8 (3.85)
beauty	7 (3.90)	6 (3.75)	9 (3.74)	3 (4.04)	6 (3.66)	6 (3.92)
creativity	12 (3.73)	3 (3.86)	7 (3.79)	7 (3.78)	10 (3.57)	9 (3.85)
perspective	10 (3.76)	14 (3.58)	10 (3.74)	10 (3.65)	9 (3.60)	7 (3.87)
social intelligence	21 (3.49)	9 (3.64)	11 (3.73)	11 (3.62)	13 (3.42)	13 (3.79)
leadership	15 (3.64)	13 (3.60)	15 (3.64)	9 (3.70)	12 (3.42)	14 (3.78)
teamwork	23 (3.43)	18 (3.50)	19 (3.55)	15 (3.50)	14 (3.42)	17 (3.52)
learning	2 (4.04)	2 (3.97)	3 (4.00)	2 (4.05)	3 (3.72)	2 (4.03)
bravery	18 (3.53)	10 (3.64)	13 (3.71)	18 (3.40)	17 (3.40)	12 (3.81)
forgive	17 (3.57)	19 (3.47)	14 (3.67)	12 (3.58)	21 (3.31)	16 (3.56)
hope	13 (3.71)	16 (3.56)	18 (3.57)	19 (3.14)	15 (3.42)	20 (3.33)
industry	11 (3.75)	20 (3.33)	12 (3.73)	24 (3.09)	20 (3.35)	21 (3.32)
religiousness	20 (3.51)	21 (3.23)	22 (3.46)	20 (3.13)	24 (3.07)	24 (2.92)
zest	19 (3.72)	17 (3.51)	23 (3.40)	22 (3.12)	22 (3.22)	18 (3.45)
prudence	14 (3.66)	23 (3.07)	20 (3.55)	13 (3.51)	18 (3.39)	19 (3.38)
modesty	22 (3.48)	24 (3.06)	21 (3.53)	21 (3.53)	19 (3.37)	22 (3.28)
self-regulation	24 (3.41)	22 (3.19)	24 (3.32)	21 (3.13)	23 (3.20)	23 (3.21)

Notes: Figures in parentheses are raw mean scores. Ranks shown in table do not reflect tie scores, although ties were used in calculating the reported ρ coefficients. Country abbreviations are as follows: AE = United Arab Emirates, AR = Argentina, AT = Austria, AU = Australia, AZ = Azerbaijan, BE = Belgium, BH = Bahrain, BR = Brazil, BS = Bahamas, CA = Canada, CF = Central African Republic, CH = Switzerland, CL = Chile, CH = China, CV = Cape Verde, CZ = Czech Republic, DE = Germany, DK = Denmark, ES = Spain, FI = Finland, FR = France, GR = Greece, HK = Hong Kong, HR = Croatia, HU = Hungary, IE = Ireland, IL = Israel, IN = India, IS = Iceland, IT = Italy, JP = Japan, KY = Cayman Islands, MX = Mexico, MY = Malaysia, NG = Nigeria, NI = Nicaragua, NL = Netherlands, NO = Norway, NZ = New Zealand, PH = Philippines, PL = Poland, PT = Portugal, SE = Sweden, SG = Singapore, TR = Turkey, TW = Taiwan, UK = United Kingdom, US = United States, UY = Uruguay, UZ = Uzbekistan, VE = Venezuela, VU = Vanuatu, ZA = South Africa, ZW = Zimbabwe.

　　仅以中美为例，我们可以发现，在美国学生中排序第 8 的 curiosity 在中国学生中排序第 1，在美国学生中排序 13 的 learning 在中国学生中位列第 3，还有 leadership, humor 两项，中美学生差异亦很大。显然，英语教育有必要引导学生把握英语国家学生的品格取向。

本章小结

英语课程的文化意识教育包括了文化教育与品格教育，尤其是从跨文化视角开展品格教育，更是其基本内涵要求。

基于英语课程的跨文化教育特性，英语课程所规定的文化知识内容，是英语课程的文化意识教育的基础，但并非品格教育本身，而是属于英语课程的知识教育。

文化意识的发展，既可以在课堂之内进行，也需要在课堂之外进行，既需要整合到语言学习之中，也可以独立进行，其中很多品格教育活动可能是无声胜有声。

推荐阅读材料

蔡春 . 2010. 德性与品格教育 [D]. 上海：复旦大学 . 60~80

鲁子问 . 2001. 英语教育的动态原则与真实原则论 [M]. 北京：外语教学与研究出版社 . 1

鲁子问等 . 2012. 英语教学论 [M]. 上海：华东师范大学出版社 . 9

苏蓉 . 2012. 我国中学生品格教育的现代性审视 [D]. 苏州：苏州大学 . 7

Lickona, Thomas. 2001. What Is Effective Character Education? [Z]. Presented at The Stony Brook School Symposium on Character (October 6).

Park, N., Peterson, C., Seligman, M., 2006. Character strengths in fifty-four nations and the fifty US states [J]. *The Journal of Positive Psychology*, 1(3): 118-129

第二章　高中英语文化意识教育的基本方法

第一节　高中英语文化意识教育的理论基础

一、教育学基础

高中英语学科的文化意识教育首先是一种教育，所以其理论基础首先应是教育学。在教育学层面，由文化意识教育本质上是文化教育与品格教育的内涵可知，文化意识教育的教育学基础也应是文化教育与品格教育。

如前所述，文化意识中的文化教育包括文化知识教育、文化理解能力与传播能力教育、文化自信的态度建构等。

从本质上说，品格教育是一切教育的价值基础和方向性前提，是学校教育的立场，也是社会教育、家庭教育的基础。在教育领域中，品格教育由学校所引领，但家庭教育的作用更为显著，社会教育的示范性作用也远远大于学校教育。学校品格教育需要家庭教育、社会教育的通力协作，单凭学校教育，品格教育目标不可能真正实现。高中英语课程的文化意识教育，属于学校教育，但基于品格教育的教育特性，作为学校教育组成部分的英语课程的文化意识教育，也需要家庭教育、社会教育的全力参与与通力协作。基于此可知，品格教育的理论基础应是学校教育、社会教育、家庭教育的基础，而不应单是学校教育的理论基础。

当然，正如本书第一章所言，英语课程的文化意识教育具有跨文化教育的特性，中外文化理解与传播的教育是英语课程品格教育的基础。所以，文化教育，尤其是跨文化教育，也是英语课程文化意识教育不可或缺的理论基础。

无论是品格教育，还是跨文化教育，其学校教育都是基于学校课程和学校活动而进行的。英语课程是学校的基础课程，不过英语课程的文化意识教育的活动，则不仅是学校的英语活动，还包括与英语教育相关的各种活动。所以，英语课程的文化意识教育，在学校教育层面，是基于学校的英语课程与英语教育相关活动而进行的教育，如在学校组织的全民阅读活动中介绍我国名著，甚至在升旗仪式的国旗下讲话，也会促进学生加深对中国文化的理解，从而促进其国家情怀与文化自信的养成。在家庭教育与社会教育层面，英语课程相关的文化意识教育往往不以课程形式出现，而以相关教育活动形式出现，如父母带孩子看外国电影、出国旅游，本地承办国际体育文化活动等等。

基于品格教育与跨文化教育的理论基础，我们可以确定英语课程的文化意识教育本质上是以学校英语课程和相关活动为基础，通过家庭与社会相关的教育活动，引导和促进学生获得英语课程文化意识所规定的核心价值，发展学生良好的道德意识、道德情感和道德行为，形成社会需要的积极品质的教育实践活动。

基于我国德育教育的基本原则、美国品格教育通行的 11 项基本原则与跨文化教育的基本原则，我们可以确定，英语课程文化意识教育的基本原则应包括：

原则 1：英语课程的文化意识教育应以促进学生的积极品格（包括但不仅限于课程标准所规定的文化意识）的建构与发展为基础。

原则 2：作为学校教育组成部分的英语课程的文化意识教育应以学校教育为主，但应积极寻求家庭教育、社会教育的积极参与和支持。

原则 3：英语课程的文化意识教育应包括品格意识、情感和行为，尤其是促进文化意识落实的行为。

原则 4：英语课程的文化意识教育应采取一种目的明确的、课程与活动有机整合的方法，促进学生在各阶段学校生活中发展相应的品格。

原则 5：英语课程的文化意识教育应是学校教育，尤其是学校品格教育的组成部分，学校必须是一个充满关怀的群体，应建立全面、全程、全域品格教育的校园。

原则 6：学校的各项活动，尤其是英语课程的课堂教学等教育教学活动，要为学生发展积极的品格创造环境、条件和机会。

原则 7：学校所有员工，首先是英语教师，必须成为英语课程的文化意识教育所倡导的积极品格的实践者和教育者。

原则 8：英语课程文化意识教育目标，尤其是具体内容，应成为学校教育，尤其是英语课程的重要评价内容。

对于英语课程文化意识教学，首先应聚焦英语课程所要求的文化意识内容，即本书第一章所总结归纳的两类目标。

同时，英语课程的文化意识还应促进以下 24 项优秀品格的发展（见下表）（Peterson, C. & M.E.P. Seligman, 2004）：

表 2-1　优秀品格

类别	你应拥有的优秀品格
一、智慧与知识：知识的获得和应用	1．好奇心。你对世界充满好奇和兴趣，你对任何事物都感到好奇。你经常发问，对所有话题和题目都感到着迷。你喜欢探索和发掘新事物。
	2．喜好学习。你喜欢学习，不管是在课堂上或自学，你都喜爱学习新事物。你喜爱上学、阅读、参观博物馆和任何有学习机会的地方。
	3．创造力。你有创造力、独立思考的能力，能够想出新方法做事是你拥有的重要特质。如果有更好的方法，你决不会满足于用传统方法去做同样的事。
	4．开放的思想。你有判断力、批判性思维和原创力，能从多角度思考和考证事物是你重要的特质。你不会妄下结论，只会根据实际的证据作决定。你能够变通。
	5．智慧和知识。包括社会智慧、个人智慧、情绪智慧。你明白别人的动机和感受。在不同的社交场合，你知道该做什么，也知道要做些什么，才能使其他人感到自在。
	6．独特视角。有统揽全局的洞察力和观点见解。你不认为自己有智慧，但你的朋友却认为你有。他们重视你对事物的洞察力，并向你寻求意见。你对这个世界的看法，无论对自己和别人来说，都具有意义。

（续表）

类别	你应拥有的优秀品格
二、勇气：面对不同立场誓达目标	7．勇敢。英武、勇敢和勇气。你无所畏惧，绝不会在威胁、挑战、困难或痛苦前畏缩。即使面对暴力，你仍会为正义疾呼。你会根据自己的信念而行动。
	8．坚持不懈。坚持性、努力、勤奋和坚毅。你努力完成自己的工作。无论怎样的工作，你都会尽力准时完成。工作时，你不会分心，而且在完成工作的过程中获得满足感。
	9．真实性。正直、诚实、真实。你是个诚实的人，不只说实话，还会以真诚和真挚的态度生活。你实事求是，不虚伪，是个"真心"的人。
三、仁慈和爱：人际交往的品质	10．仁慈、善良、慷慨。你对别人仁慈和宽宏大量。别人请你做事，你从不推搪。你享受为别人做好事，即使那些人和你认识不深。
	11．爱与被爱的能力。你重视和别人的亲密关系，特别是那些互相分享和关怀的关系。那些给你最亲密感觉的人，他们同样感到跟你最亲密。
四、正义：文明的品质	12．精神。责任、团队精神和忠诚。指公民之间的关系、公民的权利和义务、团队精神、忠诚。作为团队的一分子，你的表现突出，是个忠心和热心的队员。你对自己分内工作负责，并为团队的成功而努力。
	13．公平。平等、正义。对所有人公平，是你坚持不变的原则。你不会因为个人的感情，而对别人作出偏差的判断。你给予每个人平等的机会。
	14．领导能力。你在领导方面表现出色。你鼓励组员完成工作，让每位组员有归属感，并能维持团队的和谐。你在筹划和实践活动方面表现良好。

（续表）

类别	你应拥有的优秀品格
五、修养与节制：处世的品质	15. 自我控制。自我控制和自我管理。你自觉地规范自己的感觉与行为，是个自律的人。你对自己的食欲和情绪有自制力，不会反被它们支配。
	16. 谨慎小心。你很小心，一贯审慎选择。你不会说些将来会令自己后悔的话，或是做会后悔的事。
	17. 适度和谦虚。你不追求别人的关注，但喜欢让自己的成就显而易见。你不认为自己很特别，而你的谦逊是公认和受重视的。
六、心灵超越：个体与整体人类相联系的品质	18. 欣赏美和完美。对美的欣赏和领会。生命中的一切，从大自然、艺术、数学、科学等到日常生活体验，你都有注意到和欣赏到其美丽、优秀之处。
	19. 感激、感恩。你留意到发生在自己身上的好事，但从不会视为理所当然。由于你常常表达谢意，你的朋友和家人都知道你是个懂得感恩的人。
	20. 希望、乐观。对未来充满期望。你对未来有最好的期望，并为此努力达成心愿。你相信未来是掌握在自己手中。
	21. 有心灵上的目标和信仰。你对崇高的人生目标和宇宙的意义有着强烈和贯彻的信念。你知道自己怎样在大环境中作出配合。你的信念塑造了你的行为，也成了你的慰藉之源。
	22. 宽恕、怜悯。你宽恕那些开罪你的人，也经常给别人第二次机会。你的座右铭是慈悲，而不是报复。
	23. 风趣、幽默。你喜欢大笑和逗别人开心。对你来说，为别人带来欢笑很重要。在任何情况下，你都尝试去看事物轻松的一面。
	24. 热情。热心、激情、热情、精力充沛。

上述品格是积极的品格，是品格教育的内涵，也应是英语课程文化意识教育的内涵。

二、语言学基础

英语课程的文化意识教育本质上是品格教育，是跨文化教育，但其英语课程的特性依然要求其必须具有语言学的基础。同时，英语课程是语文类课程，语言学是其不可或缺的基础，尤其是英语课程文化意识所规定的感知所学内容的语言美和意蕴美、建构跨文化的敏感性等，都是其不可缺少的语言学基础。

基于语言学基础，英语课程的文化意识教育应该关注语义，尤其是语义的文化内涵，如 red、dragon 等词汇在英语和汉语中的不同文化内涵，以及 there be 与 have 在英语和汉语中的语义关联性异同等引发的对文化内涵的理解。当然，英语课程文化意识教育还应关注语音知识、语篇知识、语用知识等的文化内涵，如英语韵律的特征带来的英语诗歌特征和英语学术论文结构的文化特征等等。

发展跨文化敏感性等英语课程文化意识，更需要基于语言学基础而展开，如对英语语音的区域差异的敏感、对英语单词线性书写特征与汉字中心聚焦的书写特征所呈现的文化差异的敏感、对英语单词前缀与后缀和汉字偏旁所呈现的文化共性的敏感等等，都充分说明英语课程的文化意识发展不可缺少语言学基础。

第二节　高中英语文化意识教育的基本方法

一、2017 高中英语课标中的文化意识教学建议

2017 高中英语课标强调整合式学习，文化意识教学也应采取促进学生整合式学习的活动，在整合式学习中开展文化意识教育，实现其目标。

2017 高中英语课标明确倡导指向学科核心素养的英语学习活动观和

自主学习、合作学习、探究学习等学习方式，要求教师设计具有综合性、关联性和实践性特点的英语学习活动，使学生通过学习理解、应用实践、迁移创新等一系列融语言、思维、文化为一体的活动，获取、阐释和评判语篇意义，表达个人观点、意图和情感态度，分析中外文化异同，发展多元思维和批判性思维，提高英语学习的能力和实际运用语言的能力。

对于文化意识的发展，2017 高中英语课标指出，文化意识的发展是一个内化于心、外化于行的过程，涉及几个步骤的演进和融合：

感知中外文化知识——分析与比较

认同优秀文化——赏析与汲取

形成文化理解——认知与内化

具备文明素养——行为与表征

所以，从 2017 高中英语课标的规定看，文化意识发展应渗透在日常教学之中，尤其是教师的行为举止的潜移默化。文化知识的教学应以促进学生文化意识的形成为目标。文化学习不仅需要知识的积累，还需要深入理解其精神内涵，并将其进一步内化为个人的意识和品行。在语篇教学的各个教学环节之中，我们都可以基于最佳时机开展文化意识的教育，促进学生文化意识发展。

二、中外文化理解与传播能力发展的基本教学方法

对于文化意识的发展，跨文化教育已有相应的长期研究。结合跨文化教育的基本方法和 2017 高中英语课标，我们认为，发展学生理解与传播中外文化的能力的基本方法如下图所示：

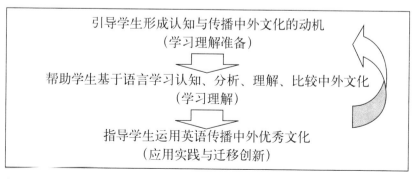

引导学生形成认知与传播中外文化的动机
（学习理解准备）

帮助学生基于语言学习认知、分析、理解、比较中外文化
（学习理解）

指导学生运用英语传播中外优秀文化
（应用实践与迁移创新）

图 2-1　高中英语课程促进中外文化理解与传播能力发展的基本教学方法

　　基于此可知，理解与传播中外文化首先必须具有开放的文化心态，形成认知与传播中外文化的动机。在英语课程中认知外国文化是课程的基本内容，而认知外国文化的同时，可以促进我们对中国文化的认知，强化我们自身的文化身份与特性认同。我们中国人学习外语，然后运用外语传播中国文化，是当然之理；但同时传播外国优秀文化，尤其是我国社会文化发展所需的外国文化，学习世界文化的先进成分，也应是当然之理。

　　认知、分析、比较、理解中外文化，是一个层层递进的过程，也是文化知识教学的基本过程。英语课程中的这一过程，应是基于英语语言学习的。这也就是说，英语语言的教学应自始至终是文化教学的组成部分，文化教育也应自始至终是语言教学的组成部分，二者相互组成，不可分离。即使是字母 A 的教学，本质上也存在文化认知、分析、比较、理解，如：为什么字母 A 如此书写（大写字母 A 起源于牛角的象形）；西方文字为什么放弃了最早的象形起源而转向拼音；中文的象形传统与西文的拼音特征及其后续对中西文化的影响比较、分析；为什么字母 A 排为第一个字母，由此形成的字母 A 有哪些诸多比喻；字母 A 的诸多其他社会意义等等。上述这些都非常显著地说明文化教育与语言教育有着密不可分的关联性。

　　传播中外文化还需要相应的语言表达能力，这也是英语语言能力发展与文化意识教育共有的当然之理。

　　以下案例较为显著地展示了高中英语课程促进中外文化理解与传播能力发展的教学方法与过程。

案例主题

　　语篇学习内容：1. 欧洲四座城市（巴黎、巴塞罗那、佛罗伦萨、雅典）的历史文化特点介绍。2. 姊妹城市（sister cities）制度文化介绍。

　　（说明：因教材内容可能出现变化，此处不呈现教材内容。）

第一课时：课前学习方案

第一步：学习理解准备——形成理解与传播中外文化的动机

让学生阅读以下短文，读后回答：你打算在学习本单元过程中完成的任务是基于本单元所学内容，介绍欧洲某地历史文化？还是基于本单元所学介绍某地历史文化的方式，介绍我国某地历史文化？

Few places can be compared with Europe, which has more historical and cultural sights than any other continent on earth. From its Northern Lights to its Southern shores, this drama queen, who enjoys amazing wealth of sights, sounds, peoples and parties, keeps making people surprised and confused. Once you go on your trip across this continent, you will have to be prepared for many surprises, which give your eyes and ears the trip of a lifetime.

Of course, for many people Europe is all about history, and oh, what a history! Even experts on history will be astonished to find that this place is full of surprises. There are famous places like Florence with historic buildings and art and Venice with the graceful canals. There are also less expected sites, among which are the remains of one of the Seven Wonders of the World in Turkey and the haunting buildings in Poland.

While Europe takes pride in its extraordinary heritage, it is certainly not one to be limited by it. Indeed, the continent leads the world in fashion, art, music, and design, examples of which are the street styles and music scenes of London and Berlin.

教师引导学生基于自己的优势选择合适的学习目标。告诉学生：凡事预则立。做好计划、设定合适的学习目标，是提高学习成效的关键。对于目标，教师要让学生清楚，每个人学习英语的目标不同，即使都很关注分数，分数的目标也不相同。如何为自己设计合适的目标呢？应先了解可以选择的学习目标。

本单元目标为（学生可以从以下目标中选择适合自己的学习目标，也可以自己重新确定学习目标）：

表 2-2　单元目标

分类	目　标
语言能力	1. 理解介绍欧洲四座城市历史文化的语篇及相关语句、语词，理解介绍姊妹城市（sister cities）制度的语篇及相关语句、语词，尤其是用于描述地理位置的介词用法、介绍特征的形容词用法； 2. 根据语用目标，运用恰当的语言介绍所知欧洲城市的历史文化，姊妹城市制度，或者所想介绍的中国某地历史文化。
文化意识	1. 进一步发展积极的跨文化态度，乐意理解与传播中外文化； 2. 理解欧洲四座城市的历史文化，传播所愿传播的欧洲历史文化； 3. 加深对中国某地历史文化的理解，并进行传播。
思维品质	分析基于目的的介绍，把握内容与目的的指向性。
学习能力	进一步发展学习计划能力，进一步体验基于语言基础、风格优势选择任务的能力。

　　教师在指导学生选择适合自己的学习目标（任务）时，不仅需要考虑兴趣，更需要考虑语言能力发展目标。在以上语言运用能力发展目标中，介绍欧洲城市历史文化的语言运用能力目标主要是基于对阅读语篇的理解，对语篇所介绍欧洲城市的历史文化信息进行整理；而介绍中国某地历史文化则属于表达，要求基于所学的语言进行自主表达。学生应基于自己的基础和发展可能，确定适合自己的学习目标。

　　除了根据自己的语言能力基础、兴趣选择任务之外，学生更应该基于自己的学习风格选择任务，因为基于风格开展学习活动可以快速地提高他们的学习成效。

　　以下是一份著名的学习风格调查表（限于篇幅，此处内容从略，需要者可在网上搜索学习风格量表而获得），请学生如实填写，然后总结；得出结论后，找出他们自己的学习风格。

　　下面，让学生选择符合他们自己的学习风格的任务吧。

表 2-3　学习任务

任　务	风格说明
任务 1：制作海报或写短文，介绍你乐意介绍的欧洲某地的历史文化，或中国某地的历史文化。	适合视觉型风格显著的学习者。
任务 2：进行演讲，介绍你乐意介绍的欧洲某地的历史文化，或中国某地的历史文化。	适合言语型风格显著的学习者。
任务 3：表演情景剧，介绍你乐意介绍的欧洲某地的历史文化，或中国某地的历史文化。	适合动觉型风格显著的学习者。

第二步：学习理解——基于语言学习，认知、分析、理解、比较中外文化

第 1 课时学习过程（本书聚焦文化意识教育，教学案例中教学设计形式保持原样，其他教学活动与语言可能存在或此或彼的不足。若使用，请注意甄别。）：

表 2-4　第 1 课时学习过程

预设时间	学习步骤	学习目的	教师支持	学生学习	学习资源
	预习	大体了解欧洲总体情况。	教师引导学生学会设计适合自己的学习目标。教师引导学生学会选择任务。教师引导学生通过预习，了解所介绍城市的地理位置，分析文章写作目的。教师要求学生预习至少一篇介绍欧洲总体情况的文章。	学生学习如何分析自己的起始水平，如何确定适合自己的学习目标。学生学习如何根据自己的风格特征、兴趣选择任务。学生确定学习目标。学生确定任务。学生预习 Introduction，总结其介绍地理位置的语句。学生阅读至少一篇介绍欧洲总体情况的文章，找出其介绍地理位置的语句。	学习策略短文：合理确定学习目标的小技巧。学习策略短文：基于风格与兴趣选择任务。教材 Introduction 内容。介绍欧洲总体情况的短文。欧洲人文地理的短文。

（续表）

预设时间	学习步骤	学习目的	教师支持	学生学习	学习资源
第1—2分钟	教学热身与启动	激活已有知识结构，进入本课时主题。	教师首先引导学生感知整个世界，再将学生兴趣集中在欧洲，告诉学生：自己的一位朋友刚刚从捷克回来（选择捷克是因为大多数学生对其地理位置不清楚，有信息差），简单介绍捷克历史名城布尔诺(Brno)。问学生是否知道捷克在哪里，布尔诺在哪里。随后展示欧洲地图，引导学生用in, on, to描述捷克以及布尔诺的地理位置。	学生看图片回答问题。	捷克与周边国家地图。归纳总结描述地理位置为主的常用介词的短文。
第3—13分钟	任务呈现与讨论	了解任务。	教师让学生介绍自己选定的任务，请学生说明自己的选择。从学生的说明引出讨论：如何确定学习目标、选择任务。分析一位学生案例，分析其目标是否合理、任务是否适合。告诉学生，这类反思每月应该自己进行一次，以后老师不再进行统一说明。自己若没有把握，可与老师讨论。教师告诉学生：无论选择以什么方式介绍什么地方，都需要描述这个地方的地理位置特征。今天先学习如何描述一个地方的地理位置特征。	学生与同伴讨论自己选定的任务，听同伴意见：自己选定的任务是否适合自己的学习风格和学习优势。	任务的不同要求。教材的多篇语篇，各有不同要求的任务。

（续表）

预设时间	学习步骤	学习目的	教师支持	学生学习	学习资源
第14–23分钟	运用能力学习	引入部分和功能部分结合起来进行学习,通过示意图直观地呈现介词的含义,利于理解。	教师告诉学生：为了解如何描述地理位置特征，先学习Introduction部分。先让学生浏览活动1方框里的词，再让学生读这些词，用简单英语解释这些词，最后让学生完成表格。完成活动1后，让学生浏览活动2中的6个词或短语，再让学生浏览语句，圈出每句中的这些词或短语。然后逐句说出句中相关的词或短语的意思，并填写地图。最后教师小结如何用介词说明地理位置。	学生复习和学习一些欧洲国家、首都、语言的词汇。认真结合地图、示意图以及教师的讲解熟悉欧洲各国的地理位置以及描述方法，学会准确地用介词描述地理位置。在听课过程中，必要时要做笔记。	教材的Introduction部分的内容。补充相应的资源。
第24–26分钟	任务准备	发现现有语言能力与完成任务的差距。	教师请基础较好的学生尝试描述所介绍地方的地理位置特征。发现问题，引导学生更好地掌握语言以准确表达。	学生写出1-4个句子，描述所介绍地方的地理位置特征。	同伴作业。
第27-36分钟	语言学习	学习巩固地理位置特征的描述方法。	教师指导学生学习Function部分，按顺序完成活动1–5中的所有内容。	学生根据发现的问题，进一步巩固介词与介词短语描述地理位置特征的用法，以及其他描述地理位置特征的方法。	教材Function部分。

（续表）

预设时间	学习步骤	学习目的	教师支持	学生学习	学习资源
第37–42分钟	任务展示	强化热爱家乡、热爱祖国的情感。学会用英语描述地理位置，同时为任务完成作准备。	教师指导学生写出至少四句话，描述所介绍地方的地理位置，为任务作准备。	学生尝试用学到的英文写出至少4个语句，描述自己所介绍地方的地理位置，并争取机会，向全班和教师展示自己完成的语句。	介绍资源，例如文字与图片等。
第43–44分钟	任务评价	强化语言运用意识。	教师指导全班进行一两个案例的评价，为学生互评提供案例。	学生根据各自选定的标准，两人一组，与同伴相互讨论各自完成的任务情况。	各种评价标准的范文。
第45分钟	布置作业	巩固说明地理特征的语句，预习课文。	教师布置课后作业：阅读短文 Prague，巩固说明地理特征的语句。预习课文，掌握课文中的语言特征，了解被动语态的用法。	学生预习课文，掌握课文中的语言特征，了解被动语态的用法。	短文 Prague。课文。

Introduction to Brno, Czech

Brno is the second largest city in the Czech Republic, located in the southeast of the country. It was founded in 1243, although the area had been settled since the 5th century. As of December 2009 the population is 405,337. Brno is the capital of the South Moravian Region.

Brno is a city with a fame of architectures. The city's skyline is dominated by the Špilberk castle, where an early-Gothic palace with two chapels is still standing. The Petrov hill is topped by the Gothic cathedral of Sts. Peter and Paul. At the beginning of the 16th century, the Old Town City Hall portal  was built, featuring a late Gothic peculiarity – a crooked pinnacle. Worth at least a brief mention are other historical buildings – the monastery and convent buildings of religious orders, the Parnas fountain in the Baroque-naturalist style, the bishop's court, the Renaissance palace of the Lords of Lipá and Kunštát, church of St. Jakub (James), and the Hausperg Palace, nowadays the seat of the Goose on a String Theater.

Brno is also a major center of modern architecture. The late-19th century Klein Palace was among the first structures built with modern technology (cast iron features, flushable toilets); the Mahen Theater was the first theater in the country to use electricity throughout the building. Among other prominent buildings are Art Nouveau, early modernist and functionalist structures. German architect Mies van der Rohe's 1929 villa Tugendhat is an outstanding example of functionalist architecture and a milestone in the development of modern architecture worldwide. Among other modernist landmarks is the Brno Exhibition Center, whose set of buildings (built over the period of forty years, from 1930s to 1960s) makes up a harmonious whole; over 50 fairs and exhibitions take place here annually.

The most famous Czech writer Milan Kundera was born on April 1st, 1929 in Brno. He has been nominated as candidate of Nobel Prize for several times. One of his popular novel is *Unbearable Lightness of Being*.

表 2-5　第 2 课时学习过程

预设时间	学习步骤	学习目的	教师支持	学生学习	学习资源
第1–5分钟	热身导入	激活活动的目的性。	教师请学生展示自己完善后的介绍某地的语句。对于某些语用目的不够明确的语句，教师进行指导。	学生展示自己完善后的介绍某地的语句。	同伴完成的语句。
第6分钟	任务呈现	了解任务。	教师告诉学生：介绍某地的目的不同，选择的介绍内容就不同，语句结构也会有些不同。今天学习课文，大家可以学到如何根据语用目的介绍某地，之后再确定各自介绍某地的语用目的，以便进一步完善自己的介绍。	学生了解任务的目的性。	教师讲解话语。
第7–15分钟	阅读活动	理解课文的语用目的。	教师指导学生学习课文，了解语用目的。引导学生阅读课文并回答问题：1) What is the purpose of the four passages to introduce those cities? 2) Why did the author write such an introduction? 3) Which sentences support your finding?　教师通过下面问题启发学生把握这篇文章的语用目的：1) 如果这篇文章发表在报刊、杂志上，会发表在什么报刊、杂志上？2) 什么人会读这篇文章？3) 读了这篇文章会产生什么行为动机？	学生阅读课文，思考：四篇短文介绍这些城市的目的是什么？从短文中寻找语句说明自己的观点。	学习方案。

（续表）

预设时间	学习步骤	学习目的	教师支持	学生学习	学习资源
第16—30分钟	阅读活动	深入任务：捕捉具体信息并进行归纳分类。	教师指导学生完成活动2-5。教师指导学生第二遍阅读，完成活动2，就理解猜测词义方法进行指导。教师指导学生第三遍阅读，完成活动3-4，教师可以建议学生在阅读中列出信息表，然后就很容易回答和选择了。全班完成活动5时，教师可以提出问题，学生回答。	学生第二遍阅读文章，完成活动2。小组活动：分享各自的方法。学生第三遍阅读，完成活动3-4，完成信息表。小组活动：相互检查表格填写是否正确，相互问答完成活动3，相互检查活动4答案是否正确。全班活动：完成活动5，根据实际情况回答。	课文。
第31—35分钟	任务准备		教师让学生确定自己介绍某地的语用目的，并与同伴交流，讨论自己设定的语用目的是否合理。	确定自己介绍某地的语用目的，与同伴交流，讨论自己设定的语用目的是否合理。	课文与已读语篇。
第36—44分钟	任务展示与评价	进一步强化学生的语言运用能力。	教师请不同的学生说明各自介绍某地的真实语用目的，指导全班同学讨论其目的是否合理。	学生说明自己的语用目的，全部同学讨论其目的是否合理。	

（续表）

预设时间	学习步骤	学习目的	教师支持	学生学习	学习资源
第45分钟	布置作业	扩展阅读，培养学生阅读能力，开阔视野，增长知识。	教师布置学生课后阅读课文并发现作者是如何使其介绍显得客观的。教师布置学生课后阅读一篇含有检测被动语态语句理解的介绍某地的文章，完成练习并学习如何介绍某地，为任务作准备。教师布置学生课后阅读更多短文，训练学生把握语用目的，理解词义、信息列表的能力。	学生预习语法的运用，理解使用被动语态可以使描述介绍更加客观。学生巩固所学的阅读技能。	教材第5页活动1–3，以及第67–68页活动1–5。

表2-6　第3课时学习过程

预设时间	学习步骤	学习目的	教师支持	学生学习	学习资源
	预习	了解问卷设计的目的性。	教师提供 How to make a questionnaire 材料，让学生预习。	学生阅读 How to make a questionnaire 并完成教材第71页表格中"YOU"部分的内容。	课前学习方案及教材。
第1分钟	任务呈现	了解任务。	教师询问学生上一课时确定的语用目的。向学生说明今天的任务是完成自己对某地的介绍，语用目的要明确，介绍要与语用目的相符。今天学习听力材料，了解如何根据语用目的选择内容。	学生根据各自选择了解任务。	教师话语。

（续表）

预设时间	学习步骤	学习目的	教师支持	学生学习	学习资源
第2–10分钟	听力训练	增加新的欧洲城市文化信息，提供更多选择。	教师提出预测问题：西班牙人 Carlos 来到英国伦敦，他会对什么信息感兴趣？告诉学生："预测"对听力理解很有帮助。历史和地理知识对本次"预测"很有用。同时，要充分利用教材中的图片和文字信息。	学生通过听力材料了解更多的欧洲著名城市的知识，巩固学过的相关知识，提高语言运用能力。学生第一次听对话，完成活动 1。学生第二次听对话，完成活动 2–3。学生第三次听对话，听懂并说明 question tags 的语调所表达的信息。全班讨论：外国人 Carlos 对英国的什么信息感兴趣？	教材第 6 页的听力材料。
第11–25分钟	听力训练	通过有趣的竞猜活动提高学生的听说能力。深入任务：捕捉具体信息，掌握 Note-taking 的技能。	教师提出预测问题：如果要通过知识竞赛吸引游客，应该问游客什么问题？教师即时评价并确定在第一次听对话后回答问题最快的前五名学生。	学生利用听力材料进一步巩固欧洲的城市文化知识，为下一步的听说活动作准备。听对话并思考：Jill 和 Sam 的答案与自己的一样吗？听的过程中，要记录关键信息。学生第一次听对话，利用已有的历史和地理知识回答问题（限时竞猜）。第二次听对话，捕捉 Jill 和 Sam 的答案。之后两人小组活动：核对答案，商讨解决其中的差异，比较二人笔记的异同及其对于答题的有效性，完善笔记。全班讨论：Are the questions good for attracting tourists?	教材第 71 页的活动。

（续表）

预设时间	学习步骤	学习目的	教师支持	学生学习	学习资源
第26—35分钟	讨论设计	进一步强化学生的语言运用能力。	教师指导学生进行小组活动，设计五个中国知识问答题，以吸引游客来中国旅游（You are asked to make a questionnaire to attract tourists to China. What questions would you like to ask?）。	学生展开小组活动：评价教材中设计的问题，设计五个问题。	课中学习方案。
第36—44分钟	成果展示	明确语用目的。	每组呈现本组设计的问题，教师指导学生讨论是否达到吸引游客的目的。同时评价学生的语言，鼓励根据需要使用的tag questions。	各组呈现讨论结果，评价活动。	各组设计的问题。
第43—45分钟	作业布置	巩固强化。	教师布置课后作业：根据自己确定的语用目的，完成对某地的介绍。	学生完成任务并复习巩固。	阅读材料。

第三步：应用实践与迁移创新——运用英语传播中外优秀文化

表 2-7 第 4 课时学习过程

预设时间	学习步骤	学习目的	教师支持	学生学习	学习资源
第 1 分钟	任务呈现	了解任务。	教师告诉学生，今天的任务是讨论各自的任务成果，并进一步完善，尤其是语用目的是否明确，介绍是否与目的一致。	学生了解任务。	教师话语。
第 2–10 分钟	阅读		教师针对部分学生在阅读时看不出文章有明确语用目的这一现象，比如预习 The European Union 时，就看不出文中有明确的语用目的的情况，指导学生分析这篇文章的语用目的。 首先请学生阅读这篇介绍性文章，然后讨论以下问题：如果这篇文章发表在网站上，会发表在什么网站？什么人会读这篇文章？他们为了什么目的获得文章中的信息？	学生阅读课文，按照教师的引导，学习分析文章的语用目的。	课中学习方案活动1。
第 11–15 分钟	讨论		教师提出讨论问题：文章中哪些内容支持了文章的写作目的？ 教师提出反思问题：你的介绍中的内容是否支持你的写作目的？	学生按照问题展开思考，找出支持写作目的的内容，陈述自己的观点。了解其他同学的陈述，并进行评价。反思自己对某地介绍的内容与目的是否一致。	

（续表）

预设时间	学习步骤	学习目的	教师支持	学生学习	学习资源
第16—20分钟	讨论		教师提出讨论问题：在刚才的阅读中，你是如何处理生词的？如何处理难句的？这些方法能否帮助你的读后讨论？教师教会学生一种学习策略：Reflection（反思）。告诉学生可以经常反思自己的学习，不过反思要有明确的目的、科学的方法。	学生按照问题进行思考，分析自己处理生词的方法，并进行陈述。听同学们介绍自己的方法。反思自己的方法是否科学、合理。	
第21—25分钟	阅读		教师指导学生阅读另一篇文章，分析写作目的并讨论下面的问题：如果这篇文章发表在网站上，会发表在什么网站？什么人会读这篇文章？他们为了什么目的获得文章中的信息？	学生阅读并思考。	课中学习方案活动2。
第26—30分钟	讨论		教师提出讨论问题：文章中哪些内容支持了文章的写作目的？文章中的被动语态对于写作目的有怎样的支持作用？教师提出反思问题：你的介绍中的内容、语句结构是否支持你的写作目的？	学生按照问题开展思考，分析被动语态对于写作目的的支持作用，陈述自己的观点。学生了解其他同学的陈述，并进行评价。学生反思自己对某地的介绍中的语言：内容与目的是否一致。	

（续表）

预设时间	学习步骤	学习目的	教师支持	学生学习	学习资源
第31–35分钟	讨论		教师指导学生再次运用反思策略。提出讨论问题：在刚才的阅读中，读前的问题是否能帮助你阅读理解？读中你是否做了笔记？读后的讨论对你理解被动语态有怎样的作用？	学生根据老师安排进行反思。听其他同学的反思，并进行评价。	
第31–35分钟	任务完成		教师指导学生修改完善他们对某地的介绍。	学生根据本单元所学内容和所获得的能力，修改完善自己对某地的介绍。	
第40–44分钟	任务展示与评价	强化语用意识和交流意识。	教师公布学生相互评价标准：1.介绍的目的是否明确；2.介绍的内容是否支持介绍的目的；3.介绍的语句结构是否支持介绍的目的。	学生选择评价标准，参与评价。部分学生按照自己选择的任务内容和完成形式展示自己的介绍。	课中学习方案活动3内容。
第45分钟	总结作业布置	突出学习策略。	教师布置课后反思内容：今天的反思策略是否帮助了你的阅读？教师布置课后作业：总结本单元学习成效和有效的学习策略。	学生总结本单元学习成效和有效的学习策略。	

　　以上案例说明，在高中英语课程中，中外文化理解与传播能力的发展，具有广泛的可能性和现实的实践性。从引导学生形成认知与传播中外文化的动机开始，基于语言学习，在学习理解、应用实践、迁移创新的学习过程中，通过认知、分析、理解、比较中外文化的学习活动，最终发展学生运用英语传播中外优秀文化的能力，这一方法具有操作性。

这一方法在不同教学条件下，针对不同教学内容的广谱性实践，以及每一环节的实践方法，将在随后展开讨论和分析。

三、品格教育的基本教学方法

对于品格教育的方法，2017 高中英语课标没有明确的专门规定，所以我们从品格教育的一般方法进行讨论。

品格教育需要更为强有力的内在动力，但也需要强有力的外在引导与约束。无论是优秀品格的发展，还是不良品行的控制，都需要内力与外力的双重作用。尽管外力最终是通过内力而起作用，但外力的引领与约束是不可或缺的基础性力量。在品格教育中，外力是环境，是示范，是引领，其影响促进内力发展，呈现为内外共生的形态，这也是品格教育的基本教学方法。

在品格教育中，人类自身的生存性先于一切而起作用，无论是在意识尚未形成之前，还是意识形成之后，皆是如此。所以，在内外共生的形态之中，内力本质性地先于外力而出现，尽管在可观测形态上，可能外力有时先于内力出现，但其实仍然是内力接受外力作用之后外力才起作用，所以，实质上依然是内力先于外力呈现。分析这一起源，有助于我们准确把握品格教育的基本教学方法。

基于此，我们可知，品格教育的基本方法可以是：

图 2-2　高中英语课程促进品格教育的基本教学方法

以下案例较为显著地展示高中英语促进品格教育的基本教学方法与过程。

表 2-3　高中英语促进品格教育的基本教学方法与过程

单元主题	The Danger of a Single Story
对象	高一新生
时间	高一学生进校后第二个月开始
教学过程	
（一）把握学生品格教育内力呈现形态与时机	教师向学生展示学校最近的一项调查，调查发现，高中新生中，偏见现象给一些同学带来严重的心理负担。现在我国极少有高中只招收来自同一所初中的学生，高中学生中经常出现对来自不同的初中，尤其是来自乡镇的初中同学的偏见，还存在对不同家庭背景、不同成绩的同学的偏见。 教师呈现一位高一学生黄某所反映的具体问题，并呈现教师观察中发现本班出现的偏见现象〔如有学生说"A 县的人就是坏""B 乡的人就是土""那些成绩好的就是聪明（而不是因为会学习，也不是因为刻苦)"，"他块头大，就是爱欺负人"〕等，最近本校或本地学生生活中出现的偏见导致的问题、冲突，或者新闻中出现的地域偏见导致的冲突，甚至悲剧，让学生分析原因，引导学生得出结论：partiality。 教师以案例方式介绍社会中还有更常见的跨文化、跨民族偏见，以及地域偏见，甚至一定程度上的性别偏见。 教师告诉学生，调查中，绝大多数学生希望所有同学都能学会克服偏见。
（二）创造品格教育外在环境与条件，形成对内力的促生作用	外语教育的一个重要功能就在于引导学生学习不同国家、不同民族的文化和语言，亦即：发展学生尽可能降低偏见的意识，是外语教育的重要责任之一。 教师找到一个可以引导学生克服偏见的著名演讲视频，演讲人是非洲年轻女作家 Chimamanda Adichie，她在演讲中介绍了她所遇到的偏见，以及她自己表现出的偏见。 教师向学生播放演讲，让学生感知其内容，然后引导学生阅读理解演讲词，深度理解其内涵。整个演讲大约 12 分钟，将近 3000 词，需要分多个课时完成学习（后附演讲全文）。 演讲词需要具有一定的冲击力，对语句结构的语用要求相对更高。本篇演讲词的语用特点非常明确，可以成为语言学习的材料。

（续表）

（二）创造品格教育外在环境与条件，形成对内力的促进作用	语用知识指在特定语境中准确地理解他人和得体地表达自己的知识。具备一定的语用知识，有助于学生根据交际的目的、交际场合的正式程度、参与人的身份和角色，选择正式或非正式、直接或委婉、口头或书面语等语言形式，得体且恰当地与他人沟通和交流，达到交际的目的。因此，学习和掌握一定的语用知识有利于提升高中学生有效运用英语的能力。 必修阶段，高中学生应掌握的语用知识为： 1. 选择符合交际场合和交际对象身份的语言形式，如正式与非正式语言，表达问候、介绍、告别、感谢等，保持良好的人际关系； 2. 运用得体的语言形式回应对方观点或所表达的意义，进行插话、打断或结束交谈，并在口语交际中有效运用非语言形式，如目光、表情、手势、姿势、动作等身势语； 3. 根据交际具体情境，正确理解他人的态度、情感和观点，运用得体的语言形式，如礼貌、直接或委婉等方式，表达自己的态度、情感和观点。 在教学中我们需要基于以下理解开展语用知识的教学。语言的得体使用必须考虑交际参与者所处的语境。也就是说，语言形式和语体风格会因交际场合的正式程度、行事程序、交际参与人身份的不同而不同。具体而言，语境主要涉及交际的时间、地点、情境、参与人员等环境因素，也涉及参与人的交际目的、交际身份、所处处境及心情等个体因素。 因此，在教学中，教师要增强语用意识，在设计口头和笔头交际活动时，努力创设接近真实世界的交际语境，明确交际场合、参与人的身份及其之间的关系，帮助学生认识到语言形式的选择受到具体交际情境的影响。针对语用知识的教学，教师可以通过讲解、观看视频、模拟实践等方式开展，增强学生对交际场合的正式程度、行事程序以及对交际参与人身份的感知，根据交际场合的正式程度选择正式或非正式的语言表达形式开展交流。同时，教师要注意增强学生对交际对象情感距离的感知，并根据这一知识，判断是否要使用正式或非正式、直接或委婉的表达方式，体现对交际对象应有的尊重和礼貌，确保交际得体有效。例如，教师在布置口语交际任务时，要明确交代交际各方的身份、年龄及其之间的关系，描述交际的场合及交际的主题等，使学生明白要根据交际场合的正式程度，选择得体的礼貌用语和身势语开展交际。此外，教师还需要在教学中有意识地帮助学生学习不同的书面文体，如记叙、说明、新闻、论述等，及其特有的文体结构和语言表达特征。了解和学习这些结构和特征，有利于学生恰当地

（续表）

（二）创造品格教育外在环境与条件，形成对内力的促生作用	使用书面语篇形式进行交流。同时，教师还要帮助学生了解不同文化的价值观和社会习俗，在交际时，避免冒犯对方的文化禁忌，从而有效地实现与他人的沟通与合作。在本演讲中，语句结构的得体性表现得比较突出。演讲者来自非洲的尼日利亚，曾在美国接受教育，此演讲为演讲者面对美国听众而讲。从语句结构上看，本演讲词很有张力，很得体，是学习语句结构的语用特性的较好材料。 　　演讲词学习过程中的品格教育目标为通过阅读演讲词，理解只听片面之词的危险，发展学生在跨文化交往中尽可能减少偏见的跨文化意识与思维能力。 　　学习过程中的任务要求学生面对自己思想意识中的偏见（每个人都存在这样或那样的偏见，因为人类迄今尚无法真正做到"全见"），为自己制定尽可能减少偏见的行动清单。 　　偏见无处不在，在跨文化交往中尤其突出。发展学生尽可能减少偏见的品格和思维能力，是外语教育的责任之一。高一新生中也广泛存在对地域（学生来自不同乡镇、街区）、家庭、成绩等的偏见。

The Danger of a Single Story
By Chimamanda Adichie

　　I'm a storyteller. And I would like to tell you a few personal stories about what I like to call "the danger of the single story." I grew up on a university campus in eastern Nigeria. My mother says that I started reading at the age of two, although I think four is probably close to the truth. So I was an early reader. And what I read were British and American children's books.

　　I was also an early writer. And when I began to write, at about the age of seven, stories in pencil with crayon illustrations that my poor mother was obligated to read, I wrote exactly the kinds of stories I was reading. All my characters were white and blue-eyed. They played in the snow. They ate apples. And they talked a lot about the weather, "How lovely it was that the sun had come out." Now, despite the fact that I lived in Nigeria, I had never been outside Nigeria. We didn't have snow. We ate mangoes. And we never talked about the weather because there was no need to.

My characters also drank a lot of ginger beer because the characters in the British books I read drank ginger beer. Never mind that I had no idea what ginger beer was. And for many years afterwards, I would have a desperate desire to taste ginger beer. But that is another story.

What this demonstrates, I think, is how impressionable and vulnerable we are in the face of a story, particularly as children. Because all I had read were books in which characters were foreign, I had become convinced that books, by their very nature, had to have foreigners in them, and had to be about things with which I could not personally identify. Now, things changed when I discovered African books. There weren't many of them available. And they weren't quite as easy to find as the foreign books.

But because of writers like Chinua Achebe and Camara Laye, I went through a mental shift in my perception of literature. I realized that people like me, girls with skin the color of chocolate, whose kinky hair could not form ponytails, could also exist in literature. I started to write about things I recognized.

Now, I loved those American and British books I read. They stirred my imagination. They opened up new worlds for me. But the unintended consequence was that I did not know that people like me could exist in literature. So what the discovery of African writers did for me was this: It saved me from having a single story of what books are.

I come from a conventional, middle-class Nigerian family. My father was a professor. My mother was an administrator. And so we had, as was the norm, live-in domestic help, who would often come from nearby rural villages. So the year I turned eight we got a new house boy. His name was Fide. The only thing my mother told us about him was that his family was very poor. My mother sent yams and rice, and our old clothes, to his family. And when I didn't finish my dinner, my mother would say, "Finish your food! Don't you know people like Fide's family have nothing?" So I felt enormous pity for Fide's family.

Then one Saturday we went to his village to visit. And his mother showed us a beautifully patterned basket, made of dyed raffia, that his brother had made. I was startled. It had not occurred to me that anybody in his family could actually make something. All I had heard about them is how poor they were, so that it had become impossible for me to see them as anything else but poor. Their poverty was my single story of them.

Years later, I thought about this when I left Nigeria to go to university in the United States. I was 19. My American roommate was shocked by me. She asked where I had learned to speak English so well, and was confused when I said that Nigeria happened to have English as its official language. She asked if she could listen to what she called my "tribal music," and was consequently very disappointed when I produced my tape of Mariah Carey. She assumed that I did not know how to use a stove.

What struck me was this: She had felt sorry for me even before she saw me. Her default position toward me, as an African, was a kind of patronizing, well-meaning, pity. My roommate had a single story of Africa. A single story of catastrophe. In this single story there was no possibility of Africans being similar to her, in any way. No possibility of feelings more complex than pity. No possibility of a connection as human equals.

I must say that before I went to the U.S., I didn't consciously identify as African. But in the U.S. whenever Africa came up, people turned to me. Never mind that I knew nothing about places like Namibia. But I did come to embrace this new identity. And in many ways I think of myself now as African, although I still get quite irritable when Africa is referred to as a country. The most recent example being my otherwise wonderful flight from Lagos two days ago, in which there was an announcement on the Virgin flight about the charity work in "India, Africa and other countries."

So after I had spent some years in the U.S. as an African, I began to understand my roommate's response to me. If I had not grown up in Nigeria, and if all I knew about Africa were from popular images, I too would think that Africa was a place of beautiful landscapes, beautiful animals, and incomprehensible people, fighting senseless wars, dying of poverty and AIDS, unable to speak for themselves, and waiting to be saved, by a kind, white foreigner. I would see Africans in the same way that I, as a child, had seen Fide's family.

This single story of Africa ultimately comes, I think, from Western literature. Now, here is a quote from the writing of a London merchant called John Locke, who sailed to west Africa in 1561, and kept a fascinating account of his voyage. After referring to the black Africans as "beasts who have no houses," he writes, "They are also people without heads, having their mouth and eyes in their breasts."

Now, I've laughed every time I've read this. And one must admire the imagination of John Locke. But what is important about his writing is that it represents the beginning of a tradition of telling African stories in the West. A tradition of Sub-Saharan Africa as a place of negatives, of difference, of darkness, of people who, in the words of the wonderful poet, Rudyard Kipling, are "half devil, half child".

And so I began to realize that my American roommate must have, throughout her life, seen and heard different versions of this single story, as had a professor, who once told me that my novel was not "authentically African." Now, I was quite willing to contend that there were a number of things wrong with the novel, that it had failed in a number of places. But I had not quite imagined that it had failed at achieving something called African authenticity. In fact I did not know what African authenticity was. The professor told me that my characters were too much like him, an educated and middle-class man. My characters drove cars. They were not starving. Therefore they were not authentically African.

But I must quickly add that I too am just as guilty in the question of the single story. A few years ago, I visited Mexico from the U.S. The political climate in the U.S. at the time, was tense. And there were debates going on about immigration. And, as often happens in America, immigration became synonymous with Mexicans. There were endless stories of Mexicans as people who were fleecing the healthcare system, sneaking across the border, being arrested at the border, that sort of thing.

I remember walking around on my first day in Guadalajara, watching the people going to work, rolling up tortillas in the marketplace, smoking, laughing. I remember first feeling slight surprise. And then I was overwhelmed with shame. I realized that I had been so immersed in the media coverage of Mexicans that they had become one thing in my mind, the abject immigrant. I had bought into the single story of Mexicans and I could not have been more ashamed of myself. So that is how to create a single story: show a people as one thing, as only one thing, over and over again, and that is what they become.

It is impossible to talk about the single story without talking about power. There is a word, an Igbo word, that I think about whenever I think about the power structures of the world, and it is "nkali." It's a noun that loosely translates to "to be greater than another." Like our economic and political worlds, stories too are defined by the principle of nkali. How they are told, who tells them, when they're told, how many stories are told, are really dependent on power.

Power is the ability not just to tell the story of another person, but to make it the definitive story of that person. The Palestinian poet Mourid Barghouti writes that if you want to dispossess a people, the simplest way to do it is to tell their story, and to start with, "secondly." Start the story with the arrows of the Native Americans, and not with the arrival of the British, and you have an entirely different story. Start the story with the failure of the

African state, and not with the colonial creation of the African state, and you have an entirely different story.

I recently spoke at a university where a student told me that it was such a shame that Nigerian men were physical abusers like the father character in my novel. I told him that I had just read a novel called *American Psycho* – and that it was such a shame that young Americans were serial murderers. Now, obviously I said this in a fit of mild irritation.

But it would never have occurred to me to think that just because I had read a novel in which a character was a serial killer that he was somehow representative of all Americans. And now, this is not because I am a better person than that student, but because of America's cultural and economic power, I had many stories of America. I had read Tyler and Updike and Steinbeck and Gaitskill. I did not have a single story of America.

When I learned, some years ago, that writers were expected to have had really unhappy childhoods to be successful, I began to think about how I could invent horrible things my parents had done to me. But the truth is that I had a very happy childhood, full of laughter and love, in a very close-knit family.

But I also had grandfathers who died in refugee camps. My cousin Polle died because he could not get adequate healthcare. One of my closest friends, Okoloma, died in a plane crash because our firetrucks did not have water. I grew up under repressive military governments that devalued education, so that sometimes my parents were not paid their salaries. And so, as a child, I saw jam disappear from the breakfast table. Then margarine disappeared. Then bread became too expensive. Then milk became rationed. And most of all, a kind of normalized political fear invaded our lives.

All of these stories make me who I am. But to insist on only these negative stories is to flatten my experience, and to overlook the many other stories that formed me. The single story creates stereotypes. And the problem with stereotypes is not that they are untrue, but that they are incomplete. They make one story become the only story.

Of course, Africa is a continent full of catastrophes. There are immense ones, such as the horrific rapes in Congo. And depressing ones, such as the fact that 5,000 people apply for one job vacancy in Nigeria. But there are other stories that are not about catastrophe. And it is very important, it is just as important, to talk about them.

I've always felt that it is impossible to engage properly with a place or a person without engaging with all of the stories of that place and that person. The consequence of the single story is this: It robs people of dignity. It makes our recognition of our equal humanity difficult. It emphasizes how we are different rather than how we are similar.

So what if before my Mexican trip I had followed the immigration debate from both sides, the U.S. and the Mexican? What if my mother had told us that Fide's family was poor and hardworking? What if we had an African television network that broadcast diverse African stories all over the world, what the Nigerian writer Chinua Achebe calls "a balance of stories?" What if my roommate knew about my Nigerian publisher, Mukta Bakaray, a remarkable man who left his job in a bank to follow his dream and start a publishing house? Now, the conventional wisdom was that Nigerians don't read literature. He disagreed. He felt that people who could read, would read, if you made literature affordable and available to them.

Shortly after he published my first novel I went to a TV station in Lagos to do an interview. And a woman who worked there as a messenger came up to me and said, "I really liked your novel. I didn't like the ending. Now you must write a sequel, and this is what will happen ..." And she went on to tell me what to write in the sequel. Now I was not only charmed, I was very moved. Here was a woman, part of the ordinary masses of Nigerians, who were not supposed to be readers. She had not only read the book, but she had taken ownership of it and felt justified in telling me what to write in the sequel.

Now, what if my roommate knew about my friend Fumi Onda, a fearless woman who hosts a TV show in Lagos, and is determined to tell the stories that we prefer to forget? What if my roommate knew about the heart procedure that was performed in the Lagos hospital last week? What if my roommate knew about contemporary Nigerian music? Talented people singing in English and Pidgin, and Igbo and Yoruba and Ijo, mixing influences from Jay-Z to Fela to Bob Marley to their grandfathers. What if my roommate knew about the female lawyer who recently went to court in Nigeria to challenge a ridiculous law that required women to get their husband's consent before renewing their passports? What if my roommate knew about Nollywood, full of innovative people making films despite great technical odds? Films so popular that they really are the best example of Nigerians consuming what they produce. What if my roommate knew about my wonderfully ambitious hair braider, who has just started her own business selling hair extensions? Or about the millions of other Nigerians who start businesses and sometimes fail, but continue to nurse ambition?

Every time I am home I am confronted with the usual sources of irritation for most Nigerians: our failed infrastructure, our failed government. But also by the incredible resilience of people who thrive despite the government, rather than because of it. I teach writing workshops in Lagos every summer. And it is amazing to me how many people apply, how many people are eager to write, to tell stories.

My Nigerian publisher and I have just started a non-profit called Farafina Trust. And we have big dreams of building libraries and refurbishing libraries that already exist, and providing books for state schools that don't have anything in their libraries, and also of organizing lots and lots of workshops, in reading and writing, for all the people who are eager to tell our many stories. Stories matter. Many stories matter. Stories have been used to dispossess and to malign. But stories can also be used to empower, and to humanize. Stories can break the dignity of a people. But stories can also repair that broken dignity.

The American writer Alice Walker wrote this about her southern relatives who had moved to the north. She introduced them to a book about the southern life that they had left behind. "They sat around, reading the book themselves, listening to me read the book, and a kind of paradise was regained." I would like to end with this thought that when we reject the single story, when we realize that there is never a single story about any place, we regain a kind of paradise. Thank you.

（续表 2-8）

（三）引导学生理解品格内涵、体验品格教育情境	让学生阅读课文演讲词，在阅读过程中，引导学生回答语言理解与内容理解问题。 语言理解问题： 1. What is the "danger"? [The danger of partiality (the single story)]. 2. Where is Nigeria? What do you know about Nigeria? [In Africa. ...]（可以让学生上网获取相关信息，然后分享；也可以让学生课前准备，此时介绍。） 3. What does "my poor mother was obligated to read" mean here? [My mother had to read them because I forced her to do so.] 4. What does "all my characters" mean here? [All the people in the stories she wrote at that age.] 5. What does "a desperate desire" mean here? [A hopeless want.] 6. Who/What made her "become convinced"? [The books she read.] 7. What does "girls with skin the color of chocolate" mean here? [Girls with dark skin.] 8. What does "stir my imagination" mean here? [Make me imagine.] 语句结构的语用理解问题： 1. I tell stories. [*I'm a storyteller* gives stronger support to the purpose of the talk, because it is about the qualification and status of the author, not about action.]

（续表）

| （三）引导学生理解品格内涵、体验品格教育情境 | 2. And I would like to tell you a few personal stories about "the danger of the single story". ["*And I would like to tell you a few personal stories about what I like to call 'the danger of the single story'*" gives stronger support to the purpose of the talk, because it clearly states that "the danger of the single story" is her personal finding.]

3. So I started to read early. ["*So I was an early reade*" gives stronger support to the purpose of the talk, because it describes that she could read at her early age and often read then. "*So I started to read early*" does not have the meaning that she often read at that age.]

4. And I began to write stories in pencil with crayon illustrations at about the age of seven. My poor mother was obligated to read my stories. I wrote exactly the kinds of stories of my reading. ["*And when I began to write, at about the age of seven, stories in pencil with crayon illustrations that my poor mother was obligated to read, I wrote exactly the kinds of stories I was reading*" gives stronger support to the purpose of the talk, because the clauses show that the author has good abilities of using English in writing and speaking which implies that she is well-educated.]

5. All my characters who were white and blue-eyed played in the snow and ate apples. ["*All my characters were white and blue-eyed. They played in the snow. They ate apples.*" gives stronger support to the purpose of the talk, because it means that all the characters played in the snow and ate apples, but the sentence 'All my characters who were white and blue-eyed played in the snow and ate apples.' implies that there are some characters who are nor white or blue-eyed. And the short sentences "*They played in the snow. They ate apples.*" are powerful in such a passage in which most sentences are compound sentence (sentences with clauses).]

6. And we never talked about the weather. There was no need to. ["*And we never talked about the weather, because there was no need to.*" gives stronger support to the purpose of the talk, because it is powerful to use a compound sentence after three simple sentences "*I had never been outside Nigeria. We didn't have snow. We ate mangoes.*" |

（续表）

（三）引导学生理解品格内涵、体验品格教育情境	7. I had no idea what ginger beer was. Never mind. ["*Never mind that I had no idea what ginger beer was*" gives stronger support to the purpose of the talk, because "Never mind that I had no idea what ginger beer was" means "*although I had no idea what ginger beer was.*" But "*I had no idea what ginger beer was. Never mind.*" means that I had no idea what ginger beer was. Please don't mind this.] 8. This demonstrates the following. We are very impressionable and vulnerable in the face of a story, particularly as children. ["*What this demonstrates, I think, is how impressionable and vulnerable we are in the face of a story, particularly as children.*" gives stronger support to the purpose of the talk, because it makes the beginning of the sentence more focused and attractive.] 9. Now, things changed. I discovered African books at that time. ["*Now, things changed when I discovered African books.*" gives stronger support to the purpose of the talk, because it makes the time clearer and more accurate. 10. I realized the following. People like me could also exist in literature. I am a girl with skin the color of chocolate. My kinky hair could not form ponytails. ["*I realized that people like me, girls with skin the color of chocolate, whose kinky hair could not form ponytails, could also exist in literature.*" gives stronger support to the purpose of the talk, because "*I realized that*" could get audience more focused on the following information, and the attributive clause can make the sentence more of literature.] 11. So what the discovery of African writers did for me was that it saved me from having a single story of what books are. ["*So what the discovery of African writers did for me was this: It saved me from having a single story of what books are.*" gives stronger support to the purpose of the talk, because it makes a longer pause in the middle of the sentence and "*this*" can make it stressed so that the audience may focus more on the following: ① What is the purpose of this talk? (To persuade the audience to believe that the single story is dangerous.) ② How did she support her purpose? (To use some stories which show the danger of the single story.)

（续表）

（三）引导学生理解品格内涵、体验品格教育情境	③ What kind of English, educated or casual, can make the audience believe her stories more? and Why? (Educated English, because education can guarantee that her findings and analysis are more academic so that they are more trustworthy.) ④ What are the basic standards of educated English? (More compound sentences for clearer and more accurate information with some simple but powerful sentences for balance.) ⑤ What are the features of the sentences in the talk? How do they give strong support to the purpose of the talk? (There are more compound sentences than simple sentences. There are more sentences with action verbs than those with nouns of status. The compound and simple sentences are properly intersected. It makes the talk powerful. The quality and status descriptive sentences are seldom but properly used. This makes the talk full of the feature of literature.)] 同时，让学生阅读有关 impartiality 的文献，如：The Concept of Impartiality，形成对这一问题的理论性认识。然后阅读 Impartiality in Journalism，让学生形成对克服偏见的方法的认识。

The Concept of Impartiality

It is all too easy to assume that the word "impartiality" must denote a positive, unitary concept – presumably a concept closely linked with, if not identical to, morality. This, however, is simply not the case. Rather, there are various sorts of behavior that may be described as "impartial", and some of these obviously have little or nothing to do with morality. A person who chooses an accountant on the basis of her friends' recommendations may be entirely impartial between the various candidates (members of the pool of local accountants) with respect to their gender, their age, or where they went to school. Yet if her choice is motivated solely by rational self-interested considerations then it is clear that the impartiality she manifests is in no way a form of moral impartiality. To take a more extreme case, consider an insane serial killer who chooses his victims on the basis of their resemblance to that of some celebrity. The killer may be impartial with respect to his victims' occupations, religious beliefs, and so forth, but it would be absurd to regard this as a form of moral impartiality.

It is also worth noting that some types of impartiality may in themselves be immoral or morally questionable. Suppose that I decide to pass along a treasured family heirloom to one of my two sons, Bill and Phil. Flipping a coin would constitute one type of impartial procedure for choosing between the two. But suppose that I have already promised the heirloom to Phil on several occasions. In this case it would be quite wrong to allow a coin toss to determine whether he gets it. Deciding by means of a coin toss would be an impartial procedure, but it would be the wrong sort of impartiality here, for it would ignore the moral obligation created by my previous promises.

The word "impartiality", then, picks out a broad concept that need not have anything to do with morality. In this broad sense, impartiality is probably best characterized in a negative rather than positive manner: an impartial choice is simply one in which a certain sort of consideration (i.e. some property of the individuals being chosen between) has no influence. An analysis along these lines has been proposed by Bernard Gert, who holds that "A is impartial in respect R with regard to group G if and only if A's actions in respect R are not influenced at all by which member(s) of G benefit or are harmed by these actions" (Gert, 1995). Thus, for Gert, impartiality is a property of a set of decisions made by a particular agent, directed toward a particular group.

Gert's analysis captures the important fact that one cannot simply ask of a given agent whether or not she is impartial. Rather, we must also specify with regard to whom she is impartial, and in what respect. Gert's analysis, then, permits and indeed requires that we make fairly fine-grained distinctions between various sorts of impartiality. This is necessary, since one and the same agent might manifest various sorts of partiality and impartiality towards various groups of persons. Consider, for instance, a university professor who is also a mother of five children, and who is currently acting as a member of a hiring committee. Such an agent might be impartial between her children with respect to the care they receive (while preferring her own children over others in this respect), and also impartial between the various job candidates; but it is clear that these two uses of the word 'impartial' denote very different practices. In particular, the idea of merit applies in one case but not the other: to be impartial between job candidates is presumably to select between them on the basis of merit, whereas to be impartial between one's children is not to think of merit at all, but rather to provide equal protection and care to all.

Many attempts to characterize impartiality fail to respect the distinction between the broadest, most formalistic sense of the notion, and a more specifically moral impartiality. To say, for instance, that an impartial choice is one that is free of bias or prejudice is to presuppose that we are dealing with a certain sort of impartiality, that which is required or recommended by morality, or at least worthy of moral approbation. 'Bias' and 'prejudice' are loaded terms, suggesting not only that some consideration is being excluded, but also that the exclusion is appropriate and warranted. Similarly, the idea that impartiality requires that we give equal and/or adequate consideration to the interests of all concerned parties goes well beyond the requirements of the merely formal notion. (In the coin toss case, it is quite clear that Phil's claims to the heirloom are not being given equal or adequate consideration.) As a characterization of moral impartiality, however, this suggestion is perhaps more promising, at least in some contexts.

Impartiality in Journalism
By David Brewer

What it means to be impartial?

Being impartial means not being prejudiced towards or against any particular side. All journalists have their own views, and yet, to deliver comprehensive and authoritative coverage of news and current affairs, they must rise above their own personal perspectives. Only by reflecting the diversity of opinion fairly and accurately can we hope to offer a true picture of what is really happening.

Impartiality in news

News is about delivering facts that have been tested, sourced, attributed and proven. Impartiality is essential for robust news coverage. It's not about being soft and bland. It's about stripping out the personal, and allowing the audience the dignity of drawing their own conclusions free from any thought pollution injected by the journalist. It means we must strive to:

reflect a wide range of opinions;

explore conflicting views;

ensure that no relevant perspective is ignored;

avoid any personal preferences over subject matter or choice of interviewees;

be honest and open about any personal interests/history.

Editorial freedom

In terms of editorial freedom, journalists should be free to:

cover any subject if there are good editorial reasons for doing so;

report on a specific aspect of an issue;

provide an opportunity for a single view to be expressed;

cover stories that might offend part of the audience.

When we invite people such as academics, industry experts and social support workers to comment on issues, we need to take into account that they may have their own agendas for cooperating with us. They will probably not be offering an impartial perspective. They are the voices who can help us include multiple perspectives.

The choice of who we invite to contribute to our journalism is important. Here we must be fair. Ideally, we should try to find time to include all perspectives, but that may not be realistic.

We will need to choose who we talk to. And it may not be possible to offer equal time for all views. Again, we need to make choices. But with all these challenges we need to be true to ourselves, our colleagues, our editor and, most importantly, our audience in order to demonstrate that we have been fair and that we have not ignored any significant voices.

We might know someone involved in the story. It could be a friend or a relative. We might have covered a similar story before, and there might be some historical issues that we are aware of that could compromise our ability to report accurately and fairly. In all cases we need to share these with our senior editorial team.

Sometimes we may not be able to see the possible conflict of interests or areas that could lead to accusations that we have not been open and impartial. It's always best to talk these things through with senior colleagues. Keeping quiet is not an option and certainly never the solution.

Editorial discussions with colleagues will help formulate this policy case by case. A journalist should not struggle alone.

Controversial subjects might cover politics, religion, sexual practices, human relationships and financial dealings. In all cases, we must ensure that a wide range of views and perspectives are aired.

Opinion and fact

We also need to ensure that opinion is clearly distinguished from fact. We might also need to ensure that some views are reflected in our output, even if we find some repulsive. We have a duty to inform the public debate regardless of our own personal points of view and preferences.

When our own media organisation becomes the story, perhaps bad financial news, a sacking, a drugs scandal, poor ratings, etc, we need to ensure that we are prepared to report on news affecting us as we would on news affecting others.

Sometimes journalists talk about offering 'balanced' reporting.

That is not realistic. Life is not balanced and nor is the journalism that reports on life.

It might be that a story is so one-sided that to try to offer so-called 'balance' makes a mockery of the report. In such cases, we should aim to offer other perspectives later in the programme or in a later bulletin. We can ensure we offer all sides in our online coverage.

Personal views offering one side of a story can often add fresh public understanding of an issue and encourage debate. These can include the views of victims and those who feel that they, or others, have been wronged. Such personal views can be highly partial. In such cases, it is important we make it clear to the audience that the views being expressed offer one side only.

Alternative points of view

It is our responsibility to find alternative points of view within the same programme strand or within the next bulletin. In all cases we must:

retain a respect for factual accuracy;

fairly represent opposing points of view except when inappropriate, defamatory or incendiary;

provide an opportunity to reply;

ensure that a sufficiently broad range of views and perspectives is included;

ensure that these are broadcast in similar output, measure and time of day.

With online debates we need to protect the audience from being led to believe that the views being discussed are endorsed by our media organisation. To do so we must:

not endorse or support any personal views or campaigns;

make a clear distinction between our content and that created by the audience;

make clear what resources we are providing.

（续表 2-8）

（四）实现品格教育	在这一阶段，让学生就本班，尤其是自身存在的偏见展开讨论、分析，列出克服偏见行为的清单，以此约束自己的行为，并请全班同学进行监督，以此实现自己品格的发展。

这一案例说明，高中英语课程促进学生品格教育不仅是课程标准的本质要求，也是英语课程实践不可或缺的内涵与目标，在学习理解、应用实践、迁移创新的学习过程中发展学生的品格，具有可操作性。对于这一方法每一环节的实践，本书第五、六章将展开讨论和分析。

本章小结

高中英语课程对于文化意识发展有两大要求：中外文化理解与传播能力发展和品格教育。为实现英语课程文化意识发展目标，本章提供了基本方法。

发展中外优秀文化的理解与传播能力，其基本方法包括三个环节：形成认知与传播中外文化的动机；基于语言学习，认知、分析、理解、比较中外文化；运用英语传播中外优秀文化。

发展学生优秀品格，其基本方法则由四个环节组成：把握学生品格教育内力呈现形态与时机；通过语言材料学习活动，创造品格教育外在环境与条件，形成对内力的促进作用；引导学生在语言学习活动中，理解品格内涵、体验品格教育情境。实现品格教育基本方法的实践需要更加具有操作性的分析，将在随后章节进一步讨论。

推荐阅读材料

Gilness, Jane. 2003. How to Integrate Character Education into the Curriculum

[J]. *Phi Delta Kappan*, 85(3) 243–245

The Jubilee Centre for Characters and Values. 2014. Framework for Character Education in Schools [R]. Birmingham: University of Birmingham.

Bialik, M., Bogan, M., Fadel, C., et al. 2015. Character Education for the 21st Century [Z]. Boston: Center for Curriculum Redesign.

王华容，蒋波 . 2006. 课堂教学中的品格教育——以人为本的心理学思考 [J]. 教育科学研究 . (2)：50–53

郑富兴 . 2001. 德育情境的建构 [J]. 比较教育研究 . (4)：29–35

第三章　高中英语中外文化理解能力发展实践

第一节　高中英语中外文化理解能力发展设计原则

理解中外文化属于跨文化教育中的跨文化理解。基于跨文化理解的研究，结合高中英语课程标准与内容可知，通过高中英语课程促进学生理解中外文化的基本原则主要有以下四项：

1. 最近发展区原则

最近发展区原则是有效教学的基本原则，低于或高于最近发展区，则会导致学习目标、内容、活动、方法难度太低或太高，学生可能不感兴趣，或者"吃不饱"，或者不能"消化"，从而难以达到学习目标，浪费学习时间、精力等，导致教育低效、无效，甚至负效。因此，用于发展学生中外文化理解能力的中外文化内容、理解方法与发展理解能力的方法，作为发展目标的中外文化理解能力，均应在学生认知水平、语言能力、文化积累等所形成的理解中外文化的最近发展区之内。

一种主流高中英语教材中有"牛郎织女"一课，对于高中一年级学生来说，内容过于简单，远远低于学生最近发展区，学生学习中对阅读内容根本不感兴趣，反倒是对牛郎偷看织女、拿走织女衣服是否道德，有着激烈的讨论。显然，教师不能只是要求学生理解故事本身，而是需要引导学生对中国文化中为什么有这样的故事和这样的节日，这一节日属于什么类型、表达什么价值取向等，进行更有深度的理解，方才可以进入到学生对中国文化理解的最近发展区。

一篇高一课文中引用了 *Hamlet* 中的下面这段对话，作为对于 treat others as you want to be treated 的例证：

> Hamlet: Good my lord, will you see the players well rewarded? Do you
> hear, let them be used, for they are the abstract and brief
> chronicles of the time; after your death you were better have a
> bad epitaph than their ill report while you live.

Polonius: My lord, I will use them according to their characters and merits.

Hamlet: For God's sake, man, you are clever. Treat every man after his character and merits, and you shall escape whipping. Why not treat them after your own honour and dignity? The less they deserve, the more merit is in your bounty. Take them in.

教学中发现，这一观点的文化理解，对于学生来说具有较大难度，尤其是对 treat others after your own honour and dignity 而不是 after his character and merits 时，发现我国学生理解难度较大。显然，这段对话的观念与话语逻辑超出了学生的最近发展区。教师需要给学生搭建更为紧密的"支架"，才能促进学生对这段对话蕴藏的文化内涵有基本的理解。

上述二例说明，发展学生理解中外文化的能力应基于学生最近发展区进行。若内容、活动或方法低于最近发展区，则需要增加内容、活动或方法的难度，以适应学生的发展；若内容、活动或方法高于最近发展区，则需要增加相应的"支架"，以适应学生的发展。无论是增加难度，还是增加"支架"，都是不得已而为之。我们应首先选择在学生最近发展区之内的以发展学生中外文化理解能力的内容、活动、方法，在不得已选择低于或高于最近发展区的内容、活动、方法时，才采取适当的调整方法。

2. 聚合与分散有机结合原则

在高中英语课程中，有不少单元的内容本身就是中外文化，如 Festivals Around the World, History of Cambridge, Tang Poems, Nelson Mandela, Mystery of the Stonehenge 等等。这些部分的教学，本身就是在开展中外文化理解活动，丰富学生中外文化知识，发展学生理解中外文化的能力。

但是，这种单元的教学往往由于过度集中于文化理解教学，理解强度较大，重复进行同一话题也需要较多注意力，导致难以进行多个单元连续发展中外文化理解能力的教学，因此需要不同话题的单元交替进行。尽管不一定是逐一单元交替，但最起码需要在一个阶段之内进行必要的主题交替。这就是高中英语课程促进学生中外文化理解能力发展的聚合与分散有机结合的原则。

这一原则不仅表现在不同单元之间，还表现在一个单元、一节课或一项活动之内。一个单元多个课时，不同课时之间要进行聚合与分散的有机结合，一节课或一项活动之内的不同环节、不同时间，也应该遵循聚合与分散有机结合的原则。

3. 课堂与生活中随机进行原则

文化理解需要条件，甚至需要机缘。在条件成熟、机缘符合之时，促进学生理解中外文化，可以事半功倍；反之，则事倍功半。在冬天之时让学生理解 If winter comes, can spring be far behind? 肯定比在夏天进行教学时条件更为合适。

在进行"Keep it up, Xie Lei"这个单元的教学中，对于课文中出现的外国教师给中国学生的论文打低分一事，有学生提出这可能是一种跨文化歧视，然后有多名学生附和这一观点。这是课堂生成出来的文化理解时机，而非教师所能预设的。教师应抓住时机，让学生讨论如何理解与判断西方人对中国人的歧视，形成分析与判断的标准，然后再让学生讨论谢蕾的老师给谢蕾打低分是否属于西方人歧视中国人的文化现象，学生最后得出结论：课文所给的材料不能说明谢蕾的英国老师对谢蕾存在文化歧视。

这种发展学生理解中外文化能力的时机在课堂上广泛存在，而且一旦抓住，则教学成效十分显著，但这种时机也总是稍纵即逝。抓住这种时机需要教师有敏锐的判断力、丰富的知识与能力储备、充满机智和耐心的课堂组织能力和师生交往能力。

发展学生中外文化理解能力，不仅可以在课堂上随机进行，也可以在生活中随机进行，如在某部西方电影在我国上映之际，可以组织学生就此电影的文化内涵、背景、情节、人物性格、语言、画面、音乐等展开讨论，并与中国文化相关内容进行比较、分析，发展学生的中外文化理解能力。

4．指向品格原则

根据《普通高中英语课程标准（2017年版）》对文化意识素养的要求，中外文化理解与传播能力应该是品格教育能力的基础，理解过程中应该把握品格，或者说是对中外文化中的品格的理解，尤其是从跨文化的视角把握品格，使英语课程的品格内涵不同于其他课程的品格内涵，成为英语学科育人与其他学科育人不同的学科特性。

高中英语课程的中外文化理解与传播能力应该具有显著的品格指向，比如在诸多中外作品中，很多作品都涉及诚实、勇敢等积极品格，这些都是理解中外文化中可以发现的人类共有的品格，即使是单词学习，也可以关注单词记忆中的意志力发展，培养坚毅学习的品格，这里的意志力、坚毅品格不直接来自中外文化，但来自英语课程对中外文化理解与传播的学习。

以"Nelson Mandela"课文为例，这一课文首先要求我们理解非洲文化、欧美殖民主义文化，然后在文化理解的基础上，尤其是在理解曼德拉所表现出的胜利者对失败者宽容的这一态度上，发展学生的领导力和宽容的品格。

再以"Festivals Around the World"课文为例，这一课文首先要求我们理解世界各地的节日文化特性，尤其是节日文化的共性，如Harvest Festival就是人类共有的庆祝活动，只是庆祝形式不同而已。然后，基于这一理解，我们则需要发展学生从本质上理解人类文化差异表象，尊重和理解人类文化差异的品格。

显然，中外文化理解是指向学生文化意识发展这一根本目的的。

第二节　高中英语中外文化理解能力发展具体方法

一、高中英语课程中外文化理解能力构成

在高中英语课程中，发展学生的中外文化理解能力需要首先把握中外文化内涵分析理解能力的基本框架，基于这一框架，方可开展相应的

能力发展活动，方可发展对英语课程呈现的中外文化内涵的理解能力。

基于跨文化研究可知，英语课程的文化内涵分析理解框架的基本形态首先应该是语言维度的理解，在语言之外还有其他理解维度。基于此，我们认为，高中英语课程中外文化理解能力的基本框架应如下：

中外文化内涵分析理解能力
{
语言维度的文化内涵分析理解能力
{
语音维度的文化内涵分析理解能力
语词维度的文化内涵分析理解能力
语句维度的文化内涵分析理解能力
语篇维度的文化内涵分析理解能力
}

其他维度的文化内涵分析理解能力
{
历史社会维度的文化内涵分析理解能力
文学艺术维度的文化内涵分析理解能力
政治经济维度的文化内涵分析理解能力
医疗军事维度的文化内涵分析理解能力
科学技术维度的文化内涵分析理解能力
}
}

这一框架的每一能力要素均有其复杂内涵，不过在高中英语课程中，我们并不需要发展这些能力中的全部，而只需要基于高中英语课程，发展相应的能力。

以语音维度的文化内涵分析理解能力为例。我们首先需要清晰把握高中英语课程标准对语音发展的能力要求，即：发展学生根据重音、语调、节奏等的变化，感知说话人的意图和态度的能力；借助重音、语调、节奏等的变化，表达意义、意图和态度等的能力；运用重音、语调、节奏等比较连贯和清晰地表达意义、意图和态度等的能力；运用恰当的重音、语调、节奏等有效地表达意义、意图和态度等的能力；发现并欣赏英语诗歌、韵文等文学形式中语言的节奏和韵律的能力；根据节奏和韵律创作英文诗歌；与不同地域的人进行交流时，可以识别出其发音和语调的不同的能力。然后，我们需要理解把握这些能力要求相关内容的文化内涵，即：重音、语调、节奏及其变化的文化内涵，所表达意义、意图、态度等的文化内涵，英语诗歌与韵文等的节奏与韵律的文化内涵，不同地域的人的语音、语调的文化内涵等。这其中每一项均需要深度理解，方可准确把握其文化内涵。

对于这一框架中每一能力的内涵此处限于篇幅无法展开，我们可以阅读相关的专业书籍，获取相关的信息，发展相关的能力。

基于这一能力结构，我们可知基于此框架分析获取相应的中外文化的内涵，其文化内涵构成与此能力框架结构完全对应，即：

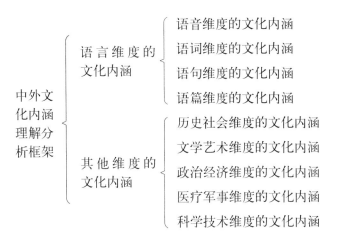

基于前述分析能力框架，采用这一文化内涵构成，我们即可形成对中外文化的理解。以《卖花女》（Pygmalion）为例，我们可以基于以上分析框架分析发现其以下文化内涵(限于篇幅，此处只能展示部分案例，不能全面分析该单元全部文化内涵)：

表 3-1　文化内涵理解分析案例

《卖花女》（Pygmalion）中的文化内涵理解分析		
语言维度的文化内涵	语音维度的文化内涵	Eliza 口音的社会阶层、地域特性所呈现出的语音的阶级性、地域性，以及 Higgins 所代表的对劳动者阶层的口音的歧视及其本质上的阶级性歧视。
	语词维度的文化内涵	Higgins 与 Pickering 的 bet 的英国文化特性(《百万英镑》中也有一个 bet，其实 bet 在英国日常生活文化中普遍存在)。

（续表）

《卖花女》（*Pygmalion*）中的文化内涵理解分析		
语言维度的文化内涵	语句维度的文化内涵	在话剧结束时，Eliza 与 Higgins 就 bet 发生争执， LIZA: *breathless* … I've won your bet for you, haven't I? That's enough for you. I don't matter, I suppose. HIGGINS: You won my bet! You! Presumptuous insect! I won it. 这里对同一事件两人使用的时态完全不同，Eliza 使用完成时，是强调过去事件对现在的影响，而 Higgins 刻意不继续使用 Eliza 的完成时，有意识地破坏语用中的合作原则，是因为他不想突出这一事件对现在的影响，而刻意突出这只是过去的事件。这一文化现象在中文表达中存在一定困难，这一段在《萧伯纳戏剧选》中的中文翻译版本是这样： 莉莎：[上气不接下气]……你打的赌我给你打赢了，对不对？这对你就足够了。我是无关紧要的，我想。 悉金斯：你给我打赢了！你！狂妄的毛毛虫！是我自己打赢的。 显然，这里的翻译"我给你打赢了"和"你给我打赢了"，更说明英文原文的语句结构特性的文化内涵，以及由此可以发现的英文语句结构，尤其是时态特性的文化内涵。
	语篇维度的文化内涵	话剧整体的语篇结构特性、冲突，尤其是结束之时 Eliza 的出走，都是非常典型的英语话剧冲突，是英国文学的经典结构形式与冲突表现形式。
其他维度的文化内涵	历史社会维度的文化内涵	这一话剧的时代背景、英国的语音歧视现象以及相关的阶级与地域歧视现象，及这些现象在中国同样存在。
	文学艺术维度的文化内涵	作者萧伯纳是获得诺贝尔文学奖的作家，其作品具有非常显著的代表性和影响力，其中话剧更是其文学作品的代表，这部话剧改编成为电影后影响力巨大。
	政治经济维度的文化内涵	这部话剧所表达的阶级性、女性独立、社会改造思想、结尾中的商业思想等等，都是萧伯纳及其所在时代的重要政治与经济思想。

《卖花女》（*Pygmalion*）中的文化内涵理解分析		
其他维度的文化内涵	医疗军事维度的文化内涵	这部话剧中 Colonel Pickering 的身份（上校、英国驻印度殖民地军官）具有显著的军事文化的特性，而且萧伯纳对其形象的描述，以及 Pickering 对 Eliza 像女儿一般的爱，都具有丰富的文化内涵。
	科学技术维度的文化内涵	这部话剧强调了语音的科学研究成果，正如 Higgins 在第一幕结束前对 Pickering 所作的解释：Simply phonetics. The science of speech. That's my profession; also my hobby. Happy is the man who can make a living by his hobby! You can spot an Irishman or a Yorkshireman by his brogue. I can place any man within six miles. I can place him within two miles in London. Sometimes within two streets. 这显然是语言科学，尤其是语音学发展的文化特性。

显然，这一文化内涵构成说明，前述高中英语课程的中外文化理解能力架构符合而且能满足高中英语课程教学需要，促进学生中外文化理解能力发展。

二、跨文化理解所需的跨文化态度

基于鲁子问在《中小学英语跨文化教育理论与实践》中所介绍的他的研究，我们知道，人类的跨文化实践告诉我们，各种积极的跨文化态度，如开放、平等、尊重、宽容、客观、谨慎等，有利于促进跨文化理解，形成积极的跨文化交往。因此，跨文化教育的态度目标就是培养开放、平等、尊重、宽容、客观、谨慎等积极的跨文化态度，消解故步自封、妄自尊大、妄自菲薄、歧视、偏见、狭隘、盲动等消极的跨文化态度。

1. 开放

开放即敞开，是双向的敞开，既包括主动走出去，也欢迎走进来。开放性是人类社会实践的要求，是人的本质特性，人的生存需要，也是人类历史发展的必然。

开放是向一切其他民族文化敞开文化胸襟，学习其他民族文化的优秀元素，并以一切其他民族文化为镜鉴来观知、认识本民族文化自身，对其他民族文化不妄加排拒，不封闭守成，不锁国自固。

开放的跨文化态度是人类生存的条件，因为人类历史表明，没有任何人类群体可以在完全与其他文化群体隔绝的情形下良性地发展，人类所有文化群体都不可规避地接受其他文化群体的文化元素。

在当前这个世界上不同文化广泛接触的时代，对其他民族文化的开放就是对世界的开放，而且，对世界的开放为每一个人类群体的生存发展提供了广泛的选择空间。开放是对文化多样性的认同与承诺。当然，开放不是无原则、无基准的，其基准就是人类文化的和谐发展与人类不同民族的文化更和谐地发展。

2．平等

"平等是人在实践领域中对自身的意识，也就是人意识到别人是和自己平等的人，人把别人当作和自己平等的人来对待。"（马克思、恩格斯，1957）

在文化意义上，平等是指一切人类文化群体在本质上无尊卑贵贱、高低上下之别，是本质尊严上的平等。

尽管人类不同群体的文化有着不同形态与特征，不同文化有着不同的历史与成就，但任何文化都是人类某一群体的生存方式，人类不同群体在人格本质上的平等诉求规定了人类不同群体文化在本质上的平等诉求。平等是文化多样性存在与发展的社会伦理基础，平等是文化之间和平共存的价值基础，平等是尊重其他民族文化的前提，文化平等是这个多文化的星球可持续存在的基础。

在跨文化交往中，平等是走向世界性交往的伦理前提。缺乏平等的态度就会滋生各种形态的文化沙文主义。因此，平等应是双向、多向的平等，是所有文化之间的平等。若平等地对待其他民族文化却不能够获得其他民族文化平等地对待本民族文化，这样的单向平等则可能导致很多的跨文化冲突。基于平等态度的跨文化理解，可以使我们以尊重的态度理解外在文化与本民族文化不同之处，也可以基于自信的态度从不同文化之间的共性理解外在文化。

3．尊重

对其他文化的尊重是联合国教科文组织长期倡导的一种跨文化态度，因为这是和谐的跨文化交往的基础。

对文化的尊重，首先是对呈现这一文化的人的尊重，对这些人的生命的尊重，然后是对这些人所呈现的文化的尊重，因为人的生命存在是人的文化存在的最基本形态。

尊重是对其他民族文化给予充分的注重，并尊重其他民族文化的生存方式，特别是与本民族文化有巨大差异的民族文化。

尊重特别强调对于那些与本民族文化有较大差异，甚至截然相反的文化也应持有尊重的心态，因为，尊重其他文化是人类更自在地生存发展所必需的心态要素。

尊重就是不歧视，就是对于任何其他民族文化，特别是那些与本民族文化截然相反的文化，不因任何原因（民族、种族、地域、肤色、宗教、服饰、饮食、婚葬风俗等）而歧视。对其他民族的歧视很多都有着深刻的传统心理因素，当然也有政治、经济、社会、宗教因素。应该说，前一种歧视比后一种歧视更难消解。

尊重就是承认各民族文化自身的价值，特别是对于那些社会发展阶段还比较落后的其他民族的文化，尤其应该尊重，尊重其文化自身的价值，尊重文化的多样性，而不以社会发展形态来否定文化的价值，更不是以经济发展形态来否定文化的价值。

尊重其他民族文化有利于避免因为文化差异而导致的文化歧视，任何理由的不尊重都可能导致跨文化冲突。尊重使人见异不怪，特别是若其他民族倡导那些与本民族文化截然相反的文化形态之时，跨文化的尊重则显得非常重要。如汉族文化倡导死者入土为安、反对暴尸荒野，而有的民族、宗教则倡导天葬、火葬。显然，只有尊重一切其他民族文化，才能理解这些不同的丧葬文化形态。

我国当前的跨文化教育主要在传授跨文化知识，对跨文化态度的教育仍需更加系统、深入，对如何引导学生形成开放、尊重、宽容、无偏见等积极的跨文化态度，应建立更明确的规范和寻找更有效的方法。

跨文化实践告诉我们，尊重其他民族文化有利于跨文化理解，形成积极的跨文化交往，不尊重其他民族文化则导致跨文化冲突。

4．宽容

宽容是基本的文化态度，是跨文化尊重的必然。宽容的本质是对不同于本民族文化的其他民族文化的公正肯定，特别是对与本民族文化截然相反的其他民族文化形态的公正认可，以及对这种对立性、否定性的接受。

宽容是对文化差异的体认，是文化多样性的基准要求，是要求其他民族文化尊重本民族文化的逻辑前提，是克服任何形式的文化偏见、消解任何形态的文化冲突的伦理价值起点。

宽容是建立在尊重的基础之上的，对其他民族文化的价值、特征、历史的尊重和理解是宽容的前提。在基于跨文化理解的跨文化交往中，宽容要求宽大为怀，求同存异，暂时退让以求长期和解与未来发展。

但是宽容是有条件的，那就是文化的存在与发展。所以，宽容不应该导致对罪恶的妥协与退让，更不应该导致文化差异性的灭绝，同时宽容也不得以灭绝任何文化差异性为前提。任何形式的文化专制主义、假借道德之名的恐怖主义和践踏生命的文化借口都不被宽容。

简言之，我们不宽容"不宽容"，即：对于那些不能以宽容的态度对待其他民族文化的态度，我们不宽容。

同时，我们也不宽容"对宽容的玷污"，宽容不是软弱，若有人试图玷污我们对他人的宽容，我们应毫不迟疑地捍卫我们的宽容精神。今天的世界，面临许许多多的跨文化冲突，诸多都是因为缺乏宽容心。显然，只有宽容的态度，才能促进跨文化的交往，促进本民族文化的发展，同时促进不同民族文化的共同发展。

5．客观

客观的态度对于走向世界性的基于跨文化理解的跨文化交往是非常重要的，因为这是准确地认知与合理地选择的前提。

客观就是在跨文化理解、跨文化交往中摒弃自己的主观视点，而从其他民族文化的观点，或者是从第三者的眼光、从全人类的眼光，认知、理解其他民族文化，分析跨文化实践，总结跨文化实践的经验教训，把握跨文化实践的方向，实现世界性的跨文化理解，形成积极的跨文化交往。

客观还意味着克服本民族文化存在的对其他民族文化的偏见。很多偏见是传统文化的痼疾，或者有着深刻的心理原因。克服自己对其他民族文化的偏见是对自己的挑战，而这也恰恰是走向世界性的跨文化理解，形成积极的跨文化交往的关键态度。

客观要求在跨文化理解、跨文化交往中不歧视，不带有偏见，不只是从自己的立场出发去认识、反思和处理与其他民族的历史与现实的跨文化冲突。

当然，偏见不同于歧视，偏见是偏狭的、片面的对其他民族文化的错误认识，而歧视是对其他民族文化的贬低与不尊重。偏见可以通过确立客观的态度来克服，而歧视则应该通过养成尊重其他民族文化的态度和通过实施政治措施、经济措施来消灭。由于人的认知能力是有限的，偏见可能长期难以克服，但歧视则是应该明确反对的。

那么我们可知，在跨文化理解、跨文化交往中，客观的态度能促进各民族文化的共同发展，而不客观的态度则会导致跨文化冲突，影响人类文化的共同发展。

6．谨慎

谨慎就是认真、细致而周全的态度，是指我们与其他民族文化交往中应该非常认真、细致、周全地而不是简单、贸然地处理各种问题，特别是不应贸然地以为自己对其他民族文化的认识是绝对正确的，或者认为自己已经准确地把握了其他民族文化，或者以简单化、想当然的态度来对待其他民族文化，因为文化是复杂的，我们可能对其他民族的认识是不准确的，我们想当然的态度可能恰恰导致对其他民族文化的不尊重。

谨慎是以充分的认知、深入的思考为基础的。之所以谨慎，是因为我们需要准确地认知其他民族文化，是因为我们应该非常谨慎地尊重其他民族文化。因此，当我们与不甚了解的其他民族文化交往时，我们就应该更加谨慎。

谨慎不是封闭，谨慎是对我们的一种警示，告诉我们应该总是在跨文化理解、跨文化交往中尊重其他民族文化。

基于以上分析，我们可以确立跨文化教育的态度目标：通过跨文化教育，培养学生在跨文化交往中坚持开放、平等、尊重、宽容、客观、谨慎等积极的跨文化态度，引导学生尽可能消解故步自封、妄自尊大、妄自菲薄、歧视、偏见、狭隘、盲动等消极的跨文化态度。

三、高中英语课程中外文化理解能力发展方法

确定高中英语课程发展学生中外文化理解能力的能力框架之后，则需要采用合理的方法和恰当的活动发展这些能力。基于高中英语课程的特点，这些方法通常分为课堂教学方法和主题活动方法。

1. 英语课程中外文化理解目标

无论是课堂教学，还是主题活动，都需要以《普通高中英语课程标准（2017年版）》所规定的课程目标为指向。

通过英语课程进行中外文化理解教育，属于跨文化教育，这一内容一直是英语学科的隐性课程（hidden curriculum），因为文化理解一直是英语课程的重要任务，英语语言本身也是英语民族文化的基本而且重要的组成部分，同时英语语言能力也是中外文化理解与传播能力的前提与条件。

实际上，理解中外文化，尤其是理解外国文化（主要是英语国家文化），一直是外语教育的主要内容，语言与文化同时教学，语言作为文化内涵进行教学。根据《礼记》中的记载，我国在周朝时期就设有"四夷之学"。希腊人是在学习腓尼基人语言的基础上创造了希腊字母。1862年京师同文馆开设的英文馆的课程都是采取语言与文化并行的课程形式。20世纪20年代，我国出现了专门以介绍外国文化为内容的英文教科书。西方的第一份有关外语教学必须进行文化教育的文件在1900年出现。当前，几乎没有一个国家不在基础教育阶段开设外语课

程，不进行对于其他民族文化的研究，不学习外来文化。目前全球外语教育界都公认，外语教育必然涉及其他民族文化教育，语言教育不可能离开文化教育而进行。实际上，单纯的外语教育就是一种发展中外文化理解能力的活动，因为即使单纯的外国语言教学也不可避免地要涉及关于外语本身所凸现的思维方式的教育。

自 1862 年英语开始作为外语课程到现在，我国一直在尽可能地开展中外文化理解教育。

1862 年，我国第一个国家兴办的近代外语学校——京师同文馆在北京成立，外语开始作为国家课程出现，这时的外语课程专门规定了传授外国文化知识的内容。

我国的外语教育从那时开始，到现在，一直强调在外语学习中的外国文化教学，只是程度有些不同，内容有些差异。

当我国的外语教学刚刚开始时，社会首先需要的是语言人才，同时外国文化也为清政府所不容，因此这一时期，外语教学中的外国文化教学并没有受到应有的重视。1902 年的《钦定中学堂章程》规定了中学开设外国文课。1904 年的《中学堂章程》中明确指出，学习外语要"知国家、知世界"，不过这些文件过于简略，关于外语教学的通常只有百余字。

1913 年—1923 年是外语教学中外国文化教学的发展时期。民国初始，新的教育理念开始形成，但这一时期军阀混战，教育发展受到制约。1913 年，《中学校课程标准》中首次明确将"（外国）文学要略"列为教学内容。1923 年的《新学制课程纲要初级中学外国语课程纲要》中不仅规定学生要"选读文学读本"，并明确规定了一些读本（如《天方夜谭》、《鲁滨孙[1]漂流记》等）。同年的《新学制课程纲要高级中学公共必修的外国语课程纲要》所规定的外语课程的主旨第一条就是"养成学生欣赏优美文学之兴趣"，规定学习内容要包括外国的小说、戏剧、传记等。

1　此为当时译名。——本书注

1929 年—1932 年，外语教学进入了一个新的外国文化教学时期，这一时期的外语课程标准都非常突出地强调了外国文化教学。

这一时期的初中、高中英语课程标准所规定的中学英语的教学目标中都包括"使学生从英语方面加增他们研究外国文化的兴趣"，要求教材中包括"外国人民生活习惯等类的事实——尤其是英语民族的"（初中）、"外国文化的事实和意义——尤其是英语民族的"（高中）；对学生的毕业要求中也包括了文化方面的要求："（明了）关于英语民族生活文化的事实"（初中）、"（明了）关于西洋民族生活文化的事实和意义"（高中）。

显然，这一阶段不仅明确了中外文化理解教育的内容，而且依据学生认知规律提出了不同程度的教学要求。

1936 年—1948 年，外语中的中外文化理解教育发展到了新的阶段，外语课程中的文化教育的目的更加符合中国文化发展的要求。

这一时期的中学英语课程标准，从 1936 年到 1941 年都没有变化，教学目标基本一样。1948 年的课程标准有些增加与明确，初中英语教学目标规定了"认识英美民族精神与风俗习惯，启发学习西洋事物之兴趣"，高中英语教学目标规定了"从英语方面加增其对于西方文化之兴趣，从语文中认识英语国家风俗之大概，从英美民族史迹记载中，激发爱国思想及国际了解"。这一变化使中外文化理解教育的目标更加明确，特别是将中外文化理解教育的目标直接与国内的社会政治发展需要结合起来，以文化理解促进品格教育。

这一时期的中学英语课程标准有关教材内容中中外文化理解教育的部分有了意义深刻的变化，要求英语教材包括"外国人民生活习惯等类之事实——尤其关于英语民族者及有益于我国民族精神之培养者"（初中）、"外国文化之事实与意义——尤其关于英语民族者及有益于我国民族精神之培养者"（高中）。这里明确提出了中外文化理解教育的目的是培养学生的民族精神，这是跨文化教育目的的深化。

1951 年—1963 年，这一时期的外语教育受到意识形态的直接影响，外语教学中的中外文化理解教育出现了新的特征：在教学目标上，不再将学习外国文化列入其中，但列入了一些新的跨文化教育的目标；在教学内容上，对外国文化进行有选择的学习。

1951 年，新的课程标准不再有直接的中外文化理解教育的目标，但内容上仍规定了要求学生阅读"英文小说"，不过没有明确规定内容。1954 年—1959 年，初中英语课停开。

1956 年的高中教学大纲规定学习外语是因为"需要吸取世界各国最新的科学和技术的成果"，学习外语能"使学生们更好地了解祖国语言，发展他们的思考能力，扩大他们的眼界"，同时明确要求教学内容要包括"资本主义国家人民的生活，美国黑人儿童的生活"这些内容。

这里的变化使中外文化理解教育的目的更加指向社会发展的需要，并出现了对跨文化参照的规定（通过学习外语更好地了解自己的母语）。

1963 年的中学英语教学大纲在教学目的上强调学习外语"进行国际交往、促进文化交流、增进与各国人民之间相互了解"，"向友好国家和人民介绍我们的经验"，"加强与各国人民之间的联系，团结各国人民共同对帝国主义做斗争"。在教学内容上，继续强调以意识形态为标准进行选择，但又同时兼顾文化自身的特点，要求课文反映"英语国家人民的阶级斗争和生产斗争、风俗习惯、文化和历史传统"，在选择课文时，"有进步意义的作品，自然可以选用。虽然没有积极意义，但也无害的作品，只要语言方面确实有值得学习的地方，也可以选用。应该把一般人民的生活风习与资产阶级的腐朽生活方式区别开来。对于别国人民的生活和风俗习惯应该予以尊重，至于内容反动的、宣扬资产阶级生活方式、思想观点的文章，对学生有害，当然不应入选"。大纲还就不同年级的教学内容中的外国文化的内容都作出了明确的规定。

这里对外语教学中中外文化理解教育有很多积极的发展，不仅强调对外国文化的学习，更强调向外国介绍我们自己的文化，包含了跨文化传播能力的要求。

1966 年—1976 年，中国的教育基本处于停顿时期，外语教育也基本处于停顿时期。1972 年，中国恢复了在联合国的席位，外语教育受到一定重视，但由于国内的政治形势又很快处于停顿状态。

1978 年—2000 年，中国进入改革开放时期。外语教育得到恢复，外语教学中的中外文化理解教育也进入了新的时期。

1978 年的《全日制十年制中小学英语教学大纲（试行草案）》在教学目的中规定外语学习是为了"国际阶级斗争、经济贸易联系、文化技术交流和友好往来"，在教材中要"有选择地编入一些反映英美等国情况的材料和浅易的或经过改写的原著"，课文要包括"反映外国（主要是英国、美国和其他英语国家）的政治、经济、社会、文化、史地等方面情况的文章"。这里对教学目的和教学内容的选择已经不再具有强烈的意识形态因素了，文化自身的规定性内涵重新成为外语教学中中外文化理解教育的主导因素。

1993 年的英语教学大纲在教学目的中规定，外语教学要"增进对所学语言国家的了解"，在教学原则中强调要"处理好语言教学与文化的关系"，指出"语言是文化的重要载体，语言与文化密切联系"，强调"通过英语学习使学生了解英语国家的文化和社会风俗习惯"，而且指出跨文化教育"有助于他们（学生）理解本民族的文化"。这是在中国的中小学外语教学大纲中第一次明确提出要处理好语言与文化的关系。

1996 年，中学英语教学大纲指出："外国语是学习文化科学知识、获得世界各方面信息和进行国际交往的重要工具。通过学习他国的语言，加深对他国文化的认识和理解，学会尊重他国的语言和文化，进而更好地认识并热爱本民族的语言和文化，培养和提高学生的人文素质。"教学目的包括"增进对外国文化，特别是英语国家文化的了解"，在教学原则的"处理好语言和文化的关系"一节中强调学习外国文化有助于学生"增强世界意识"。

2001 年，我国的外语教学中的中外文化理解教育进入了一个新的时期，中外文化理解不仅作为一个教学目标得到单独的确认，而且中外文化理解教育的内容与教学要求都非常明确地单列在《英语课程标准(实验稿)》之中。

2001 年，我国颁布的英语教育文件《英语课程标准（实验稿）》明确地将跨文化教育的内容作为一个单项列出。这份文件规定：英语教育的目标包括"文化知识、文化理解、跨文化交际意识和能力"，并具体规定了各级不同的中外文化理解教育的目标。

《英语课程标准（实验稿）》规定，在基础教育的小学、初中、高中不同阶段，英语学科中外文化理解教育的目标分别是：

表 3-2　英语学科中外文化理解教育的目标

级别	标准描述
二级（小学阶段）	1. 知道英语中最简单的称谓语、问候语和告别语； 2. 对一般的赞扬、请求等做出适当的反应； 3. 知道国际上最重要的文娱和体育活动； 4. 知道英语国家中最常见的饮料和食品的名称； 5. 知道主要英语国家的首都和国旗； 6. 了解世界上主要国家的重要标志物，如：英国的大本钟等； 7. 了解英语国家中重要的节假日。
五级（初中阶段）	1. 了解英语交际中常用的体态语，如手势、表情等； 2. 恰当使用英语中不同的称谓语、问候语和告别语； 3. 了解、区别英语中不同性别常用的名字和亲昵的称呼； 4. 了解英语国家中家庭成员之间的称呼习俗； 5. 了解英语国家正式和非正式场合服饰和穿戴习俗； 6. 了解英语国家的饮食习俗； 7. 对别人的赞扬、请求等做出恰当的反应； 8. 用恰当的方式表达赞扬、请求等意义； 9. 初步了解英语国家的地理位置、气候特点、历史等； 10. 了解常见动植物在英语国家中的文化涵义； 11. 了解自然现象在英语中可能具有的文化涵义； 12. 了解英语国家中传统的文娱和体育活动； 13. 了解英语国家中重要的节假日及主要庆祝方式； 14. 加深对中国文化的理解。

（续表）

级别	标准描述
八级（高中阶段）	1. 理解英语中常见成语和俗语及其文化内涵； 2. 理解英语交际中常用典故或传说； 3. 了解英语国家主要的文学家、艺术家、科学家的经历、成就和贡献； 4. 初步了解主要英语国家的政治、经济等方面的情况； 5. 了解英语国家中主要大众传播媒体的情况； 6. 了解主要英语国家与中国的生活方式的异同； 7. 了解英语国家人们在行为举止、待人接物等方面与中国人的异同； 8. 了解英语国家主要宗教传统； 9. 通过学习英语了解世界文化，培养世界意识； 10. 通过中外文化对比，加深对中国文化的理解。

《义务教育英语课程标准（2011 年版）》对中外文化理解能力的培养作出更为明确的规定。具体内容为：

表 3-3　对中外文化理解能力培养的要求

级别	标准描述
二级（小学阶段）	1. 知道英语中最简单的称谓语、问候语和告别语； 2. 对一般的赞扬、请求、道歉等做出适当的反应； 3. 知道世界上主要的文娱和体育活动； 4. 知道英语国家中典型的食品和饮料的名称； 5. 知道主要英语国家的首都和国旗； 6. 了解主要英语国家的重要标志物，如英国的大本钟等； 7. 了解英语国家中重要的节假日； 8. 在学习和日常交际中，能初步注意到中外文化异同。
五级（初中阶段）	1. 了解英语交际中常用的体态语，如手势、表情等； 2. 恰当使用英语中的称谓语、问候语和告别语； 3. 了解、区别英语中不同性别常用的名字和亲昵的称呼； 4. 了解英语国家的饮食习俗； 5. 对别人的赞扬、请求、致歉等做出恰当的反应； 6. 用恰当的方式表达赞扬、请求等意义； 7. 初步了解英语国家的地理位置、气候特点、历史等； 8. 了解英语国家的人际交往习俗；

（续表）

级别	标准描述
五级 （初中 阶段）	9. 了解世界上主要的文娱和体育活动； 10. 了解世界上主要的节假日及庆祝方式； 11. 关注中外文化异同，加深对中国文化的理解； 12. 能初步用英语介绍祖国的主要节日和典型的文化习俗。

《普通高中英语课程标准（2017 年版）》对此有更加明确、系统的规定，见本书第一章表 1-1 与 1-3。

从以上简述中我们可以看出，我国外语课程大纲中对跨文化教育的目标的规定具有这样的特点：中外文化理解教育的教育目标逐步扩展，逐步明确。

以上所有的课程大纲都提出了中外文化教育的相关内容，跨文化教育一直是我国外语课程的基本内涵。

2. 发展中外文化理解能力的课堂教学方法

基于课程标准的规定，我们应在课堂教学中系统实施其规定，从而达到其目标。根据我国目前的跨文化教育实践经验，参考借鉴英美多元文化教育的四种课程模式与教学方法，笔者认为，在英语课程发展学生中外文化理解能力的教育实践中，我们可以采取以下主要方法：

（1）单元主题融合法

高中英语课程强调基于单元主题的整合式学习，中外文化理解可以融合到单元主题之中。把中外文化理解教育的知识目标、态度目标、能力目标等全部系统地融入外语教学之中进行教学，让学生在学习语言中不知不觉地发展中外文化理解能力。

这一方法就是编写以文化为课文题材的语言材料，采取文化会话、文化合作、文化表演、文化交流等方式进行外语课堂教学。

这一方法要求在教材和教学方法中适当地将跨文化知识融合到课文与教学中去。由于语言知识与能力教学有着自身的规律（比如我们需要先学名词单数形式，再学习名词复数形式等），这往往难以同时全面体现中外文化知识、态度、能力目标。

因此，运用融合法的时候，可以与其他方法结合使用，如用附加方式全面地呈现不同的文化，用融合方式将跨文化态度的教育目标融合到课文中去，将跨文化能力与运用外语的能力结合起来，或者开展实践体验活动。

由于现行高中英语教材基本都有大量的中外文化专题内容，有专门的中外文化理解单元，这一方法可以在这些单元的学习中全面、深度使用。

（2）增加法

增加法就是在外语教学中系统地增加补充一些跨文化的内容，作为课堂教学与教材的组成部分或附加部分，尤其是当教材内容不足以帮助我们开展中外文化理解能力发展时，我们可以使用这一方法。

这一方法就是在教材中专门设立中外文化理解单元主题（每册若干单元确定为跨文化理解单元主题），或者每单元设置文化理解专栏，如Culture Section，Around the World 等，或者在教学中给学生举办中外文化专题讲座，组织参观中外文化展览，组织有关讨论，组织欣赏中外文化的表演、活动等。这样，通过增加的中外文化知识，让学生系统地掌握所学外语国家的基础文化知识。附加的中外文化知识可以附加在外语教材之中，也可以是单独的中外文化选修课、文化知识读本。

我们还需要附加相应的活动与能力培养方面的内容，可能是一些问答讨论题，或者是一些相关的活动。

（3）厘清讨论法

对于一些有疑惑，甚至有歧见与冲突的中外文化现象、问题，尤其是一些热点问题，可以采用讨论的方式，厘清相关文化知识，促进中外文化理解。这一讨论可以是教师与学生作为不同文化表现者的互动讨论，可以是学生之间的讨论，也可以是其他人士参与的讨论，如家长、专家等，使学生在与老师的中外文化互动中感知外来文化。通过讨论某一文化现象（不一定是外来文化的），使学生在探讨中感知到自己与老师文化的不同，然后形成自我判断。可以采取的方法有文化疑惑解析、文化冲突化解、文化专题研究等。

厘清互动讨论特别适合跨文化教育态度目标的教学。通过开放式的、平等性的、交流式的讨论，让学生在讨论中自觉地形成开放、平等、尊重（不歧视）、宽容、客观（无偏见）、谨慎的跨文化态度。因此，在互动讨论中，教师也应特别注意以开放、平等、尊重（不歧视）、宽容、客观（无偏见）、谨慎的态度组织讨论，只有将这些跨文化态度渗透到整个教学活动中，才能真正有助于学生形成相应的中外文化理解所需的态度。

当然，厘清互动讨论应该只给材料，而不直接给观点。教师引导学生对材料进行广泛、深入的讨论，引导他们形成合理的跨文化态度。

（4）文化体验法

文化体验法就是让学生在中外文化理解活动中通过自身的充分体验来理解中外文化知识，养成积极的跨文化态度，形成中外文化理解能力。

在外语教学中，体验法有两种形态：直接体验、间接体验。

直接体验就是让学生直接与外在文化接触（比如学习独立的外国文化单元的课文，听外国文化专题讲座，观看外国电影，与外国人直接交往等），在这些接触中学生直接了解外国文化，认知外国文化的知识内容，发现自己的跨文化态度，了解到何种态度有利于了解外国文化、有利于与外国人交往等等，从而形成积极的跨文化态度，并通过直接的交往获得跨文化的能力。

间接体验是将教学内容隐含在常规的教学活动之中，让学生在不知不觉中潜移默化地了解外国文化的相关知识，养成积极的跨文化态度，形成有效的跨文化能力。

应该说，间接体验特别适合小学的外语教学，因为小学生主要是通过感知来学习文化，特别是跨文化态度的养成。直接体验则更适合跨文化知识的明确传授，适合中学外语教学中的跨文化教育。

（5）亲身实践法

亲身实践法就是让学生在外语教学中直接参与到中外文化理解实践、跨文化交往实践之中，在亲身参与的跨文化实践中获得跨文化的知识，形成合理的跨文化态度和中外文化理解能力。

实践法就是引导学生对跨文化实践进行分析，特别是对跨文化实践的热点（如新闻事件）、难点（如历史问题）进行专项的分析，通过分析引导学生形成跨文化认知、比较、参照、取舍、传播的能力。

外语教育中的跨文化教育活动可以在本体文化的环境（中国老师在中国教中国学生）中开展，但更可以充分运用外语教育的独有特点，让学生通过各种形式（特别是网络形式，这种形式成本低、方便快捷，又能与外国人直接交往）与外国人直接交往，在与外国人的直接交往中直观地获得跨文化知识，在交往的成功与失败中形成合理的跨文化意识和能力。

为了充分利用与外国人直接交往的机会，提高跨文化教育的有效性，在学生与外国人直接交往之前，教师应该引导学生进行必要的知识、意识、能力准备。同时，在与外国人直接接触之后，教师应组织学生进行相关的专题讨论，让学生总结他们获得的跨文化知识，形成或强化跨文化态度与能力。

与外国人的直接交往，可以采取面对面交往的形式，也可以采取更便捷的网络交往形式。在与外国人交往时，可以专门与有一定跨文化交往经历的外国人（比如曾经访问过中国，或者在其他国家生活过的外国人）进行交往，以提高教学效率。也可以采取与和学生同龄的外国学生交往的形式，因为学生通常更容易与同龄人交往。不过，同龄外国人存在缺乏权威性的问题，因此，学生与同龄的外国人交往时可以适当安排外国老师在场（或者在线），以在必要的时候给予一定的权威性支持。

直接体验也可能是一种亲身实践，但直接体验更强调体验，而体验之后可能形成亲身实践。

（6）学科融合法

除了外语学科包含着中外文化理解教育之外，其他学科也同样存在着中外文化理解教育的成分，尤其是人文学科。这些学科也可以开展基于英语的中外文化理解教育。

中外文化教育具有鲜明的人文色彩，因此，几乎所有的人文学科都具有中外文化理解教育的可能。语文课程中有一定比例的外国优秀文学作品的学习，是开展文化意识教育的基础性材料。与外国历史、外国社会相关的历史、社会学科也是跨文化教育的主要学科。在教育部制定的历史与社会课程标准、历史课程标准中，都有一定程度的中外文化理解能力发展的内容要求。这些新的课程标准都为中外文化理解教育带来新的机遇。按照课程标准，这些学科的教学将明确地传授跨文化知识，培养学生的跨文化态度和跨文化能力。

艺术（音乐与美术）是联合国教科文组织倡导的展开跨文化教育的重要课程，课程中必然要介绍外国艺术作品，让学生从外国艺术中感知外国文化。因此这些学科也是开展中外文化理解教育的基础学科。

中国当代的科学教育几乎完全是包含了西方文化的中外文化理解教育活动，数学、物理、化学、生物、地理等学科的教学内容中包含了大量来自西方的科学思想、归纳演绎的思维方式、因果关联的逻辑思维、科学人物（牛顿、伽利略、爱因斯坦、瓦特、焦耳等）和科学事件（牛顿的苹果故事、伽利略的重力实验故事以及哥白尼坚持"太阳中心说"受到宗教迫害等等）。

甚至体育学科中也同样包含了大量外国体育活动、外国体育人物等的介绍与评价，如篮球、排球、现代足球、乒乓球、体操。特别是当代西方体育文化的核心——游戏规则意识，更是西方文化的重要内涵。这都是直接的中外文化理解教育活动。

在不同学科中进行中外文化理解教育的实践可以采取附加、融合、互动、实践的方法。也就是在历史、历史与社会、语文、艺术等学科中明确地附加其他民族文化（外国文学、外国艺术）方面的内容，采取融合的方法将其他民族文化中的科学精神、规则意识等融合在相关学科中进行，采取参观、社会与历史专题探究、科学实验等互动的、实践的方法培养学生的跨文化意识和中外文化理解能力。

这些内容的中外文化理解教育在非外语学科中当然可以运用汉语（或学生的母语）进行，我们英语教师应主动参与这些学科的中外文化理解教育。我们可以在英语课堂教学与课外活动中，运用这些学科的材料，基于这些学科所发展的学生的中外文化理解能力，进一步发展学生的中外文化理解能力。我们还可以主动为这些学科的教学提供英文的补充学习材料，供这些学科的教师使用，或者供学生学习这些学科时使用。

需要特别说明的是，以上方法都是具体方法，其基础应是《普通高中英语课程标准（2017年版）》所倡导的整合式学习路径，亦即：无论采取哪种具体方法，都应是基于整合式学习路径的方法。

3. 发展学生中外文化理解能力的主题实践法

主题实践活动（thematic project）就是集中于一个主题的实践型的教学活动，这些实践活动基于学生的直接生活与学习体验，联系学生的自身生活和社会生活，体现对知识能力的综合运用。主题实践活动是一种体验式学习（experiential learning）。

根据钟启泉等人的研究（钟启泉等，2001），主题实践活动的最大特点在于其实践性、生成性、开放性。主题实践活动涉及很多文化类的主题活动，如：

A. 少数民族文化探讨：少数民族饮食文化研究，少数民族音乐与经济，少数民族的文化传统的保护，宗教信仰、古代建筑、文化遗产遗址研究等。

B. 国际文化交流：外国文化教育、国际理解教育等。

在主题实践活动中，学生通过亲身实践直接体验教育内容，有利于达到良好的教学效果，特别有利于培养情感态度、实践能力等。

（1）中外文化理解主题实践活动类型

显然，中外文化理解应该是当前一个重要的实践的主题系列。依据笔者的分析，中外文化理解的主题实践活动的类型包括：

① 主题探究活动

这是就一个中外文化理解的主题进行信息的搜集、比较、分析等探索研究活动，比如对不同民族的饮食文化与生活环境及其生活哲学的探究、对不同的中外文化认知途径的分析研究等。

在中外文化理解活动中，主题探究活动所探究的主题可以包括对其他民族文化知识的获得探究与获得方法探究（方法探究更为重要，因为知识是无限的，学生可以通过获得方法而自己主动地探究知识）、对其他民族文化的态度与观念的比较探究（比较的方法有利于跨文化态度与观念的形成），在探究过程中获得中外文化理解能力。

② 主题社会实践活动

这是直接对社会生活中的中外文化现象进行考察，直接参与中外文化理解的社会实践活动，包括主题性的社会考察与主题性的社会参与，如考察少数民族的官方语言与民族语言的双语教育，考察社会对少数民族生活风俗、宗教活动的支持，参与接待外国来访学生的活动，参与大型的国际化活动（如奥林匹克运动会、国际电影节、国际展览会等）。

社会考察能帮助学生直观地获得中外文化知识，形成直接的中外文化理解体验，从而促进跨文化意识和中外文化理解能力的养成，而社会考察之后就考察内容进行的专题讨论，也有利于形成积极的跨文化态度与中外文化理解能力。

社会参与是指学生参与社会问题的讨论与解决，比如对社区垃圾问题的解决。在社会参与中，我们可以鼓励学生从不同的文化视点探讨同一问题，比如了解其他人是如何解决他们的垃圾问题的，从而展开跨文化教育，发展中外文化理解能力。也可以直接参与社区的跨文化交往活动，如接待访问的外国人，开展有关的讨论等。

③ 主题生活学习活动

我们也可以通过学生自己生活（学校生活与社会生活）中的跨文化活动，来展开跨文化教育，发展学生的中外文化理解能力。

在跨文化教育中，生活学习就是通过对社会生活的观察、分析、讨论等，获得跨文化的知识、态度与中外文化理解能力。

显然，主题实践活动有助于整体地展开跨文化教育，发展学生的中外文化理解能力。

在实践活动中，我们要让学生获得专题的跨文化知识。这样的知识比较系统，同时学生通过自我探究（查找资料、访谈、分析文献等）获得专题的跨文化知识，这更有利于他们理解与掌握，就如流行的外语教育口号所说的："Tell me, I forget. Show me, I remember. Involve me, I understand."（你告诉我，我就忘了。你给我看，我记住了。让我参与其中，我理解了。）

主题实践活动可以涉及各个学科的知识，能培养学生对这些知识的综合运用能力，还能培养学生的实践能力。

这种综合的体验性的实践活动有利于帮助学生获得中外文化的知识，培养积极的跨文化态度，形成有效的中外文化理解能力。

养成积极的跨文化态度就是要帮助受教育者养成开放、平等（不歧视）、尊重、宽容、客观（无偏见）、谨慎的跨文化观念，显然，这些都可以通过主题实践活动展开。

我们应该通过实践活动让学生自己体验跨文化的交往，让学生从小养成良好的、积极的跨文化态度。这不是可以通过简单的道德说教就能完成的，我们必须让学生认知、了解外来文化，参与各种跨文化教育活动（比如在实践活动中与外国人直接交往），引导学生在这些活动中建构积极的跨文化态度。

有效的中外文化理解能力是中外文化理解教育的主要内容。跨文化教育的主要目的是让学生学会与外来文化交往，并学习外来文化的优秀成分，而这都需要有效的中外文化理解能力。

如前所析，中外文化理解能力包括中外文化认知、比较、参照、取舍、传播的能力。而主题实践活动的最大特点就在于实践性、生成性，学生可以通过参加综合实践活动在实践中生成这些能力。

根据我们的研究分析与实验，在目前的学校教育中，培养跨文化能力最有效的方法是 project（项目）这种综合性的主题实践活动。根据国外的经验，主题性的综合实践活动可以在小学、初中、高中、大学分阶段开展，也可以在每个年级开展。

（2）主题实践活动建议

在主题实践活动中，我们可以组织学生获得尽可能系统、全面、深刻的中外文化知识，具体方法包括：

① 引导学生整理从不同学科所学的其他民族文化知识，听跨文化的专题知识讲座，与外国学生进行交往（最好是面对面的直接交往，但也可以是通过网络等方式的间接交往），观看外国电视节目、外国电影等，阅读其他民族文化的书籍，访问外国网站，参观其他民族文化展览，观看外国体育比赛等，有意识地要求学生对获得的跨文化知识进行

系统、全面、深刻的整理。

② 组织学生参加有引导的专题讨论以及其他相关活动，让学生在讨论甚至辩论中分辨出正确与错误、合理与不合理，判断出我们应该学习外来文化的哪些内容，应该舍弃哪些内容，如何参照外来文化建设自己的文化，从而形成合理的跨文化意识和足够的中外文化理解能力。

③ 让学生在活动中充分体验跨文化的交往，通过跨文化交往，亲身体验其他民族文化的生活方式、价值观等，获得跨文化的知识和能力，并通过亲身体验形成积极的跨文化态度。这种体验式的学习通常有利于学生更准确地把握跨文化的知识，也更有利于形成积极的跨文化态度和有效的中外文化理解能力。

虽然跨文化知识可以在一次主题实践活动之后有明显的增加，但跨文化态度和跨文化能力则不是一两次跨学科实践活动能够养成和提高的，因此，跨文化教育需要持之以恒。

在主题实践活动中，对中外文化理解教育进行明确的指导是至关重要的。

我们在实验教学中发现：具有明确指导的主题实践活动能实现跨文化教育的目的；缺乏明确指导的主题实践活动不但没有起到跨文化教育的作用，反而很可能导致相反的效果。

因此，在主题实践活动之前，教师必须制定明确的指导方案。这个指导方案应该符合主题实践活动的要求，同时具有跨文化教育的特点。

我们依据相关研究与分析，设计了以下中外文化理解主题实践活动指南（样本）：

表3-4 中外文化理解主题实践活动指南（样本）

一、主题探究活动

1.选定要探究的中外文化理解的专题

教师可以引导学生从下列各大类专题中选择一个小专题：

大专题1：了解中外文化知识

小专题样本1：广泛而深入地认识某一外来文化的某一方面

（续表）

> 小专题样本 2：广泛而深入地认识外国饮食文化（如麦当劳）
>
> 小专题样本 3：广泛而深入地认识外国电影文化（如日本卡通片）
>
> 在老师指导下自拟其他同类小专题。
>
> 大专题 2：养成跨文化态度
>
> 　　小专题样本 1：分析中国唐代贞观之治与康乾盛世的跨文化态度差异
>
> 　　小专题样本 2：分析西方的殖民侵略历史态度
>
> 　　小专题样本 3：分析蒙古帝国的形成与瓦解
>
> 　　小专题样本 4：分析好莱坞电影中的中国形象
>
> 　　在老师指导下自拟其他同类小专题。
>
> 大专题 3：提高中外文化理解能力
>
> 　　小专题样本 1：分析当今中美关系、中日关系的文化原因
>
> 　　小专题样本 2：分析比较洋务运动与"五四运动"的文化背景差异
>
> 　　小专题样本 3：分析比较中国经济改革与苏联经济改革的文化背景差异
>
> 　　小专题样本 4：分析中国在欧美获奖电影的文化背景
>
> 　　小专题样本 5：分析中国男子足球曲折发展的历史的跨文化原因
>
> 　　小专题样本 6：直接（或通过网络）与外国学生讨论青年人与父母的关系问题
>
> 　　小专题样本 7：向外国人介绍中国的家庭关系
>
> 　　在老师指导下自拟其他同类小专题。
>
> 2. 制订探究学习计划
>
> 　　鼓励学生进行合作探究，有意识地强调合作中的态度情感、能力等问题。

（续表）

3. 实施探究学习的计划

鼓励学生相互帮助，广泛协作，利用多种渠道与媒体，有意识地强调分析、判断、比较、取舍、传播能力的形成。

4. 对探究性学习的过程与结果进行全面总结

从跨文化知识获得、跨文化态度养成、中外文化理解能力形成等不同层面，对探究活动进行全面系统的总结，要强调对过程的总结分析，强调对体验的总结分析。

二、主题社会实践活动

（一）主题社会考察

1. 确定考察的基本内容

考察的内容通常包括：观看外国电影、接待外国访问团、参观跨文化相关的博物馆(如鸦片战争博物馆)、参观外国艺术展览。

2. 制订考察计划（计划要周全，特别是要制订备选方案）

3. 准备考察需要的各种表格，各种必要的工具、时间表等

4. 进入现场进行考察，若出现问题，及时启动备选方案

5. 撰写考察报告

6. 对考察进行全面系统的总结分析

（二）主题社会参与

1. 分析社会问题，确定要参与的社会问题

2. 制订社会参与方案，特别是要规划参与程度、参与结果

3. 准备参与计划

4. 正式参与

强调让学生注意参与过程中的跨文化问题，比如不同文化背景学生的不同意见、不同处理方法、不同解决方案等

5. 撰写参与报告，进行全面总结

三、主题生活学习活动

1. 事先了解学校生活与社会生活的复杂性

（续表）

> 2. 从复杂的生活中选取自己最感兴趣的跨文化实践的话题（比如一部电影、一部流行小说、新闻以及发生在身边的事等）
>
> 3. 搜集相关生活材料
>
> 4. 在老师指导下对材料进行分析
>
> 5. 与老师、同学就这一问题进行讨论，获得相关情感体验或能力
>
> 6. 向同学展示自己的生活观察分析报告，特别说明自己的情感态度的变化

在所有的实践中，都要鼓励不同群体的学生开展跨文化对话，特别是与外国学生的对话。在对话中，要有意识地引导学生"用和善的方式""为了共同的目的"倾听他人、言说自己、相互理解，要持有平等、尊重的跨文化态度。

我们曾经为华南师范大学附属中学高一学生设计了一项中外文化理解教育的主题综合实践活动。为了让学生尽可能广泛地选择自己喜欢的专题进行研究，我们设计了一个很宽泛的主题：The world you know through English，简称 The world（世界）。

在活动开始前，我们给学生介绍了实践活动的具体要求，确定了操作步骤与所需要的表格，并提出了语言要求：英语是本活动的唯一工作语言，并明确告诉学生，最终成果形式可以是文字，也可以是图表、电子材料，或者是音像材料（如短剧、歌曲、录像节目等）。

我们允许学生独自完成课题，也可以合作完成课题（包括国际合作），同时说明学校将安排一整天的时间让学生呈现、展示、表演最终成果。

全班 50 人参加研究项目，学生自愿组合成 18 个小组。

项目成果涉及的内容主要包括：

a. 历史文化研究：美国历史、美国华人、宗教、东西方节日比较（这个案例的具体内容在下一章介绍）

b. 社会生活文化研究：广告、电子游戏、电子词典现象

c. 科学文化研究：中外垃圾处理比较

d. 国际交往活动研究：国际夏令营与英语学习

学生完成的项目成果共 18 份，其中论文报告 15 份（含各种工具的电子文本 14 份），剧本 3 份（含表演录像一份）。

很多学生在报告总结中写道："这是终生难忘的经历""更多、更深刻地了解外国文化""完成项目的过程中我们一直很开心"。

中外文化理解的主题实践活动在我国中小学教育中尚在起步阶段，随着更广泛地开展，必将形成更多的实践经验与有效方法。

第三节　高中英语中外文化理解能力发展案例分析

一、基于单元主题发展文化理解能力

现在的高中英语教材基本上每册都有部分单元以文化理解为主题，如"Festivals Around the World"就是一个介绍全世界节日文化主要类型的文化理解单元。

我们知道，文化首先是一种生活方式，所以人类文化中有很多是可以基于对生活方式的理解而形成直接理解的，如节日。这个单元就是介绍世界不同文化共同的节日类型，虽然节日不同，但节日的类型相同，这使得学生可以通过阅读而形成对节日文化的直接理解。

表 3-5　文化理解单元教学案例

教学内容	Festivals Around the World
教学内容分析	本单元是一个非常典型的中外文化主题单元，适合采用单元主题法进行教学。本单元教学力图通过对比中西节日由来、庆祝方式等的差异，使学生广泛认识世界不同国家的节日文化，加强对中国传统节日的认同，促进学生从生活方式理解文化，把握人类文化的诸多共性，寻找人类共同的核心理念。 本单元任务设定为发现人类节日文化共性，以此共性比较一组中外节日。单元教学分为 6 个课时完成，每一课时都围绕单元任务展开，以下为第二课时阅读课文的教学的主要过程。

（续表）

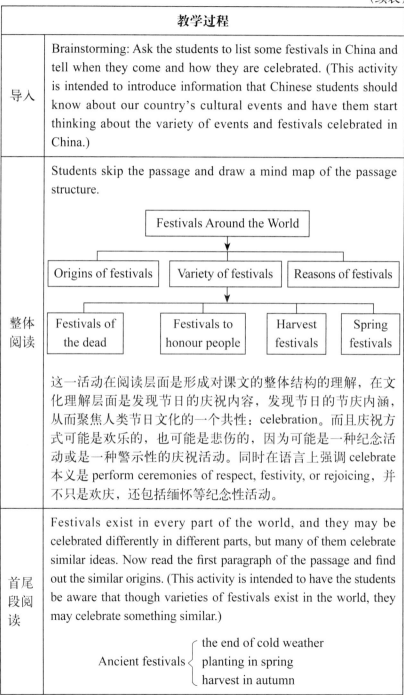

教学过程	
导入	Brainstorming: Ask the students to list some festivals in China and tell when they come and how they are celebrated. (This activity is intended to introduce information that Chinese students should know about our country's cultural events and have them start thinking about the variety of events and festivals celebrated in China.)
整体阅读	Students skip the passage and draw a mind map of the passage structure. Festivals Around the World Origins of festivals　Variety of festivals　Reasons of festivals Festivals of the dead　Festivals to honour people　Harvest festivals　Spring festivals 这一活动在阅读层面是形成对课文的整体结构的理解，在文化理解层面是发现节日的庆祝内容，发现节日的节庆内涵，从而聚焦人类节日文化的一个共性：celebration。而且庆祝方式可能是欢乐的，也可能是悲伤的，因为可能是一种纪念活动或是一种警示性的庆祝活动。同时在语言上强调 celebrate 本义是 perform ceremonies of respect, festivity, or rejoicing，并不只是欢庆，还包括缅怀等纪念性活动。
首尾段阅读	Festivals exist in every part of the world, and they may be celebrated differently in different parts, but many of them celebrate similar ideas. Now read the first paragraph of the passage and find out the similar origins. (This activity is intended to have the students be aware that though varieties of festivals exist in the world, they may celebrate something similar.) Ancient festivals { the end of cold weather / planting in spring / harvest in autumn

教学过程

<table>
<tr><td rowspan="1">首尾段阅读</td><td>

Today's festivals {
religious
seasonal
for special people or events

Human beings, regardless of races and nationalities, need festivals for some common reasons. Now please read the last paragraph and find out the reasons. And please come up with more reasons.

通过此环节的讨论，教师引导学生探讨节日在日常生活、文化、教育、政治、经济等方面的意义。第三部分的两个任务，旨在让学生了解不同的国家、文化或种族享有的共同的节日的起源和目的，解读节日的共性，把握人类文化的诸多共性，寻找人类共同的核心理念。
</td></tr>
</table>

教学过程

学生阅读文章的主体部分，找出各节日的信息并填写表格。

	Kinds of festivals	Names of festivals	Countries	How they are celebrated
主体阅读	Festivals for the dead	Bon; Day of the Dead; Halloween	Japan; Mexico; Some Western countries	Clean graves, light incense, light lamps, play music, eat food in the shape of skulls and cakes with "bones", treat or trick

（续表）

	Festivals to honour people	Dragon Boat Festival; Columbus Day; Festival to honour Gandhi	China; USA; India	Not mentioned
	Harvest festivals	Harvest; Thanksgiving Festivals; Mid-autumn Festivals	European countries; China and Japan	Decorate churches and town halls, have meals together, farm produce competition; admire the moon, enjoy mooncakes, have big meals
主体阅读	Spring festivals	Spring Festival; Cherry Blossom Festival	China; Some Western countries; Japan	Give children lucky money, get together, send best wishes, etc; carnivals including parades; admire the flowers

主体阅读部分下方：

教师提出问题：Is there anything common about how people celebrate the festivals? 引导学生分析归纳不同国家庆祝节日方式的共同点：family get-together, visiting friends, having big meals, entertainment, etc，从而发展学生分析归纳信息的能力，并把握不同文化共有的核心理念，如重视亲情友情、追求幸福安康等。然后学生思考讨论：What do you think about Mexican practice of making cakes in the shape of skulls and with "bones"? 通过此问题的讨论引导学生认识文化的多样性，培养对不同文化的尊重和接纳，发展学生尊重差异、包容不同的文化意识。

读后讨论	教师呈现来自网络的圣诞节宣传照片、反对过西方节日的照片等，引导学生思考：目前很多青少年庆祝西洋节日，如情人节、圣诞节等，却冷落中国传统节日。为了突出中华传统节日，有些高校禁止学生过西洋节，此举是否有助于保护中国传统节日？青少年该不该过西洋节？如何提高中国传统节日的吸引力？

这一课堂教学案例采用单元主题等多种方法，引导学生在学习理解、应用实践、迁移创新的学习过程中，理解中外文化的共性与差异性，发现其本质，运用其发现成果形成新的观点，从而发展学生的文化意识。

二、基于体验发展文化理解能力

当代高中学生有着对跨文化的很多体验，他们学习外语、看外国书、看外国电影、打外国游戏，甚至出国旅游、游学。这些都是我们引导学生通过体验而发展文化理解能力的基础。我们可以在学习一篇关于中国学生在国外留学而遇到跨文化理解困难的课文时，引导学生基于自身的体验和对体验的讨论，发展他们的跨文化理解能力。以下是这个单元的教学实录，这一课例是基于体验发展跨文化理解的。

1. 通过背景知识激活已有体验（本书主要从跨文化理解分析此案例，案例中的每一个环节也可从学生思维品质发展、学生生命成长发展等视角进行标注）

导入是教师基于学生已经掌握的背景知识导出新知识的活动。激活背景知识是导入的关键，而要激活背景知识，不能只是进行浅层次的讨论，还需要进行深度的讨论。但由于这是一种引导活动，不可能一开始就进入深层讨论，需要从浅层问题开始，引导学生逐步深入，直到通过深度讨论激活所需的知识。Travelling abroad 课文介绍中国学生谢蕾在英国留学期间的经历，尤其是她认为导师给她的作业打分不合理而引出的跨文化理解冲突。根据教学经验，我们知道，这很容易引发学生对英国导师是否存在文化偏见甚至文化歧视的讨论。

在这一课例的热身导入环节，教师就话题 Travelling abroad 进行提问，首先提出最浅层次的问题：What is the topic of Unit 5? (IQ1, IQ1=Initial Question 1, 起问问题 1) 以此浅层问题询问单元主题，学生看教材集体朗读出单元主题：Travelling abroad.

需要说明的是，这一课例不仅通过教师提问、学生的跨文化体验从而促进了学生的跨文化理解，而且通过教师提问，学生非常有效地发展了思维品质，并形成了积极面对挫折、分析问题、找出解决办法、克服困难进而幸福成长的积极品格。

教师接着追问：For what do people travel abroad? (FQ1，FQ1=Further Question 1，追问问题 1)

此问题不是询问学生可以从课文中读出的内容，而是询问课文中没有提及的出国旅行的目的，这一问题需要学生从不同的角度思考，从而进入深层次思维。一位学生回答 (SR1，SR1=Student Response 1，学生回答 1)：For sightseeing.（数字指学生回答问题的次数，整节课连贯标注，但不包括朗读。）

另一位学生回答 (SR2)：Learning.

另一位学生回答 (SR3)：Business.

另一位学生回答 (SR4)：Visiting family members or friends.

这一组回答充分说明，教师的追问有助于激活学生的背景知识。

此节课的授课对象是广州某重点高中的学生，他们对出国并不陌生。教师课前了解到，学生基本上都有随家人出国、出境旅游的经历，有的甚至有短期出国学习的经历。

显然，因为教师所追问的不是课文内容而是背景知识，学生给出多种回答，说出不同目的，通过背景知识提问发展深层次思维。

随后教师提问：What are the advantages of learning abroad? (IQ2) 以询问出国学习的优势，这要求学生进行一定的判断，于是出现了多种不同的回答：

一位学生回答 (SR5)：We can experience a different culture.

另一位学生回答 (SR6)：We can meet different people.

另一位学生回答 (SR7)：We can broaden our horizons.

另一位学生回答 (SR8)：We can become more open-minded.

这四种答案已经具有代表性，教师肯定学生的回答：Yes. Learning abroad has lots of advantages.

教师马上提到相反的情况：But we will definitely meet some difficulties. 于是提出问题：Can you imagine what difficulties in life you will meet if you learn abroad? (FQ2)

这一问题询问学生出国可能遇到的困难，是前一问题的反向提问，形成提问的深度。这一问题要求没有出国留学经历的学生展开想象然后回答，问题的深度到了想象的层面，学生给出各种回答：

一位学生回答 (SR9)：I will meet with cultural shock. I will come across language barrier.

另一位学生回答 (SR10)：I will become lonely and homesick.

另一位学生回答 (SR11)：I don't have anyone to take care of me if I am sick.

另一位学生回答 (SR12)：I have to adapt to a new life.

显然，从跨文化理解视角看，学生已有较为丰富的出国经历，激活他们的这些经历有助于他们基于自己的跨文化体验形成跨文化理解。从思维品质发展视角看，对于思维能力已经高度发展的高中学生，教师提出深度的问题，学生的思维深度就可以随即发展到同一深度。

教师在对不同的观点进行点评后，随即转向与学生生活、课文有关的学习问题进行提问：What about difficulties in learning? (FQ3)

一位学生回答 (SR13)：I might not understand what the professors say.

另一位学生回答 (SR14)：The way of learning might be very different.

另一位学生回答 (SR15)：There may be different academic requirements.

教师的问题转到另一领域的深度，促进学生思考这些生活问题，学生思维的深度得到了同步发展。

教师回答：Yes. You may meet with many difficulties, but I believe every problem has a solution. And today we are going to read about Xie Lei's story. 以此引导学生准备进入课文阅读理解。

这些激活文化理解的背景知识的问题，若只是对浅层信息进行提问，则难以引导学生为深度理解课文的跨文化的深层意义作准备，难以发展学生已有的思维的深刻性，也难以在随后的读中、读后活动中发展学生的跨文化理解与思维的深刻性。

本节课对出国的目的、可能的优势与困难进行深度讨论，尤其是对于困难的讨论，不仅激活有关出国遇到困难的背景知识的广度，更激活背景知识的深度，为随后引导学生体验跨文化交往中可能出现的困难、同时发展学生思维的深刻性作好准备，还加深了学生的跨文化理解，发展了学生思维的深刻性。

这一环节不仅发展了学生的思维品质，而且引导学生体验出国可能遇到的困难，为下一步寻找发现谢蕾的困难、寻找对策作好铺垫。这是基于自身体验而体验他人境遇的基础，对跨文化理解非常关键。

2．通过内容理解深化跨文化体验

在激活相关背景知识之后，教师引导学生进入课文理解。课文理解内容丰富，从词汇与语句的基本语义、逻辑联系，到言外之意，各种内容都有从浅层到深层的理解层次，教师可以通过不同层次的提问，促进学生思维深刻性的发展，进而形成深刻的文化理解。

教师首先提出最浅层的问题：What is the title? (IQ3)

学生们齐声读出课文标题：Keep it up, Xie Lei. Chinese student fitting in well. (朗读是学习活动，不是真正的回答问题，故不列入学生回答系列。)

教师接着追问：What can we learn about Xie Lei from the title? (FQ4)

一位学生回答 (SR16)：Xie Lei is learning abroad.

教师提出追问问题：Is everything going well with her? (FQ5)

学生集体回答 (SR17)：Yes.

教师马上追问：How do you know that? (FQ6)

一位学生回答 (SR18)：Because the title is "KEEP IT UP".

这一追问引导学生深度理解课文标题，不过教师没有就此止步，而是考虑到班里还有不同层次的学生，于是继续追问：What does "KEEP IT UP" mean? (FQ7) 并请英语学习有一定困难的学生回答，学生回答 (SR19)：It means "Keeping a good situation".

教师感谢这位学生，并给予鼓励。显然，这一层次的问题很适合这位学生，也能促使他更多地参与课堂的讨论。

教师引导学生进一步理解课文标题的其他部分，提出以下问题：What about "Chinese student fitting in well"? (IQ4)

一位学生回答 (SR20)：It means she has adapted to the life there.

以上一组对于课文标题的提问，不仅加深了学生对课文标题的理解，为学生理解随后的课文奠定了很好的基础，而且这种追问也发展了学生思维的深刻性，使学生意识到对课文标题不能只是一扫而过，而是要加深理解。

教师呈现以下文章结构，引导学生理解段落大意。

表3-6　课文结构分析

Part	Paragraphs	Main idea of each part
1		It is a brief _____ to Xie Lei.
2		It is about _____ in life and learning and how she _____ .
3		It is about _____ she has made and her _____ .
4		It is about _____ to Xie Lei.

教师让学生扫读课文并回答：How many parts does the text include? (IQ5)

学生扫读后给出一致答案 (SR21)：4.

教师马上追问：What are they? (FQ8)

一位学生给出答案 (SR22): Paragraph 1 is Part 1. Paragraph 2 to 5 is Part 2. Paragraph 6 is Part 3 and Paragraph 7 is Part 4.

教师再追问学生是否有不同的意见：Do you all agree? Are there any different divisions? (FQ9)

全班同意其分段，无人给出不同的意见。尽管这一追问没有出现不同的意见，但追问本身的作用依然是非常显著的，因为可以引导学生形成精准阅读、精准回答的好习惯。

然后，教师要求学生全面通读课文，并写出段落大意。学生填写了不同的内容，教师引导学生展开讨论，形成以下共识的答案：

表 3-7　课文段落大意分析

Part	Paragraphs	Main idea of each part
1	1	It is a brief introduction to Xie Lei.
2	2-5	It is about the difficulties in life and learning and how she overcame them.
3	6	It is about the progress she has made and her plans.
4	7	It is about the wishes to Xie Lei.

这一活动是对段落意义的总体把握，是随后深度提问的基础。正是在此基础上，学生思维的深刻性品质可以得到发展。此文较长，情节虽不复杂，但对学生而言比较陌生。对于这类课文，若直接进入深度提问，不先进行整体把握，难以真正进入深度理解，学生思维的深刻性则难以发展。

在学生准确把握段落大意之后，教师随即开始引导学生讨论文章内容。

教师问：Where do you think this article might have been published? (IQ6)

学生答不上来，教师追问：Can you find a sentence to help us in Paragraph 2? (FQ10)

学生回答 (SR23)：Xie Lei, who is 21 years old, has come to our university to study …

教师追问：So? (FQ11)

学生回答 (SR24)：It might have been published in a college newspaper.

教师追问：I agree on that. From which words did you get it? (FQ12)

学生回答 (SR25)："Our university."

正是这一连串的追问使得学生可以准确地获得相关信息。教师肯定学生的答案，引导之后开始理解文章内容。教师问：According to Para 1, how did Xie Lei feel when she got her visa? (IQ7)

学生回答 (SR26): She was very excited and nervous.

教师马上追问：Why did she feel nervous? (FQ13)

学生回答 (SR27)：Because she didn't know what to expect.

教师进一步追问：What does "She didn't know what to expect" mean? (FQ14)

学生回答 (SR28)：It means she didn't know what would happen in future.

教师追问：Yes, it means she didn't know what her future would be. But were there any other reasons for her nervousness? (FQ15)

学生回答 (SR29)：She left her families and friends and went to London alone. She had no families and friends there.

这一组追问使得学生对基于语篇的语义形成深层理解，这种追问引导学生准确获得相关信息，从而发展学生思维的准确性，形成对文化交往的背景的准确理解。

教师问：Yes. Did she use to go abroad? (IQ8)

学生回答 (SR30)：No. It was her first time.

教师追问：What was Xie Lei's difficulties in her new life (FQ16)?

学生回答 (SR31)：She had to get used to a whole new way of life, which can take up all her concentration.

教师问：What does "take up" mean? (IQ9)

学生回答 (SR32)：It means she used a lot of time to get used to the new life.

教师追问：We don't use time, we spend time. She spent lots of time getting used to the new life. That means adapting to the new life took up lots of her time. Then, here "take up" means? ... (FQ17)

学生回答 (SR33)：Occupy.

教师追问：Good. So how did she overcome the difficulties in life? (FQ18)

学生回答 (SR34)：She learned almost everything again.

教师进一步追问：Yes, and from where did she get help? (FQ19)

学生回答 (SR35)：From a host family.

教师追问：What help did she get from the host family? (FQ20)

学生回答 (SR36)：She got lots of good advice.

学生回答 (SR37)：She had the chance to learn more about the new culture.

学生回答 (SR38)：She had a substitute family.

这一组追问对内容的深度讨论，引导学生形成丰富的认知，从而通过准确获得相关信息而发展思维的深刻性，加深跨文化理解。

教师问：What can the substitute family offer her? (IQ10)

学生回答 (SR39)：They can offer her comfort.

教师追问：What do you think the substitute family cannot offer her? (FQ21)

学生回答 (SR40)：They cannot offer her the warmth of a real family.

学生回答 (SR41)：They cannot offer selfless love.

教师问：Yes. Maybe they cannot offer unconditional love. I think no one will offer us unconditional love except our parents, for which we should be grateful. And why was learning also difficult for Xie Lei? (IQ11)

学生回答 (SR42)：Because studying here is quite different from studying in China.

教师问：Who helped Xie Lei with her learning difficulty? (FQ22)

学生回答 (SR43)：Her tutor.

教师追问：What did her tutor help her with? (FQ23)

学生回答 (SR44)：Her tutor helped her with how to write an essay.

教师追问：How did she finish her first essay? (FQ24)

学生回答 (SR45)：She found an article she wanted on the Net, made a summary of the article, revised the draft and handed in.

教师提问：How did her tutor grade her essay? (FQ25)

学生回答 (SR46)：An E.

教师追问：Do you think Xie Lei's way of finishing her essay has something to do with the education in China? (IQ12)

学生回答 (SR47)：Maybe.

教师就相关性提问：How is it relevant? (FQ26)

学生回答 (SR48)：Students in China are not encouraged to express our own opinion. We are passive learners.

教师给予学生回应：Yes. So I always encourage you to be a critical learner.

显然，不断的追问使学生可以通过深度的思考发现问题的本质，从而形成更为深刻的、准确的跨文化理解。

课文随后一段用较大篇幅介绍了外国教师给谢蕾的建议，但这一段文章的语篇标识词（Discourse Markers）对语义理解干扰较大，这种干扰或许是作者有意为之。深度分析这一组标识词与准确的语义关联，是发展学生思维深刻性非常难得的机遇，更是引导学生基于他人体验而形成深刻的跨文化理解的难得机遇。这种有深度的讨论，既发展了学生的思维品质，同时形成了准确、深刻的跨文化理解，发展了学生基于体验的跨文化理解能力。于是，教师就课文中一处重要内容提问：What advice did the tutor give Xie Lei? (IQ13)

鉴于学生对这一内容理解有一定困难，教师给出两种结构图，然后再问学生：Which mind map shows the structure of the advice? (IQ14) Give your reasons. Read and then discuss with your partner.

表 3-8　外国教师给谢蕾的建议

Structure 1		Structure 2		
Tutor's Advice	First of all …	Tutor's Advice	First of all …	
	Besides …		Besides …	…
	Then …			Then …
	Finally …			Finally …

学生回答 (SR49)：I agree with the second one. First of all, Xie Lei should show thanks to other authors. Besides, "what other people thought was not the most important thing. He wanted to know what I thought". That means the tutor thought Xie Lei should express her own opinion. Then the tutor explained how Xie Lei could express her own opinion. First, she should read a lot and analyse. Then she should give her opinion and explained. Finally she was encouraged to contradict other authors.

教师感谢这位学生回答，然后问其他学生：Do all of you agree with him? (FQ27) 此时教师发现一位学生举手，教师问：What is your opinion? (FQ28)

学生表示要画出自己理解的结构图，教师邀请学生到黑板上画出结构图，学生画出以下结构图 (SR50)：

$$
\text{Tutor's advice} \begin{cases} \text{First of all} \\ \text{Besides} \begin{cases} \text{Read and analyse} \\ \text{Then } \ldots \text{ give her opinion and explain} \end{cases} \\ \text{Finally} \end{cases}
$$

教师感谢这位学生的回答后，让全班关注这里最后一条建议 "contradict the authors" 不属于教授的建议，教师就此询问全班同学：Is there any different question? Do you all agree with him? (FQ29)。

另一位同学提出不同意见，学生回答 (SR51)：I don't think so. Contradicting the author is also about how to express her own opinion. And it is more difficult than "give my own opinion and explain". That is why the writer uses the word "even" here. This word tells us "Finally" should parallel "Then" instead of "Besides" ….

教师在感谢这位同学发言后询问是否还有不同意见，然后告诉学生自己同意这位同学的意见，教师展示自己理解的教授的指导结构图：

表 3-9　教师理解的教授的指导结构

Tutor's advice	First of all		Show acknowledgements
	Besides, be a critical learner, express her own opinion		Read and analyse
			Then, form her own opinion and explain
			Finally, contradict the authors' opinion

教师明确告诉学生，这里 first of all 对应的是 besides，不是 then, finally，这是很容易出现理解错误的。

尽管这一段讨论用时较长（6 分钟），但引导学生深度理解文章内容，发现语言结构关联下的语义关联，形成准确、深刻的跨文化理解，非常有效地发展了学生思维的深刻性。

在学生思维品质发展的同时，学生对学习中遇到的困难的深度分析，以及提供合理的克服困难的方法，使他们可以体验到克服学习困难，尤其是跨文化理解导致的学习困难的成就，体验成长之美，并形成克服困难的能力，实现自己的成长。

之后，教师问学生：So what is Xie Lei's progress in learning? (FQ30)

学生回答 (SR52)：She is now a more autonomous learner. 教师追问：What is "an autonomous learner" like? (FQ31)

学生回答 (SR53)：An autonomous learner should be an independent learner.

(SR54)：An autonomous learner should be an active learner.

(SR55)：An autonomous learner should be a critical learner.

(SR56)：An autonomous learner should be self-motivated.

(SR57)：An autonomous learner should be self-managed.

(SR58)：An autonomous learner should be self-disciplined.

教师总结说：Yes. So only when you are an autonomous learner can you really learn well. Ask yourself if you are an autonomous learner. See what you can improve. 同时在黑板上完成以下板书：

An autonomous learner
- an independent learner
- a critical learner
- an active learner
- a self-motivated learner
- a self-disciplined learner
- a self-managed learner
- …

这一组讨论引导学生深度分析文本，而且结合自身的英语学习经历、知识基础，深度展开讨论，形成丰富而深刻的跨文化理解，从而通过广度与精准度发展学生思维的深刻性。

3．通过建构价值与意义发展文化理解

在全面理解课文内容、尤其是形成对以跨文化冲突为现象的跨文化误解的深度理解之后，教师引导学生进入深度讨论，帮助学生理解深层意思。教师先引导学生总结课文，然后提问：At the end of the news report, the writer says "She deserves to succeed". Why does Xie Lei deserve to succeed? (IQ15)

学生回答 (SR59)：She is active to adapt to the new way of life. She learned almost everything again. She got help from the host family.

另一学生回答 (SR60)：She is brave to face a new life. Though she stayed in London without families and friends, she was not scared. She tried her best to overcome the difficulty.

另一学生回答 (SR61)：She is enterprising. When she got an E in the essay, she asked for advice from the tutor instead of just keeping silent.

另一学生回答 (SR62)：She is very adaptable. Now she feels more at home in London and has become an autonomous learner.

另一学生回答 (SR63)：She is active in after-class activities. She is going to join a few clubs and make some new friends.

然后，教师引导学生思考自己的学习：Yes. Now let's make a summary. If we want to fit in well when learning abroad, we need to be …? (FQ32)

学生回答 (SR64)：Independent.

另一学生回答 (SR65)：Psychologically strong.

另一学生回答 (SR66)：Adaptable.

另一学生回答 (SR67)：Active.

另一学生回答 (SR68)：Hard-working.

另一学生回答 (SR69)：Be an autonomous learner.

最后，教师引导学生得出结论，出国学习要学习谢蕾的做法，也要作好准备，尽可能避免遇到类似谢蕾的困难，从而取得更大成功。

这一组讨论使问题更具有丰富性和高度，从而促进学生思维深刻性的发展。

在这一课例中，教师提出的追问问题（32个）远远多于起始问题（15个），由此促成了学生给出多样的回答（对47个问题给出69次回答），从而使跨文化理解与思维深刻性的发展成为可能。

表3-10　不同类型问题数量与学生回答次数

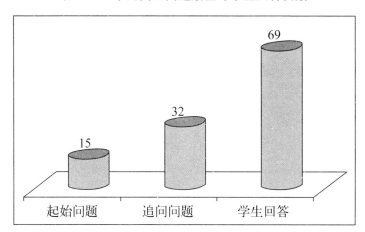

这一课例说明，在课文阅读理解教学中，教师设计的追问问题以及生成性的追问，使学生在信息获取的过程中不断发展跨文化理解与思维的深度；通过问题向深度不断发展，非常显著地促进学生跨文化理解能力与思维深刻性的发展。教师事先设计这些追问问题是基础，但课堂教学中基于教学生成性的过程出现的机会，教师凭借个人智慧而进行的追问，也是发展学生跨文化理解能力和思维深刻性的关键因素。无论是预设的追问，还是生成中的追问，都需要教师具有跨文化理解能力和思维深刻性。

这节课促使学生体验如何面对学习困难、尤其是跨文化理解导致的困难，体验如何走出跨文化理解困难，促进自己的跨文化理解与思维发展，实现自己的成长之美。这充分说明在跨文化理解主题的单元教学中，整合语言能力、文化理解能力、思维品质、品格与审美情趣发展的可能路径，也充分说明教师的提问、尤其是基于教学智慧的追问，在发展学生的阅读理解能力、文化理解能力、思维品质、品格与审美情趣等方面的重要作用。

三、基于分析文化态度发展文化理解能力

人类文化不仅是生活方式，更是价值观念，这些价值观念并不完全相同，但我们可以基于自己的价值观念理解他人的价值观念，从而发展学生的文化理解能力。以下这一案例就是基于我们自己的跨文化态度去理解其他文化不同的价值观念的案例。

Leaving some behind for birds

As we drove by a recently harvested field, I saw a flock of sandhill cranes gleaning the left-over grain. I thought of the words in a holy book to suggest people to deliberately leave some produce behind for those less fortunate—the sort of people who wouldn't have land of their own from which to harvest. No simple handout, this law guaranteed them a chance to improve their lives while maintaining their dignity as they labored in the fields.

I also remember I have read some suggestions from some Chinese ethnic minorities which encourage harvesting people to leave some grains to the birds and the wild animals which shared the same habitat with us.

The command to leave behind the left-overs for the poor was not to be taken lightly. In fact, if nothing remained in the fields following harvest, the landowner could be punished.

As I thought about leaving a little behind for those less fortunate, I remembered the words of some friends. Having no children and knowing they can't take their money with them, they've decided to spend every cent before they die. If anything happens to be left over (as I expect it will), a few well-off nieces will get it. Granted, this couple earned their money and it is theirs to dispose of as they wish. What shocked me, however, was their comment that "No charity will ever get a penny of it!" There will be no left-overs for the less fortunate from their field!

There is in fact a law from the Hebrews: Don't be too greedy with their blessings. They learned that a joyful time, like a harvest, is a time for generosity and compassion. A wise man taught us in that vein when he commanded us to share our excess and to love our neighbor as ourselves. In most human cultures today, both faiths embrace the concept of sharing with and caring for others and encourage a willingness to give up what is rightfully ours to share with those less fortunate. Not generously loving is no more an option for us as human beings than not leaving grain in the field was for the landowner.

I'm not a farmer—I have no fields, vineyards or olive trees—but I certainly have been blessed with more than I need. Remembering that time and talent are as valuable as money, I imagine most of us have plenty of something that could be shared with those less fortunate. It has been said that the best thing anyone can give someone is a chance. The bits of grain left in the field gave the cranes nourishment and a better chance of surviving their long flight south. By leaving part of the harvest, the poor were given a chance to survive and better their lives. Do you have anything, even a few left-overs, to share that could give someone a chance?

　　正如这篇文章的陈述，其表达的观点来自希伯来文化，告诉人们收获的时候不要把地里所有庄稼都收获完，而要留下一些给鸟儿和他人。这与我们熟知的把每一束稻穗、麦穗都捡回来的传统有着很大的不同，也与我们所知的西方文化中在庄稼地里树一些稻草人驱赶啄食庄稼的小鸟这一传统有着很大的不同。这似乎是很难理解的，因为我们可以把庄稼收获回来，再分享给小鸟和他人。

　　如何理解希伯来文化中这一传统？如何理解给予他们帮助之时不伤害他人的尊严？我们不能从文化现象形成直接理解，我们需要引导学生进行分析和讨论，从而形成跨文化理解。

　　我们首先引导学生讨论如何不伤害他人的尊严。这其实对学生来说更加容易理解，因为学生也肯定希望在自己得到他人帮助的同时保持自己的尊严。我们让学生讨论：如果你考试得了 59 分，你是希望老师同情你而给你施舍 1 分，还是希望老师再次批改你的试卷发现你的试卷其实可以少扣 1 分？学生选择之后，我们再让学生讨论：若你的学业需要得到经济资助，你是希望直接得到他人或机构给你的助学金，还是希望你通过自己的劳动得到助学金，或是希望通过努力学习得到奖学金？为什么？讨论之后，学生就能更加深刻地理解帮助与尊严的关系。

　　当然，我们还需要继续讨论为什么我们应给鸟儿留下一些食物，为什么人类需要鸟儿。这是人与自然的关系。我们的庄稼来自大自然，来自阳光雨露。没有大自然，单凭我们的劳作也没有庄稼。鸟儿也是大自然的一部分，鸟儿帮我们吃庄稼上的虫子，所以我们要为鸟儿留下一些粮食。

　　我们引导学生建立这样一个分析过程：

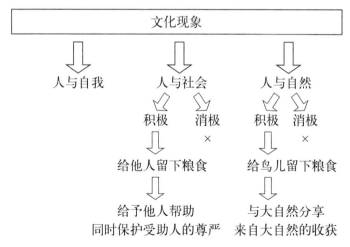

图 3-1　跨文化现象分析过程

　　经过这样的分析与讨论，学生可以基于跨文化的态度，形成文化理解。显然，我们可以引导学生通过基于跨文化态度的文化分析形成文化理解。

当然，因为这一文化价值观念与我们传统的文化价值观念差异较大，可能单就这一篇短文进行分析讨论还不足以发展学生对这一价值观念的文化理解能力，我们还可以为学生提供更为丰富的阅读材料，让学生在下一节课向全班介绍各自的理解，甚至可以组织一次班级专刊，让学生分组阅读和讨论，写出各组对这一价值观念的进一步阅读和思考。

我们可以选择以下材料供学生阅读，并引导学生进一步讨论。

这是一个为世界各地饥民提供食物的项目的发展过程介绍，我们可以基于此了解其发展的历史与现实。

Gleaning for the Hungry People Project

Gleaning for the Hungry People Project started producing food in the summer 1982 just after the Christmas in 1981 when Wally and his wife, Norma, got to know that the tons of California cull fruit thrown away annually could be used as "gleanings for the needy of the world".

During the first summer of 1982, the Wenges and local volunteers were able to process about 15,000 pounds of donated cull fruit using donated equipment in a borrowed raisin dehydration facility in Yettem. Roughly 1,500 pounds of sun-dried peaches and nectarines produced that first year were used to feed the hungry in Guatemala after a hurricane and flood occurred there. A shipping company helped transport the dried fruit to Guatemala and it was distributed by some local volunteers. The next six years all of the dried fruit was shipped to Thailand to help feed the Cambodian refugees who had no enough food there.

Through process improvements and focused volunteer recruiting bases throughout the western U.S. and Canada, production increased rapidly in the early years. In the 1986 season, over 500,000 pounds of fresh peaches and nectarines were processed. In April 1987, just nine weeks before the start of the summer fruit season, Wally got some bad news … the borrowed Yettem facility was being lost to foreclosure. With only days to remove the fruit processing equipment, things looked pretty grim. But in the eleventh hour, a 10-acre former tomato-packing facility in Sultana was given to them. Even with a delayed start, roughly 40,000 pounds of dried fruit was produced that year.

In late fall of 1988, Wally invited more volunteers to join Gleanings Project. Over 2 million pounds of fresh fruit was processed that summer. In 1991, Wally acted on an opportunity to purchase an 11.6-acre parcel adjacent to the existing facility, which allowed for expanded production and improved staff housing.

Gleanings continued to flourish even after Wally went home to be with the Lord in 1999. Len and Lois Nylin served as directors from 1999 through early 2004, and the Project continued to develop and strengthen under their influence. Soup mix production began in 2000, with 160,000 8-ounce servings produced in the inaugural season.

From 2004–2012, the Project enlarged the office and soup plant, completed the dining hall and chapel, added RV spaces, and kicked off the building of a new 10-plex.

Fritz and Cindy Meier have been serving with excellence in building, improving, and caring for this ministry, since 2012. Under their direction, the beautiful new 10-plex building was finished, as well as a 2-bay fumigation tunnel, complete with a rain canopy. The fumigation bays greatly enhance our soup production process. We have seen landscaping and building improvements, such as the 8-plex rooms being painted and redecorated. The Meiers have increased short-term outreaches, including both staff and Gleanings' volunteers in the trips. This has allowed a great opportunity for volunteers to participate in not just the start, but the completion of our mission, from production to delivery, and see first-hand the impact our product has on the world. A project to bring solar power to Gleanings was completed in 2018. The solar power will significantly reduce our cost of operation for years to come.

Gleanings has also pioneered a new program to "Backpackers", opening our lives to international travelers who seek opportunities to volunteer.

This project continues to fulfill its vision to feed the hungry of the world, both physically and spiritually. In 2015, with the help of thousands of volunteers, over 53 million servings of soup were produced and shipped to more than 30 different nations.

这是项目志愿者参与类似项目之后的感受。

Gratitude and choices with After the Harvest

After working at After the Harvest for a little over a year, I have learned many lessons. I've learned that a bushel of apples weigh about 25 pounds. I've learned how to dig potatoes, plant tomatoes, harvest chestnuts, and identify turnips. I've learned my way around Kansas City delivering to food pantries and kitchens. Of all of these lessons, I think the biggest and the one that will stay with me always is gratitude.

Gratitude for farmers. I have always loved farm fresh produce, but it wasn't until I got to know so many of the farmers in our area, that I really learned to appreciate the work that they put in to provide fruits and vegetables to feed their communities. The fact, that success of their crop (and many times their paycheck) is determined by so many variables that are out of their control, i.e. weather, pests, consumer demand. I am in awe of their ability to deal with so much uncertainty and come back each new season eager to plant again. This newly found appreciation of their work has made me focus on seeking out local food options whenever possible. With all of the hard work these farmers put in, they deserve to be chosen.

Gratitude for my ability to choose to feed myself healthy food. After delivering food to various pantries over the past year, I've realized how lucky

I am that I can buy and prepare food that is healthy (not that I always do, but I have the option!). Some people in our community don't have that luxury—they have to make do with whatever is available to them. They can't always choose to eat healthily. I however have that choice and am consciously trying to take advantage of it.

Gratitude for my coworkers. These ladies I have the pleasure of working with every day are wonderful. They will spend many dedicated hours working to get produce into the hands of those who need it. Due to an office of only four full time staff and a seasonal part time individual, all of our days are busy. We all find time to help each other out. Sandy, Mindy, Lisa, Mariah, and I have all chosen to work here ... chosen the hectic days in order to help provide more choices for our farmers and those that are hungry in our community.

These three gratitudes—farmers, coworkers and the ability to choose healthy food—are just the tip of the gratitude iceberg here at After the Harvest. I am constantly feeling gratitude for so many other people and things: the volunteers who harvest in the hot summer; the people who work at pantries making sure all of the produce we bring is distributed; my boyfriend who deals with boxes, shovels, and bags in our garage; the cool mornings we've had to harvest in this fall and my cell phone that allows me to make calls from the field. Once I start thinking about all of the things I am grateful for, the list seems to go on forever.

若学生阅读以上内容有一定语言困难，我们可以让学生阅读下面这两个可能完全虚构的故事，然后进行讨论：

Could you please move the wood for us?

One day during the Second World War, a hungry and tired man in a worn hat and an old coat hovered over the fence of a house in a German village where an old man and a little boy lived. The old man observed for a long time, and then walked up to the man and said, "Sir, would you help me to carry the pile of wood into the yard? I am too old to carry it. However, I can't pay you because I have no money. But I can cook some potato soup for you. That's what I only have now." The man's eyes were bright and repeatedly promised. The coat off, the hat off, and soon he tried to carry all the wood and stacked neatly. That night, the sweaty guest was in the kitchen to have dinner with the house owners in a comfortable mood. During the war, many people fled the city, and the elderly asked passers-by countless times to move the only pile of wood in and out of the courtyard.

The one hundredth eater

At noon, the rush hour passed, and eaters had already gone out from a small and crowded noodle shop. When the boss was going to catch a breath and read the newspaper, someone came in. It was an old woman and a little boy.

"How much is a bowl of beef noodles?" Grandma sat down to take out her purse and count the money, and ordered a bowl of beef noodles. Then she pushed the bowl to her grandson, and the little boy was ready to swallow down the noodles but looked at his grandma.

"Grandma, have you really had lunch?" "Of course," said the grandmother slowly chewing a small piece of pickled radish. Just a flash, the little boy poured the bowl of noodles into his belly.

Just then, the shop owner went to the two and said, "Congratulations to you, dear granny, you are so lucky because you are our 100th eater today, and you got that bowl of noodles for free. That's the tradition of my noodle shop." And he returned the money to the old lady.

After that day, the owner saw the little boy often squatting near his shop. But he was too busy preparing the noodles and beef. He never checked what the boy was doing there. One day over a month later, he saw the boy squatting opposite to his noodle shop as usual. He was not that busy that day because his daughter helped him in the shop. Then he went near the door of his small noodle shop and saw the boy, who was counting the eaters coming into his shop! The boy put a little pebble into the painting circle when one eater came into the noodle shop! The shop owner understood why the boy was doing that. Lunch time was almost over that time, but the number of small stones inside the circle was even less than fifty.

The boss called up all the old customers he knew, "Please come to my noodle shop and eat a bowl of noodles. It's my treat today." Soon, a lot of people came in. "Eighty-one, eighty-two, eighty-three …" The little boy was counting faster and faster and his face started to shine. At last, the moment came when the ninety-ninth small stone was put in the circle.

At that moment, the little boy hurried his grandmother, who was selling some rough sewing work at the corner of a back street nearby, and took her to the shop.

"Grandma, this time it's my treat. As a matter of fact, it's the boss's treat because you are today's 100th eater at his shop," the little boy said with pride when he came into the shop with his grandma.

"Yes, you are, Granny. You're so lucky," said the boss, who hinted other eaters waiting outside for a short while when he saw the boy running home with a big smile on his face.

Grandma shared the noodles with the little boy but the little boy had just a little and said, "I'm full, granny." And he ran out of the shop in a flash. The old lady finished the noodles and thanked the boss. The boss said, "No thanks. That's the luck of your lovely little grandson."

通过引导阅读这些内容并开展小组讨论，可以发展学生对这一价值观念更加深刻的理解，甚至可能促进他们开始思考：我们自己应该如何帮助他人？

本章小结

中外文化理解能力是中外文化传播能力的基础，进而是文化意识发展的基础。发展中外文化理解能力应以课堂教学为主，尤其是基于单元主题为中外文化的教学内容，开展单元融合的中外文化理解教学，发展学生中外文化理解能力，同时要适度开展主题实践活动。

发展学生的中外文化理解能力要遵循最近发展区原则、聚合与分散有机结合原则、课堂与生活中随机进行原则以及指向品格原则，从语言的文化内涵、非语言的文化内涵两大领域进行发展。

推荐阅读材料

鲁子问 . 2006. 中小学英语跨文化教育理论与实践 [M]. 北京：中国电力出版社 .

夏谷鸣 . 2014. 以文化为导向的外文特色教育 [J]. 英语学习（教师版）.（7）.

程良宏 . 2013. 文化理解型反思性实践者：双语教师的角色分析 [J]. 全球教育展望 .（10）.

第四章 高中英语促进中外优秀文化传播能力发展方法

第一节 高中英语促进中外优秀文化传播能力发展活动设计原则

传播中外优秀文化是高中英语课程对文化意识素养的基本要求，也是我国学生学习英语的根本目的之一，2017 高中英语课标对此有非常明确的要求，而且从文化自信的高度作出相关的规定。

基于传播学与跨文化传播的研究，我们认为，高中英语促进中外优秀文化传播能力发展应基于以下基本原则进行：

1. 积极原则

人类为了生存发展而创造文化，因此人类文化的最根本价值在于促进人类的生存发展。文化传播作为人类文化实践活动，应该以促进人类生存发展为第一原则与根本目的。所以，中外优秀文化传播应该传播一切促进人类生存的内容，而且其方法与目的也应是促进人类生存发展的。此一类内容、方法、目的可称之为积极内容、积极方法、积极目的，此一原则则为积极原则。

高中英语教材所传播的中外文化内容、引导学生传播的中外文化内容，皆已经过国家审查，其内容应该是积极的，但我们自选的中外优秀文化传播的内容，是否都是积极的，则需要加以审析，如很多来自传统的、其他时代的故事，其内容可能在本地传统和某些时代是积极的，而对其他传统、其他时代可能未必是积极的。例如，孔融让梨的故事使很多外国学生认为"让梨"不公平；愚公移山的故事也使很多外国学生认为这种方法对生态环境不利。同时，有些内容可能在我们的视角是积极的，而在其他视角则未必。例如，英语教材中牛郎织女的故事，很多外国学生认为，牛郎偷看仙女洗澡、拿走织女衣服，是不道德的。此外，我们知道，以坚船利炮、殖民奴役去传播文化，无论其文化多么先进，其方法都不是积极的，都不是促进人类生存的，而是给人类带来灾难的。

在发展学生的中外优秀文化传播能力时，我们应坚持引导学生遵循积极原则，传播积极的内容，运用积极的方法，指向积极的目的。这也是 2017 高中英语课标以及本书一直强调传播"中外优秀文化"而不只是"中外文化"的原因。

2. 主动原则

文化传播的方式很多，可以是显性的传播，也可以是隐性的传播；可以是直接的传播，还可以是间接的传播。我们直接向外国人介绍中国的"有所为有所不为"的文化观念，是显性的传播；我们在与外国人讨论如何解决问题时，采用"有所为有所不为"的立场，提出解决问题的方法和建议，则是隐性地传播"有所为有所不为"的文化观念。我们向外国人介绍中国的"天人合一"思想，是直接地传播"天人合一"的中国思想；而我们采用介绍中国中医根据一年四季变化调理身体的具体做法，则是间接地传播"天人合一"的中国思想。

无论采用哪种传播方式，作为文化传播者，我们都应有主动传播的意识，不仅英语教师应主动传播中外优秀文化，我们的学生作为英语学习者，也应主动传播中外优秀文化，这是我们学习英语的根本目的之一。

3. 共同意愿原则

如前所述，文化传播应遵循积极原则，传播积极的内容，采用积极的方法，坚持积极的目的。何为"积极"？总有一个判断标准，而这一标准，不应只是传播者的标准，也不应只是传播对象的标准，而应是双方共同的标准。

因此，在传播中外优秀文化，尤其是判断何为"优秀"上，在传播的利益、内容、方法、目的上，既不采取自我意愿（at my will）取向，也不放弃自我意愿而采取对方意愿（at your will）取向，而是建构共同意愿取向（at our will）。

以志愿者工作为例。一主流教材中有课文介绍西方志愿者在非洲从事化学教学工作，结果做化学实验时，学生吓得夺门而逃，该志愿者反思：这些非洲穷孩子不需要学化学，只需要学种地。这位志愿者教化学的想法是以传播者的意愿为取向，而认为非洲孩子不需要学化学，只需要学种地的想法，完全是以传播对象的意愿为取向。其实，非洲孩子需要把化学与种地结合起来进行学习。非洲孩子不学科学，非洲没有未来；非洲孩子不结合实际学科学，非洲的现实生存问题无法解决。二者结合，这才是双方共同的意愿。

4. 理解性原则

文化传播的基础是文化理解，准确理解文化内涵，方可准确传播文化。准确理解中外文化，把握其优秀文化，是传播中外优秀文化的基础。

除了对文化内涵的理解之外，还需要理解传播对象的话语方式与思维方式。传播中外优秀文化是一种积极的传播行为，既然是传播，自然就希望对方理解自己的传播内容，所以传播中外优秀文化，必须坚持理解性原则，即：促进对方理解的传播，可以减少对方理解的困难，保证对方理解的准确性。在向外国人传播中国优秀文化时，应该使用对方能够理解的语言，因为能够使用外语的中国人远远多于能够理解汉语的外国人。促进理解的传播还应该使用对方能够理解的话语方式和思维方式进行表达，因为即使是使用外语，若完全采用中国人才能理解的话语方式和思维方式进行表达（如 What he did is as Sima Zhao's thought.），绝大多数外国人仍然不能理解其意，因为他们可能对"司马昭之心"全然无知。在向中国人传播外国优秀文化时，则完全可以采用汉语，以及我们中国人自己的思维方式。所以，传播中外优秀文化，应尽可能使用传播对象能理解的话语方式、思维方式和语言进行，这要求传播者不仅要具有外语运用能力，能够准确理解和运用外语进行表达，更要求传播者具有准确理解和运用传播对象的话语方式和思维方式的能力。

5.品格指向原则

一如中外文化理解能力的品格指向原则，中外优秀文化传播能力的原则也应包含品格指向原则。因为根据2017高中英语课标对文化意识素养的要求，中外文化理解与传播能力应该是品格教育的基础，理解中应该把握品格，或者关键应该是对中外文化中品格的理解，尤其是从跨文化的视角把握品格，这使得英语课程的品格内涵不同于其他课程的品格内涵，成为英语学科育人与其他学科育人不同的学科特性。

高中英语课程的中外优秀文化传播能力应该具有显著的品格指向，这不仅指在发展学生中外优秀文化传播能力的过程中发展相应品格，培养传播中外优秀文化能力本身也需要，而且能够发展相应品格。应该说，传播中外优秀文化的直接目的是发展传播对象的文化意识。不过，在传播中外优秀文化过程中，传播者的文化意识也会发展。所以，高中学生无论是作为中外优秀文化的传播对象，还是作为中外优秀文化的传播者，他们的品格教育都是传播中外优秀文化的根本指向。

第二节　高中英语促进中外优秀文化传播能力发展具体方法

一、确定能力目标

基于传播学与跨文化传播能力的研究可知，高中英语中外优秀文化传播能力应以中外文化理解能力为基础，而且如前所述，传播对象的话语方式和思维方式也应成为中外优秀文化传播能力的基础，中外优秀文化传播能力则应以文化传播方式选择与运用能力、文化传播内容选定能力、文化传播内容组织与呈现能力、文化传播目的达成能力为基本构成，以图表示如下：

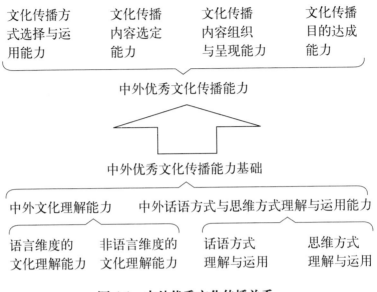

图 4-1 中外优秀文化传播关系

话语方式与思维方式是传播中外优秀文化所需的能力基础，思维方式属于思维品质范畴，此处不赘述。话语方式则需要简要说明。

就传播而言，传播对象更为熟悉的是自己群体的话语类型。所谓话语类型，是社会语言学研究的一个重要领域。话语类型理论研究始于前苏联语言哲学家巴赫金，他在 20 世纪 50 年代发表的《言语话语类型问题》（*The Problem of Speech Genres*）论文，是话语类型研究的起点。话语类型"是某个话语社团中人们为一定的语言资源和非语言资源（离散资源）做事情的社会过程的习惯"，是人们约定俗成的、被社团成员所接受的一种类型。从社会语言学的视角看，话语类型是人类不同群体的一种社会语言活动，是作者和读者、讲话者和受话者在一定的社会群体交往情景中互动建立的，这种话语经过反复使用而形成的、相对稳定的交际形式。不同的人类群体在生成、理解、解释话语类型时，基于共同的原型、框架和隐喻，形成共同理解，从而实现交际。话语类型具有比较固定的语义单位、语用单位、词汇、语法、音系、文章结构、话语逻辑等形式。

话语类型是语言运用中自然形成的。当人类群体主动基于话语类型，运用基于话语类型的特征，进行交际表达时，则创造出话语方式。

厘清话语方式这一概念，需先解析话语和模式这两个术语。话语（discourse）是语言运用的扩展性段落，也就是说，在语言实际应用中，句子连续形成的句段动态结构，是一套系统地组织起来的论述，用以描述、限定什么才是能够言说的；是一种认知方式，它是社会、历史、制度框架的产物。也有人认为，话语是思考权力、知识与语言关系的一种方法，即在现代权力系统中的一种说话权力运作方式。正如法国思想家福柯所言，话语本身就是"物"，不仅仅是对它指涉之物的再现，也就是说，话语本身具有某种物质性。正是由于如此，话语也是一种社会实践形式。话语不仅是语言，并不仅仅停留在嘴上，它还是社会性的，而不是纯粹的个人行为。"话语"一词暗示了一种特定的世界观。事实上，话语在个人身份的确立、相互关系的建构、心理过程的阐释等方面发挥着重要作用。

话语方式（或话语方式固定而形成的模式）就是从不断重复出现的事件中发现和抽象出的规律、解决类似问题的经验的总结，事实上，只要是一再重复出现的事物，就可能存在某种方式。每种方式都可以重复地使用，用于解决类似的问题。

如前所述，话语类型是总结归纳话语形成的，话语方式是通过发现话语类型，然后对话语行为进行主动干预和规范而形成的，是话语行为者为了达到话语目的，主动采用某一话语类型而表现出的话语方式。话语方式的关键是话语所依赖的话语类型。

因此可知，话语方式是发话者为了实现自身的话语目的，采用某一话语社群普遍使用的话语用词、句式、语篇结构、逻辑关系等而表现出的话语形态特征，因此存在官方话语方式、民间话语方式、学术话语方式等不同的话语方式。话语方式是发话者的主动选择，选择的依据是发话者的话语目的。发话者在选择时可能受其自身对于受话者态度的影响。

构成话语方式的要素是：发话者选择的某一话语社群的话语特征、发话者对受话者的态度、发话者与受话者的关系、发话者的话语目的，以及发话者话语意图的可理解性与受话者理解能力之间的距离，即：

$$
话语方式\begin{cases} 某一话语社群的话语特征 \\ 发话者对受话者的态度 \\ 发话者与受话者的关系 \\ 发话者的话语目的 \\ 发话者话语意图的可理解性与受话者理解能力之间的距离 \end{cases}
$$

显然，话语方式首先具有某一话语社群的话语特征，在语词、语句结构、语篇结构、逻辑表达方式等方面，都以该话语社群广泛使用、约定俗成的方式进行表达。

话语中表现出的发话者对受话者的态度是话语方式的重要组成部分，因为话语既是一种行为，必然表达话语者的态度，话语表达出的态度直接影响话语的行为效果。

话语方式还包括发话者与受话者的关系。发话者一般掌握着话语权，话语本来效果的形成应该是发话者与受话者的相互作用，但由于发话者掌握着话语主动权，所以发话者对受话者就具有社会权势，那么发话者的话语权就被放大，而受话者本应拥有的话语权则会减弱。

话语总是具有特定目的，发话者的话语目的是什么，也会影响话语行为。话语行为目的的实现需要受话者理解发话者的话语目的，所以受话者对发话者话语意图的理解力直接影响话语行为目的的实现。

当然，话语方式并不是一个封闭的结构，而是可能随着话语的变化而变化，同时在具体实施过程中会因其构成条件的变化而采取相应的策略，进而带来了话语方式的变化，产生话语方式的变化。

基于此可知，传播中外优秀文化主要应依于传播对象的话语方式，基于此的传播成效更高，更易于实现传播目的。

二、确定品格目标

传播中外优秀文化，直接目的在于发展传播对象基于中外优秀文化的品格，其品格目标是英语课程所规定的文化意识目标：能够以尊重文化多样性的方式找出并解决问题，调适交际策略；有兴趣和意愿了解和比较具有文化多样性的活动和事物，尊重和理解文化的多样性，领悟世界文化的多样性和丰富性，具有面向世界的开放态度和文化自信，具有国际视野、爱国情怀和国家认同感；分析、鉴别文化现象所反映的价值取向，汲取文化精华，具有正确的价值观、健康的审美情趣和积极的道德情感，并内化为个人的意识和品行，形成自尊、自信、自强的良好品格。

在发展中外优秀文化传播能力、形成传播中外优秀文化所需能力的过程中，可以、而且应该发展传播者开放、平等、尊重、宽容、客观、谨慎等积极品格，消解故步自封、妄自尊大、妄自菲薄、歧视、偏见、狭隘、盲动等消极品格，唯此方可真正形成传播中外优秀文化的能力。这些目标不同于前述英语课程已有的传播对象品格教育的目标，而是发展中外优秀文化传播能力过程中发展的传播者的品格目标。

基于之前分析，我们可以确立中外优秀文化传播能力发展的态度目标：通过中外优秀文化传播能力发展，培养学生在跨文化交往中坚持开放、平等、尊重、宽容、客观、谨慎等积极的跨文化态度，引导学生尽可能消解故步自封、妄自尊大、妄自菲薄、歧视、偏见、狭隘、盲动等消极的跨文化态度。

三、促进中外优秀文化传播能力发展的基本方法

高中英语课程发展学生传播中外优秀文化能力的基本方法是实践，同骑自行车的能力、游泳的能力一样。

这一实践就过程而言，为以下基本过程：

指导学生理解中外文化现象

指导学生基于中外文化现象理解、分析与比较中外文化现象

指导学生基于中外文化现象分析与比较，判断与选择中外文化成分

指导学生基于中外文化成分判断与选择，选择中外优秀文化进行传播

促进学生基于中外优秀文化传播发展品格

131

这一过程显示从中外文化理解到文化意识发展的全过程，以促进品格教育为目标的中外优秀文化传播也应基于这一过程，发展传播中外优秀文化的能力，也便是这一过程的各项能力。

1．中外文化的认知能力

一切中外文化接触必然导致中外文化的认知，这也是人类的"新奇认知偏向"天性的体现（人类的大脑具有一种新奇刺激源更容易形成大脑神经认知的机制，此即人类的"新奇认知偏向"）。

中外文化认知是指通过观察、观看、了解、访问、调查、研究、阅读、分析、对话、交流等中外文化交往形式，形成对其他民族文化的理解。

我们从对中外文化实践的分析可以看出，什么样的中外文化认知能力能够促进中外文化实践走向世界性的中外文化交往，避免或者弱化中外文化冲突。

中外文化实践告诉我们，全面、准确地认知其他民族文化的能力有助于促进中外文化实践走向世界性的中外文化交往。

那么，中外文化教育的目标应该包括培养学生全面而准确认知其他民族文化、进行中外文化对话交往的能力。

中外文化对话交流通常都是以语言为载体的，因此缺乏足够的外语能力，往往成为中外文化理解的主要障碍。在英国，很多人对美国文化有着比较全面、准确的了解，因为他们使用同一种语言。而世界上大多数国家和民族都使用不同的语言，这为理解其他民族文化带来了困难。因此，在向其他民族传播本民族文化时，使用其他民族的语言比使用本民族语言更加有效。所以，很多国家和民族总是不断地将本民族的文化翻译为外语，以此传播本民族的文化。实际上，懂得其他民族语言也能帮助我们更准确地认知其他民族的文化。同时，外语也是其他民族文化的一部分，因为语言不仅是文化的载体，也是文化的呈现形式。所以，在中外文化交往中，运用外语的能力也是一个非常重要的能力。

中外文化实践告诉我们，全面、准确地认知其他民族文化的能力有助于促进中外文化实践走向世界性的中外文化交往。那么，中外文化教育的目标应该包括培养学生全面而准确认知其他民族文化、进行中外文化对话交往的能力。

2．中外文化的比较能力

了解其他民族文化之后，必然会将本民族文化与其他民族文化进行比较，而中外文化比较能帮助我们把握本民族文化与其他民族文化的异同，这可以加深我们对本民族文化和其他民族文化的理解。

更为重要的是，中外文化比较是中外文化取舍的前提。在依据文化评价标准对本民族文化和其他民族文化进行比较之后，才可以决定是否要学习其他民族文化，或者学习哪些部分，而舍弃哪些部分。

中外文化认知的目的并不只在于中外文化比较，而是在中外文化比较基础上，基于正确的中外文化认知，与中外文化选择，通过中外文化交往促进本民族文化的发展，同时促进人类文化的发展，这才是中外文化比较的根本目的。

因此，中外文化教育必须培养学生的中外文化比较的能力。

3．中外文化的取舍能力

中外文化取舍是指在认知其他民族文化之后，选择学习或者舍弃其他民族文化或其中的某些成分。

在当今世界，没有一个人类群体能完全不学习其他人类群体的文化，很多人类群体的文化发展通常都是在与外国文化接触中获得其他民族的文化因素，从而形成本民族文化的新的发展。比如正在建构现代化文化的中国文化自然需要与已经实现现代化、并且已经认识到现代化的诸多矛盾的西方文化交往，学习西方文化中的先进成分，舍弃西方文化中的落后成分。这也正是对中国的受教育者进行西方文化教育的必然目的。

从文化的本质看，文化是一个人类群体区分于另一个人类群体的根本标识，文化的差异是文化的本质所规定的，全球文化完全一体化是不可能的，就像自然界存在生物多样性一样，人类必然地存在文化多样性。

在中外文化交往中，任何一个民族为了更为理想的社会文化，必然会吸取其他民族文化中那些有利于本民族更自在地生存发展的内容，而舍弃那些违反本民族更自在地生存发展的内容。

显然，中外文化的摄取与舍弃都是中外文化的必然形态，但如何取舍并不容易。合理的取舍依赖于开放的心态、准确的理解和比较，特别是合理的评价判断。

4. 中外文化的参照能力

中外文化参照是指在认知其他民族文化之后，不是简单地对其他民族文化进行取舍，而是以其他民族文化为参照对象，发现本民族文化应该弘扬的成分，或者应该舍弃的部分。

中外文化参照有着重要的意义，特别是在进入全面中外文化接触的当今时代。我们接触到全人类的文化，但我们不可能将全人类的所有文化吸收到本民族的文化之中，否则本民族文化就不存在了，成了全世界文化的大拼盘。但我们仍然有必要接触一切其他民族文化，因为全人类的文化是本民族文化的一面镜子，供我们进行中外文化的参照。

在人类历史上，形成更大生存可能的中外文化参照是屡见不鲜的，特别是近代以后，由于中外文化交往的层面更广泛，地域更广阔，关联性更强，不同的人类群体往往面临相同的文化环境和中外文化选择，因而中外文化参照更具意义。在当代，中外文化参照更是全人类的共识。

但是，中外文化参照并不总能促进本民族文化的发展，在其他民族文化参照下对本民族文化进行的错误变革可能带来灾难，这是中外文化取舍中的错误所致。

这些中外文化实践告诉我们，要促进中外文化实践走向世界性的交往，就必须培养学生合理依据其他民族文化审视本民族文化的能力。

5. 中外优秀文化的传播能力

中外优秀文化传播是指本民族文化在与其他民族文化的交往中，主动地展现、介绍自己的文化，从而让其他文化认知本民族文化。

人类文化历史上的中外文化传播有两种基本形式：血与火、笔与纸。血与火的传播形式给人类带来了很多的灾难，因此我们应该彻底放弃，而笔与纸的传播形式则更容易达到传播的目的。比如，佛教在中国的传播就是笔与纸的传播，而近代史上基督教在中国的传播就是血与火的传播。结果，中国文化中融入了很多佛教思想，但基督教思想却始终没有成为中国文化的组成部分。

在中外文化传播中，有两种展现介绍本民族文化的基本方法：强调与其他民族文化的差异性；承认与其他民族文化的差异性，但强调差异中的共同性。笔者把前一种称为"强差异传播方式"，把后一种称为"弱差异传播方式"。人类的中外文化实践表明，弱差异方式的传播效果优于强差异方式。

至于发展上述能力的具体方法，则如同中外文化理解能力的具体方法，依然是 2017 高中英语课标所倡导的整合式学习路径的课堂教学方法和主题项目实践活动方法。具体方法在前一章节已经说明，此处不再赘述。

第三节　高中英语促进中外优秀文化传播能力发展案例分析

如前一节所述，课堂教学和主题实践依然是高中英语促进中外优秀文化传播能力发展的具体方法，整合式学习路径依然是课堂教学的基本方法。以下是基于案例说明方法的具体运用。

一、课堂教学案例 1

我们先看基于 Robots 整个单元的五课时教学中，促进学生中外优秀文化传播能力发展的具体实践。

表 4-1　单元教学目标

教学内容	Robots	
教学对象	高二学生	
单元目标（重点突出文化意识）	语言能力	熟悉有关机器人种类与功能的话题； 能运用词汇表述自己的想法与观点。 完成单元任务：World Student for Future Organization is holding a robot design competition. You are invited to write a robot design plan to attend the pre-competition.
	文化意识	理解机器人现象背后的科学精神与技术伦理（机器人四原则等）； 基于对机器人背后的科学精神与技术伦理的理解，分析与比较机器人文化现象； 基于对机器人文化现象的分析与比较，判断与选择其中的科学精神与技术伦理； 基于对机器人相关的科学精神与技术伦理的判断与选择，选择对其中的科学精神与技术伦理进行传播； 基于中外优秀文化传播主题，发展科学精神、技术伦理等相关品格。
	思维品质	通过分析机器人种类和技术的目的性，发展思维品格。
	学习能力	发展阅读理解能力。

表 4-2　第一课时教学设计

教学内容	Listening & Speaking			
课时任务	**Task of Period 1:** Make a list of different kinds of robots and their functions and decide what kind of robots you want to design.			
教学过程				
时间	教学步骤	教师活动	学生活动	教学目的
第1—5分钟	热身导入，启动教学	教师播放最新人工智能机器人新闻，导入话题，然后让学生思考并回答问题： 1. Do we really need robots? If yes, for what do we need robots? If no, why not? 2. Do we need any ethnic rules for robots? If yes, what rules do we need to have? If no, why not?	学生分析人类制造和使用机器人的必要性并讨论制造和使用机器人的基本伦理。	深化学生对机器人相关的科学精神与技术伦理的理解。

第6分钟	呈现任务	教师呈现本单元以及本课时的任务，引导学生进行思考： **Task of Unit 2:** World Student for Future Organization is holding a robot design competition. You are invited to write a robot design plan to attend the pre-competition. **Task of Period 1:** Make a list of different kinds of robots and their functions and decide what kind of robots you want to design.	学生听教师布置任务，思考任务。	以真实任务开展教学，让学生在真实情景中有目的地进行学习。
第7—9分钟	头脑风暴	教师提出头脑风暴问题（Brainstorming）并引导学生思考：When we talk about robots, what words will you think of? (Robots: kinds/functions/parts/appearance/feelings/technology/purposes …)	学生思考有关机器人的词汇。	复习已有词汇，熟悉话题。
第10—16分钟	听前任务	教师呈现听前任务（Pre-listening task）并引导学生思考： 1. Look at the pictures on P54 and pictures in PPT. What kind of robots do you think they are? 2. Think out as many kinds of robots as you can. (Kinds of robots: robots for army/service/entertainment/agriculture/industry) 3. What can they do?	学生浏览图片，思考与之有关的词汇。	复习有关机器人种类及功能的词汇，为听力作准备。
第17—23分钟	听中任务	教师呈现听中任务 (While-listening task) 并引导学生思考： 1. Listen to the interview and number the pictures in the order that you hear them. 2. Listen to the interview again and fill in as much of the table as you can.	学生听听力，做练习题。	通过听听力材料，了解机器人种类及用途。

137

（续表）

第24–30分钟	听后任务	教师呈现听后任务 (Post-listening task) 并引导学生思考： Discuss in groups. Find out the positive and negative aspects of each robot. Use your imagination.	学生讨论四种机器人的优缺点。	培养学生的想象力及表达能力。
第31–39分钟	任务完成	教师指导学生通过准备和完成下面的表格来完成本课时的任务： **Task fulfillment**：列表比较机器人的不同种类、功能及其利弊，从而决定设计什么样的机器人。 {Kinds / Functions / Positive aspects / Negative aspects} The robot you design: _____ .	学生完成任务。	通过以上教学环节的开展和任务的准备，完成本课时任务，从而为完成本单元任务打下基础，作好准备。
第40–44分钟	反馈巩固	教师引导学生回到本节课开始的问题，让学生进一步讨论： 1. Do we really need robots? If yes, for what do we need robots? If no, why not? 2. Do we need any ethnic rules for robots? If yes, what rules do we need to have? If no, why not?	学生在学习本节课之后，进一步阐释自己的观点。	进一步深化学生对机器人相关的科学精神与技术伦理的理解。
第45分钟	布置作业	教师布置课后作业： Write a passage about what kind of robot you want.	学生听老师布置作业，并记下作业。	进一步熟悉话题。

其中任务完成一行中的表格内容：

Kinds	Functions	Positive aspects	Negative aspects

The robot you design: _____ .

表 4-3　第二课时教学设计

教学内容	Warming Up ＆Vocabulary, Reading
课时任务	**Task of Period 2:** Decide whether your robot has feelings or not, and state your reasons.

（续表）

时间	教学步骤	教师活动	学生活动	教学目的
		教学过程		
第1–5分钟	热身活动	教师先让学生就下面的问题进行讨论，再用多媒体播放 Bicentennial Man（《机器管家》）的片段，指导学生回答问题并给出原因： As we all know, there are many kinds of robots. Robots can be used in many fields. But do you think robots should think for itself? have feelings? have its own needs and desires? look and feel like a human being?	学生观看视频，对机器人是否应该有感情进行讨论。	以贴近单元内容的视频启动教学，激活学生已有的知识，再次把学生的注意力集中到本单元内容上。
第6分钟	呈现任务	教师呈现本课时任务并指导学生思考： **Task of Period 2:** Decide whether your robot has feelings or not, and state your reasons.	学生听教师布置任务，思考任务。	以真实任务开展教学，激发学生的学习兴趣，让学生在真实情景中有目的地进行学习。
第7–8分钟	读前任务	教师呈现读前任务（Pre-reading task）并引导学生思考和回答问题： Today we'll read a story about a robot that has feelings. The story was originally written by the science fiction writer, Isaac Asimov, and published in 1951. Look at the picture and the title of the passage, and think: 1. What does the title mean? 2. What do you think the story is mainly about? Then skim the passage to see if you were right.	学生讨论并回答问题。	通过讨论和回答问题，导入课文内容。

（续表）

| 第9–25分钟 | 读中任务 | 教师呈现读中任务（While-reading task）并引导学生完成任务：
1. Read the story quickly and do Comprehending 1, P12.
2. Read the story again and do Comprehending 2, P12.
教师指导学生学习文章中出现的重要词汇和结构（Language focus）：
1. Work with your partner and make a list of the useful words and structures you've noticed in the passage.
sympathy
favour
declare
it 作形式主语（It was disturbing and frightening that he looked so human.）
have sb doing
2. Finish Ex.1, P13. | 学生快速阅读课文，找出文章的主旨大意。学生阅读细节，回答问题，找出并理解文章中出现的重要短语。 | 锻炼学生快速阅读，把握中心含义的能力，培养学生细节理解能力，为以后活动的开展和任务的实现扫除语言障碍。 |
| 第26–30分钟 | 读后任务 | 教师呈现读后任务（Post-reading task），引导学生思考和完成任务：
1. Find as many of these words in the text as possible and underline the sentences. (Ex.3, P13)
2. Write a short paragraph to describe Claire using some of these words.
3. Tell a story using at least five of these words. | 学生完成阅读任务。 | 了解故事人物的情感变化。 |
第31–35分钟	讨论	教师指导学生小组讨论： Discuss in groups. Finish Ex.3 on P12. 	Characteristics	Similar	Different
Physical		
Mental				学生讨论并找出答案。	培养学生分析和比较能力，为单元任务的完成作准备。

（续表）

第36—39分钟	完成任务	教师指导学生完成本课时任务： **Task of Period 2:** Decide whether your robot has feelings or not, and state your reasons. **Task fulfillment:** Complete the following: Positive aspects of robots with feelings: Negative aspects of robots with feelings: Your decision: Your reason:	学生就机器人特性进行比较分析，并通过对比人类与机器人的差异，决定是否设计带有感情的机器人。	通过教学环节的开展和本课时任务的准备、完成，为完成本单元任务打下基础，作好准备。
第40—44分钟	随堂检测	教师布置本课时"学生随堂练习册"中的随堂检测题。	学生完成随堂检测练习。	对本课时内容进行检测，对学习效果进行评价。
第45分钟	布置作业	教师布置课后作业： 1. Find any language items you think difficult and try to solve them by, for example, referring to the dictionary. 2. Do Ex.2, P13.	学生听老师布置作业，并记下作业。	巩固所学的知识。

表4-4　第三课时教学设计

教学内容	Reading, Grammar
课时任务	**Task of Period 3:** List what your robot can do and how each part of its body works, using the passive voice.

教学过程				
时间	教学步骤	教师活动	学生活动	教学目的
第1分钟	呈现任务	教师呈现本课时任务并指导学生思考： **Task of Period 3:** List what your robot can do and how each part of its body works, using the passive voice.	学生听教师布置任务，思考任务。	以真实任务开展教学，激活学生已有的知识，激发学生的兴趣，使学生在任务的驱动下更有效地学习。

（续表）

| 第3–4分钟 | 复习导入 | 教师通过提问引导学生复习上一课时的内容，并引导学生分析机器人的四原则（从教材三原则延伸），建构技术伦理价值取向，进一步强化促进人类生存的向生存性的技术品格和文化意识：In the last lesson, we decided whether our robots have feelings or not after reading the passage *Satisfaction Guaranteed*. Why does the writer choose the title *Satisfaction Guaranteed* rather than *Tony, the Best Lover*? Let's have a revision. Answer the following questions according to the reading passage.
1. Why was Tony sent to Claire? (Her husband worked for a robot company and Tony was going **to be tested out** by her.)
2. What is the law for the robot Tony? (The robot wouldn't harm her or allow her **to be harmed**.)
3. When Tony said Claire must feel unhappy to say she was not clever, how did Claire feel? (It was ridiculous **to be offered** sympathy by a robot.)
4. By the time Tony was to leave, what did he expect? (By that time, Tony expected the house **to be completely transformed**.)
5. What would happen to Tony at last? (Tony would **have to be rebuilt**.)
教师在学生回答完问题后，呈现答案，所有问题和答案呈现完毕后，让学生注意答案中的黑体字部分。 | 学生根据课文内容回答问题，思考黑体字部分的意义。 | 通过复习，让学生在熟悉的语境中体会不定式被动语态的用法，降低了认知难度。 |

（续表）

第5—6分钟	知识拓展	教师引导学生用发现法和归纳法发现总结语法规律：Find out the same points of parts in bold and summarize the usages of the passive infinitives. Compare the two sentences and find out the usage. I often see him take physical exercise. He was often seen to take physical exercise.	学生总结不定式被动语态的构成（被动语态基本构成：be＋过去分词；不定式构成：to＋动词原形；被动的不定式：to＋be＋过去分词）。	让学生通过发现法和归纳法发现和总结语法规律，培养学生发现问题和解决问题的能力以及自主学习能力。
第7—12分钟	练习语法项目	教师布置课堂练习，引导学生练习所学的语法知识：Do Ex.2 on P14 and Ex.1 on P56.	学生做第14页及56页的练习题。	巩固所学的语法知识。
第13—18分钟	巩固语法项目	教师布置课堂练习，引导学生巩固所学的语法知识：Do Ex.3 on P14 and Ex.2 on P56.	学生做第14页及56页的练习题。	进一步巩固所学的语法知识。
第19—22分钟	运用语法项目	教师布置课堂练习，引导学生讨论并运用所学的语法知识：Do Ex.4 on P14.	学生讨论并运用语法。	在实际运用中练习语法。
第23分钟	读前任务	教师呈现读前任务（Pre-reading task）并引导学生思考和回答问题： Today we'll begin to design our robots. Now read a passage about a new robot in order to help us to design. Look at the pictures on P57 and guess what the passage is mainly about. 1. What is the soldier doing in the first picture? (He's using a metal detector to find the mines.) 2. What can the robot in the picture do? (The robot can remove landmines.)	学生了解学习目的。	激发学生的学习兴趣。

（续表）

第24—29分钟	读中任务	教师呈现读中任务 (While-reading task) 并引导学生思考： Read the passage and answer the following questions. What is the passage mainly about? What does the robot look like? How does the robot work? What function may the robot have in the future?	了解机器人的用途和工作方式。	了解扫雷机器人的样式及工作方式，为任务的完成作准备。
第30—34分钟	读后任务	教师呈现读后任务（Post-reading task），引导学生思考和完成任务： List all kinds of robots you know. List the parts of each kind. List what they can do. The following table may help you. <table><tr><td>Kinds</td><td>Structures</td><td>Functions</td></tr><tr><td></td><td></td><td></td></tr><tr><td></td><td></td><td></td></tr><tr><td></td><td></td><td></td></tr></table> Describe one kind, using passive voice when necessary.	学生总结分析所知道的机器人的种类、结构及其功能。	通过学生自我总结，为课时任务的完成作准备。
第35—39分钟	完成任务	教师指导学生完成本单元任务： **Task of Unit 2:** The Future Robot Company in America is holding a robot design competition. Design your robot and write a design plan. **Task fulfillment:** List what your robot can do and how each part of its body works, using the passive voice.	学生小组合作，完成任务。	运用所学的语法项目，小组合作，完成任务。
第40—44分钟	随堂检测	教师布置该课时"学生随堂练习册"中的随堂检测题。	学生完成随堂检测。	对本课时内容进行检测，对学习效果进行评价。

（续表）

第45分钟	布置作业	教师布置课后作业： 1. Do Ex.3 on P56. 2. Read the passage (P57) again and underline all the verbs which use the passive voice. Then summarize the passive structures of different tenses.	学生听老师布置作业，并记下作业。	巩固所学的语法项目。

表 4-5　第四课时教学设计

教学内容	Listening & Speaking			
课时任务	**Task of Period 4:** Exchange your design plan with your partner and find out the positive and negative effects that might be caused by his/her robot, and then give suggestions to the designer to improve his/her design.			
教学过程				
时间	教学步骤	教师活动	学生活动	教学目的
第1–3分钟	启动教学	教师通过提出问题，启发学生的想象力：We have designed our robots. They can help us do a lot of things, but can you imagine sometimes they also can cause some troubles for you? Please make a list of the troubles that might be caused by robots and give your reasons.	学生想象机器人带来的负面效应，为进一步学习作准备。	激发学生的学习兴趣。
第4分钟	呈现任务	教师呈现本课时任务并指导学生思考： **Task of Period 4:** Exchange your design plan with your partner and find out the positive and negative effects that might be caused by his/her robot, and then give suggestions to the designer to improve his/her design.	学生了解和接受任务。	以真实的任务开展教学，使学生的学习更有目的性，同时也增加了趣味性。

（续表）

第5–7分钟	听前任务	教师呈现听前任务（Pre-listening task）并引导学生思考：Do you remember Tony in *Satisfaction Guaranteed*? Is it a love story? Does Tony really love Claire? What trouble does Tony cause? Molly and Kate are also discussing the story *Satisfaction Guaranteed*. Can you guess which topic they will discuss?	学生讨论、分析 Tony 带来的负面效应。	通过讨论熟悉的听力话题，对听力内容进行预测，有助于听力。
第8–21分钟	听中任务	教师呈现听中任务（While-listening task）并引导学生思考：What is the discussion mainly about? Do Ex.1 & 2, P15. Listen to the tape and write down the expressions of supposition and belief. I think …　　I believe … I guess …　　I don't believe … I wonder …　　I doubt … I suppose …　　Maybe … I don't think …	学生听听力材料，做练习。	听听力，理解听力内容，锻炼学生获取听力信息的能力及从听力中学习语言的能力。
第22–27分钟	听后任务	教师呈现听后任务（Post-listening task）并引导学生完成：Do Ex.4 & 5 on P15.	学生小组针对话题进行讨论。	小组进行讨论，运用所学的内容。
第28–39分钟	完成任务	教师指导学生通过小组讨论完成本课时的任务： **Task fulfillment:** 1. Exchange your design plan with your partner. 2. Talk about and find out the positive effects and negative effects of his/her robot, using the expression of the supposition and belief. 3. Then give suggestions to the designer to improve his/her design.	学生用所学的知识完成任务。	运用所学的表达方式完成本课时任务，为完成本单元任务作准备。

（续表）

第40–44分钟	随堂检测	教师布置本课时"学生随堂练习册"中的随堂检测题。	学生完成随堂检测练习。	对本课时内容进行检测，对学习效果进行评价。
第45分钟	布置作业	教师布置课后作业：Revise your own design plan, paying attention to correcting errors in grammar.	学生记下作业。	锻炼学生的自主学习能力。

表4-6　第五课时教学设计

教学内容	Reading, Speaking, Writing
课时任务	**Task of Period 5:** Find out the best laws for robots and revise your design plan. Present your design plan in class.

教学过程

时间	教学步骤	教师活动	学生活动	教学目的
第1–2分钟	启动教学	教师通过提出问题，激发学生的学习兴趣： 1. What is a robot? (A robot is a machine designed to do jobs that are usually performed by humans. Robots are programmed and controlled by a computer.) 2. Since the robots are programmed and controlled by a computer, they must follow some laws for them. Do you remember the law for robots in *Satisfaction Guaranteed* written by Isaac Asimov? 3. Isaac Asimov wrote many books. Do you know them? (Present some of his works in PPT.)	通过同学介绍或教师展示，了解艾萨克·阿西莫夫及作品。	激发学生的学习兴趣。

（续表）

第3分钟	呈现任务	教师呈现本单元及本课时的任务并指导学生思考： **Task of Unit 2:** The Future Robot Company in America is holding a robot design competition. Design your robot and write a design plan. **Task of Period 5:** Find out the best laws for robots and revise your design plan. Present your design plan in class.	学生听教师布置任务，思考任务。	以真实任务开展教学，激活学生已有的知识，激发学生的兴趣，使学生在任务的驱动下更有效地学习。
第4—5分钟	读前任务	教师呈现读前任务（Pre-reading task）并引导学生思考和回答问题： We have learned *Satisfaction Guaranteed* written by Isaac Asimov and have watched *Bicentennial Man* adapted from a fiction of Isaac Asimov. Do you want to know something about Isaac Asimov? Please guess what the passage is mainly about? What do you want to know from the passage? Let's read the passage and learn about Isaac Asimov and the laws he developed for robots.	学生预测课文内容。	通过预测，激发学生的学习兴趣。
第6—21分钟	读中任务	教师呈现读中任务（While-reading task）并引导学生思考： 1. Read the passage and find out the main idea of the passage. 2. Answer the following questions: Which paragraph tells you when and where Asimov was born and died? Which paragraph tells you about his education? 3. Which paragraph tells you about the awards he received?	学生熟悉课文，学习课文中的语言点。	阅读课文，了解艾萨克·阿西莫夫的生平，锻炼学生从文章中获取信息的能力。

（续表）

		4. Read the passage again and finish the timeline on P17. 教师通过以下活动帮助学生学习文章中的语言点（Language focus）： 1. Underline the useful words or structures that you've noticed. Prepare to report your findings to the class. 2. Complete the following sentences with proper words. (Let Ss close their books.) Asimov had an amazing mind _____ he searched for explanations of everything. Among his most famous works of science fiction, one _____ he won an award was the *Foundation Trilogy*. He is also well known for his collection of short stories, *I, Robot*, _____ he developed a set of three "laws" for robots. (Keys: with which; for which; in which) (If the students don't understand this grammar well, give some necessary explanations.) 3. Complete the quiz below. He seemed to be looking for the words _____ he could express what he was thinking about. The novel _____ the film has been adapted for children is written by a famous American writer. The car, _____ I paid a lot of money, is now out of date. He is telling a story of a hero, _____ everyone in the town is proud. (Keys: with which; from which; for which; of whom)		学习文章中的语言点，让学生打下良好的语言基础。

（续表）

第22–30分钟	读后任务	教师呈现读后任务（Post-reading task），引导学生思考： 1. Ask Ss if they know the three laws for robots. Let Ss read the passage and find the first one out. (The first law is: "*A robot must not injure human beings or allow them to be injured*".) Ask Ss to discuss what the other two laws might be. 2. Let Ss watch *Bicentennial Man* and find out the three laws and read the laws on P18. Compare Asimov's laws with those you wrote just now and think of which set of laws is better and give your reasons. 3. Let Ss discuss what might happen in a world where there were robots if Asimov's three laws did not exist.	学生阅读课文，观看电影片段，讨论机器人的三原则，分析技术伦理的哲学基础和促进人类生存性的根本价值取向。	通过对机器人三原则的讨论，锻炼学生分析、判断、总结和归纳的能力，并为任务的完成作准备。
第31–39分钟	完成任务	教师指导学生完成本课时任务： **Task of Period 5:** Find out the best laws for robots and revise your design plan. Present your design plan in class. **Task fulfillment:** 1. Discuss in groups to find out the best laws for your robots. 2. Revise your design plan and present it in class.	学生分小组讨论，修改设计计划，完成任务。	通过讨论找出最佳三原则，小组合作，完成任务。
第40–44分钟	随堂检测	教师布置该课时"学生随堂练习册"中的随堂检测题。	学生完成随堂检测。	对本课时内容进行检测，对学习效果进行评价。

（续表）

第45分钟	布置作业	教师布置课后作业： Write a short summary of Asimov's life in 150-200 words.	学生听教师布置作业，并记下作业。	巩固所学的语法项目。

　　这一案例的中外优秀文化传播对象是本班学生，传播者也是本班学生，即：学生在教师引导下学习本单元，首先作为传播对象认知、比较与分析、判断与选择，并传播科学精神与技术伦理等，同时作为传播者，在传播过程中发展相应品格，尤其是对于技术的客观与谨慎态度得到显著发展。在学习理解、应用实践、迁移创新的学习过程中，发展学生中外文化理解意识、能力与态度，亦即：在这一案例的实施中，作为中外优秀文化传播对象的本班学生的相应文化意识（科学精神、技术伦理）得到显著发展，而在这一传播中外优秀文化的过程中，作为中外优秀文化传播者的本班学生的品格（客观、谨慎等）也得到显著发展。

二、课堂教学案例 2

表 4-7　A Short History of Western Painting 第二课时教案

教学内容	《英语》（人教版）选修六，Unit 1 A Short History of Western Painting，第二课时
教学目标	让学生通过西方和中国绘画历史的风格变化，了解其背后文化，通过对艺术反映生活、艺术形式的变化基于社会和理念的变革的理解，把握艺术、审美的价值内涵，发展学生的审美感知能力。
单元任务	为美术俱乐部高一新成员制作并介绍比较中西美术的简报（poster）。
主要教学过程	
Warming-up	Warming-up is intended to give students an opportunity to review their own knowledge and opinions about various art forms and be aware that there are differences between Chinese paintings and western paintings, though they may not be clear

（续表）

what the differences are. It also previews some of the specialist vocabulary used in the text.

Brainstorming: Art takes on various forms. Can you list some of them?

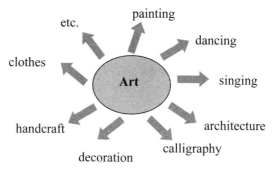

Teacher: Both pictures are about nature. Which one is western painting and which one is Chinese painting? How are they different? Which one do you like to decorate your bedroom? Why?

| Skimming the text for the gist | Ask students to read the title of the text and the headings within it. Then ask them what the topic of the text is and how the information is organized. Next ask students to skim the first paragraph to find the sentence that tells what the text is going to be about and the last paragraph to find out how the writer concludes the passage. Then show the answers with mind maps like the following: |

（续表）

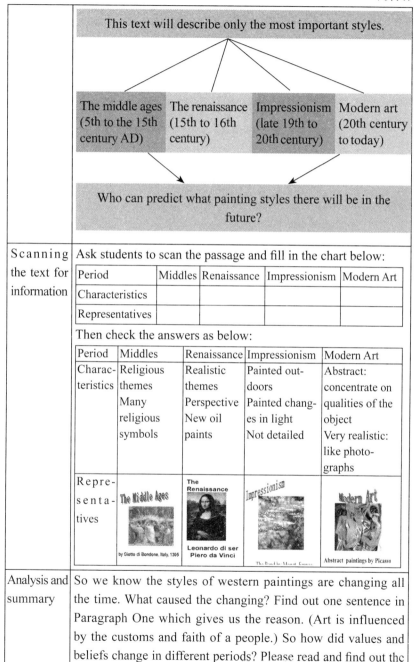

This text will describe only the most important styles.

- The middle ages (5th to the 15th century AD)
- The renaissance (15th to 16th century)
- Impressionism (late 19th to 20th century)
- Modern art (20th century to today)

Who can predict what painting styles there will be in the future?

Scanning the text for information	Ask students to scan the passage and fill in the chart below:

Period	Middles	Renaissance	Impressionism	Modern Art
Characteristics				
Representatives				

Then check the answers as below:

Period	Middles	Renaissance	Impressionism	Modern Art
Characteristics	Religious themes Many religious symbols	Realistic themes Perspective New oil paints	Painted outdoors Painted changes in light Not detailed	Abstract: concentrate on qualities of the object Very realistic: like photographs
Representatives	The Middle Ages by Giotto di Bondone, Italy, 1305	The Renaissance Leonardo di ser Piero da Vinci	Impressionism The Pond by Monet, France	Modern Art Abstract paintings by Picasso

Analysis and summary	So we know the styles of western paintings are changing all the time. What caused the changing? Find out one sentence in Paragraph One which gives us the reason. (Art is influenced by the customs and faith of a people.) So how did values and beliefs change in different periods? Please read and find out the answers.

153

（续表）

How values and beliefs influence art

Period	Themes	Values and Beliefs
the Middle Ages	religion	?
The Renaissance	people	?
Impressionism	nature	?
Modern	various	?

Ask students to search for other references if they fail to get the answer from the text. And the teacher will supplement the information when necessary. Students and the teacher work out the answer together.

Art is influenced by the customs and faiths of a people.

Period	Themes	Values and Beliefs
the Middle Ages	religion	believe in God
The Renaissance	people	more humanistic
Impressionism	nature	rebellion against academic painting
Modern	various	diverse

Can you give some examples in China where art styles are influenced by people's beliefs and customs? Students' answers may vary. If the students fail to give the answer, the teacher may present some examples to help the students better understand how beliefs and customs influence art. The following is an example: Why did ancient Chinese people choose fish? What did it symbolize?

Why fish?

Comparison between Chinese painting and western painting	We have learned some styles of western painting, now let's make a summary of how they are different and why they are different.		
		Western paintings	Chinese paintings
	Tool and material	1. Tools: painting brush, palette (调色板), easel (画架) 2. Materials: canvas, wall 3. Paint: oil paint	Writing brush, ink stick, ink slab, paper
	Content	1. Religious figures 2. History figures 3. Still object 4. Portraits 5. Life and society 6. Nature	Flower-bird painting Landscape painting Figure painting
	Feature	1. Painting realistically 2. Focus perspective: use a piece of glass 3. The way to paint (4 fixed): Same people, light, environment, angle of view 4. Light (physics) & Structure (dissection) 5. Decoration	1. Distributed view "reflecting form by spirit" 2. Subjective understanding 3. Have relationship with handwriting, poem
	Beliefs	1. Rationalism & value science 2. Humanism (renaissance) 3. Dualism (nature& man separated) 4. Religion rules: Christian	1. Monism 2. Harmony between man and nature
	This activity is intended to help the students develop some knowledge about western paintings and Chinese paintings so that they can better appreciate both.		
Making posters about western paintings and Chinese paintings for Painting Club	Ask students to choose a topic about western paintings and Chinese paintings, find some information and work in groups to make posters to introduce the topic.		

在这一案例的实施中，作为中外优秀文化传播对象的高一学生的品格（中西美术的共性与思维方式的差异性）得到显著发展，而在传播这一中外优秀文化的过程中，作为中外优秀文化传播者的高二学生的品格（开放、尊重、客观等）也得到显著发展。

三、主题实践活动案例

表 4-8　*Understanding China* 主题实践活动案例

主题内容	*Understanding China*
任务	写一篇介绍自己熟悉的关于中国文化某一元素的、较为系统的学术性文章
步骤一	教师给学生展示一篇由新加坡学者撰写的 *Understanding China* 论文，明确告诉学生：尽管作者对中国的态度比较友好，对中国的介绍总体比较客观，但其介绍与分析仍然有很多误解。向外国人更准确地介绍中国文化，让外国人准确地理解中国文化，是我们中国人的义务与责任。
步骤二	教师要求学生阅读这篇文章，然后小组集体讨论分析其产生误解的原因。
步骤三	学生单独或小组合作写一篇介绍自己熟知的有关中国文化的文章，要求符合国际学术规范，以确保读者对文章能形成客观、准确的第一印象。

步骤二论文：

Understanding China

—Kishore Mahbubani[*]

Foreign Affairs. September/ October 2005 (51–60)

The Waking Dragon

China today is like a dragon that, waking up after centuries of slumber,

---

[*]　(Kishore Mahbubani is Dean of the Lee Kuan Yew School of Public Policy in Singapore. This essay is adapted from his book *Beyond the Age of Innocence: Rebuilding Trust Between America and the World*.)

suddenly realizes many nations have been trampling on its tail. With all that has happened to it over the past 200 years, China could be forgiven for awakening as an angry nation, and yet Beijing has declared that it will rise peacefully. This good disposition stems partly from China's awareness that it is relatively weak. But it is also a sign that Beijing has endorsed the vision of progress that the United States has extolled since World War II. States no longer need to pursue military conquest to prosper, the theory goes; trade and economic integration pave a surer path to growth. And Beijing has noted how much adhering to this philosophy helped Japan and Germany emerge from the ruins of World War II.

（以下内容从略，需要阅读全文者，请在网上搜索阅读。）

本章小结

传播中外优秀文化和理解中外文化一样，是发展学生文化意识的基础。在传播中外优秀文化的过程中，学生作为传播对象，发展课程标准所规定的文化意识，同时作为传播者，发展开放、平等、尊重、宽容、客观、谨慎等文化意识。

发展学生的中外优秀文化传播能力的方法，如同所有能力发展方法一样，主要是实践法，具体方法同理解中外文化一样，主要是整合式学习路径的课堂教学和主题实践活动等方法。

推荐阅读材料

李月明. 2009. 对外文化传播与我国文化软实力的构建 [J]. 攀登，28 (1).

单波. 2011. 跨文化传播的基本理论命题 [J]. 华中师范大学学报（人文社会科学版），50 (1).

徐稳. 2013. 全球化背景下当代中国文化传播的困境与出路 [J]. 山东大学学报（哲学社会科学版），(4).

第五章　高中英语促进品格教育方法

第一节　高中英语促进品格教育的设计原则

无论中国，还是西方，品格教育都具有数千年的悠久传统，品格教育有效原则与方法也非常清晰。但囿于人性的本质性弱点，品格教育总是面临物质利益与身体享乐的巨大挑战，使得品格教育的有效原则与方法虽然清晰、明确，但时刻不能放松，唯有持之以恒、全面实践，方能实现品格教育的最基本目标。20世纪，美国进行了较为广泛的品格教育实践，形成了通行的11项基本原则和100种具体方法。参考品格教育已有的有效原则，英语课程文化意识教育中的品格教育可以确定以下基本原则：

1. 积极原则

英语课程的文化意识教育应以建构学生积极品格为目标，使用积极的方法，促进学生积极品格（包括但不限于课程标准所规定的文化意识）的建构与发展。积极原则要求我们不仅发展学生的积极品格，还要具有积极的目的、采用积极的方法。很多传统的方法，如责骂、甚至殴打等，并不具有实际成效。积极原则要求我们采用积极的方法，促进学生积极品格的发展。

2. 全面、全程、全域原则

品格教育的最大障碍是人自身，尤其是人本性中的消极因素，如享乐、疏懒等。品格教育须在人的一生中全程进行。我们不能指望高中阶段完成品格教学，甚至不能指望基础教育阶段完成品格教育。人即使到了老年，依然可能出现品格问题。所以，品格教育本质上应是一项终身事业，是人的一生皆应发展的领域。这也告诉我们，在高中英语课程中发展人的品格，是高中这一阶段的必然任务，但不是高中阶段可以完成的。高中英语课程中的品格教育，是小学、初中品格教育的继续，是高中各个学科共同促进品格教育的组成部分，是人的终生品格教育的阶段性工作。

　　同时，我们要在高中英语教学的全过程关注品格教育，在每一教学环节皆应关注品格教育，而不应只是在一节课结束时用一张 PPT 呈现品格教育的口号。

　　英语课程的文化意识教育应包括品格意识、情感和行为等品格教育的所有内容，尤其是促进文化意识落实为行为。

　　品格教育还需要学校各部门、社会各界、家庭全体成员等全体相关者的积极参与。作为学校教育组成部分的英语课程的文化意识教育，应以学校教育为主，但应积极寻求家庭教育、社会教育的参与和支持。学校的各项活动，尤其是英语课程的课堂教学等教育教学活动，要为学生实践英语课程的文化意识教育所发展的积极品格创造环境、条件和机会。英语课程的文化意识教育应是学校教育，尤其是学校品格教育的组成部分，学校应该是一个充满关怀的群体，应建立全面、全程、全域品格教育的校园。

　　3. 整合渗透原则

　　英语课程文化意识教育中的品格教育不是一种附加在英语语言学习之后的活动，而是采取一种目的明确的、课程与活动有机整合的方法，将品格教育整合到英语教学的各个方面、各个环节，从而促进学生在各阶段学校生活中发展相应的品格。以记忆单词为例，这可以促进学生毅力品格的发展、乐于助人品格的发展、自尊自信品格的发展等等。

　　4. 身教原则

　　品格不是教会的，也不是学会的，而是养成的。品格的养成需要品格发育的环境，尤其是品格教育环境中关键人的示范作用，教师的身教便是非常重要的环境因素。虽然学校所有员工都必须成为英语课程的文化意识教育所倡导的积极品格的实践者、教育者，但在英语课程发展学生品格的过程中，首先的身教者应该是英语教师。

　　5. 评价激励原则

　　唯有将品格教育积极的评价激励作为引导，方能引导学生坚持所发展的积极品格。英语课程的文化意识教育目标，尤其是其内容，应成为学校教育，尤其是英语课程的重要评价内容，不仅必须在形成性评价中坚持，还要在高考这类选拔性考试中，纳入对品格的评价。

第二节　高中英语促进品格教育的基本方法

一、促进品格教育的基本方法

高中英语课程促进品格教育的基本方法，与发展中外文化理解能力的具体方法一样，主要是课堂教学、主题活动两大类，具体内容参见本书第三章相关部分。

无论是课堂教学，还是主题活动，发展学生品格教育的基本过程依然采用本书第二章所介绍的基本方法：

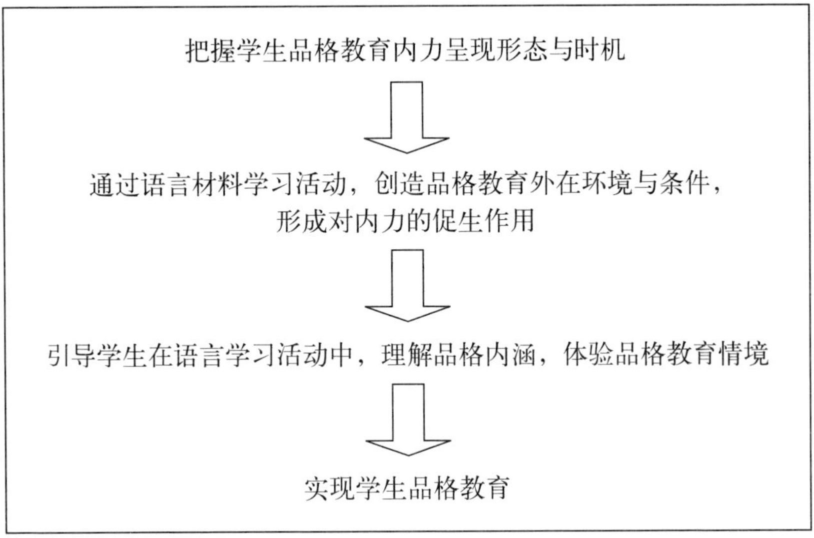

把握学生品格教育内力呈现形态与时机

通过语言材料学习活动，创造品格教育外在环境与条件，
形成对内力的促生作用

引导学生在语言学习活动中，理解品格内涵，体验品格教育情境

实现学生品格教育

图 5-1　高中英语课程促进品格教育的基本教学方法

在英语课程促进学生品格教育的教学活动中，情境创设非常重要，因为情境才能引导学生发现、理解品格的必须性与必需性，从而自主发展品格。

根据冯德正（2015）的研究，积极品格的发展可以采用以下多模态语篇建构方式开展：

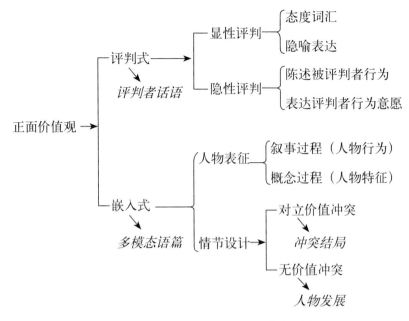

图 5-2　正面价值观的多模态语篇建构

　　冯德正（2015）还提出，英语课程的品格教育可以通过多元读写教学活动开展，具体方式为：

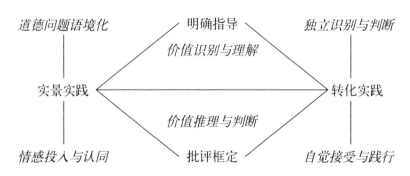

图 5-3　道德教育的多元读写教学法

　　这些方法都应融入到课堂教学、主题活动之中使用，而不是单独使用。

　　在促进品格教育的英语课堂教学与主体活动中，我们应主要通过提问的方式，引导学生自主分析、理解品格发生的情境，从而自主发展品格。在这种提问中，最有效的方法是运用苏格拉底提问法，其具体操作过程可参考如下环节：

1．分析教学内容，确定具有发展优势的品格领域，如以 Friendship 为主题的单元，显然具有发展友谊品格的优势。

2．根据学生真实生活，或者课文内容，设定预设发展的品格的情境，尤其与预设发展的品格对立的情境，如发展友谊品格，则可预设必需友谊的情境，或者友谊出现冲突的情境。

3．设计问题线，确定情境分析、品格教育的发展方向，按照问题线提问。问题线从 What do you think is ...? 开始，... thinks ... is ...，What do you think of his/her idea?（尤其是名人观点），然后设定情境 What would you do if you ...? If this happened, what would you do then? 等。

4．每一学生回答后，询问是否有不同意见。

5．学生无不同意见后，教师提出新的相反的情境，让学生讨论 If this happened, what would you do then?

可以经常使用这样的问题，引导学生深度分析、思考、理解情境。

What if the hero of a movie did that? How would you feel about the character? (Pose an objective and hypothetical situation.)

Remember, you're the hero of your own movie. (Compare the position with the students self-image.)

Would that be the right thing to do? (A consensus will probably develop. The kids will usually know what's right when pressed.)

6．就不同观点展开协商式讨论，尽可能形成共识，引导学生形成符合预设发展品格的条件，从而引导学生自主发展相应品格。

7．发现预设发展品格出现在学生行为之中后，及时提问：Why did you do that? 问其他同学 What do you think of his doing?

二、品格教育活动技巧

品格教育还有很多操作性技巧，尤其是美国品格教育研究所提出的品格教育 100 种具体方法，非常具有操作性。我们可以根据教学需要而采用。

以下为美国品格教育的 100 种操作性技巧：

1．把英雄人物的画像挂在大厅和教室里。

2．制订一个指导学生学习和道德成长的教学计划。

3．在学校里成立服务俱乐部，使学校社区化。

4．要注意不要让一个孩子代其他孩子受过。

5．制订赏识的教学计划，这些计划承认学生在学习、体育和艺术成就背后的付出。

6．对学生的日常行为及其对社区的贡献给予等级评定。

7．为你的课堂（和学校）制订一套行为规则，学生和教师经协商后都一致同意。

8．邀请家长来学校和教室进行观察，提出对你的课堂教学有所帮助的建议。

9．校长或教师选择一条自己欣赏的格言与你的学生一起分享。

10．每个月提出需要学习和宣传的品德，并在全校范围内进行学习和宣传。

11．和学生一起分享你心目中的一位英雄，告诉学生为什么他或她是你的英雄。

12．经常参加关于故事、历史和其他主题的讨论，询问"做什么才是正确的？"，通过不断讨论来加强效果。

13．帮助学生认识到"善"（美好）的品德要比学术上的成功更重要。

14．对待伦理道德问题要像对待其他知识问题一样——获得事实、收集证据、权衡后果和作出决定。

15．为你的学生在社区中进行服务创造机会。

16．校长和教师要通过榜样来进行领导。例如，把大厅里被丢弃的废纸捡起来，出于对下一位讲课老师的尊重而在上完课后主动擦黑板。

17．不允许在你的教室里出现任何不友善的行为。

18．不允许在教室里或学校的任何地方使用诅咒、粗俗和令人厌恶的话语。

19．通过写字条、打电话、走访等方式使家长关注学生的不良行为。

20．通过写信、打电话或走访家长等方式来表扬他们的孩子。

21．要使每个学生明确其在学校里努力做事的道德责任。

22．对其他教员和同事要使用道德的语言"我有责任……"，"她自信且有勇气……"，"我的疏忽导致他……"。

23．把学习"当地或身边的英雄"纳入到你的社会学习课程中去。

24．为进行测验、考试和布置家庭作业建立一种荣誉体系。

25．创立一种慈善事业。筹集捐款，并让学生决定他们的捐赠数额。

26．强化父母的道德权威，督促学生把他们的道德疑虑／困惑告诉家长。和学生们一起讨论为什么有时候不愿意把自己的道德疑虑／困惑告诉家长。

27．在墙上贴上鼓励发展良好品格的标语。例如，"不要等待将来成为一位伟人，现在就开始吧。"

28．分享与道德相悖的故事，要毫不犹豫地把它写下来，特别是学生在当前情境中的故事，并让他们把自己的观点写在纸上。

29．举行仪式庆祝英雄人物的生日，讨论他们的成就。

30．让学生在墙上记下对他们有重大意义的行为和言语。

31．对带来有关伦理和道德问题的文章的学生进行奖励。在课堂上讨论这些文章。

32．剖析和批评校园中常见的"品格问题"（破坏公共财物的行为、撒谎、作弊行为等）。

33．明确学生对课堂教学的期待，并鼓励学生说出这些期待。

34．平等对待每一位学生，避免个人感情干扰公平。

35．教师要勇于承认错误并改正。期待和鼓励学生亦如此。

36．每天在上学开始或放学时大声地朗读一段以价值观为中心的"两分钟的故事"。

37．在制定课堂教学和学校政策时，考虑其道德意义，并意识到它们会带给学生什么样的信息。

38．解释某个特殊的学校或课堂教学策略、行动或决定的理由。帮助学生理解"为什么"，而不仅"是什么"。

39．让学生们讨论成为一位好学生应具有哪些道德品质，以及应包含哪些优秀品格。

40．向学生讲解竞争的意义，让他们懂得什么时候竞争有价值，什么时候没有价值。

41．和你的学生谈谈为什么你要当教师，解释你是怎样理解教书的重要性和教育的责任。

42．让学生了解你的社会服务项目，鼓励他们志愿参加一个"食品储库"、训练小运动员或其他某项公益事业。

43．教会学生批判性地分析媒体，让他们明白媒体传播的信息在多大程度上鼓励人们过一种有品格的生活。

44．邀请最近毕业的学生回校谈谈他们是怎样成功升入大学、参加工作或参军的。

45．邀请当地的成年人谈谈他们是如何理解生活中的品格这个概念的。

46．帮助学生强化换位思考。向他们提这类问题，"如果没有人愿意和你玩，你会觉得怎么样？""如果有人拿你的名字开玩笑（或起绰号），是因为他们认为你的名字听起来很奇怪，你有什么感觉？"

47．学生在学校里发生冲突时，要教会学生坦率地承认错误、懂得尊重个人隐私以及肩负责任的重要性。

48．言谈有礼。教会学生怎样倾听别的学生和成人说话，并尽量不打断别人。

49．阅读和讨论名人传记。鼓励高年级的学生，树立正确的英雄观，如一个人外表有缺陷，但他（她）能够做出许多令人钦佩的事情。

50．让年龄大的学生帮助年龄小的学生，例如，高年级的学生领新生熟悉校园环境。

51．开学第一天就强调努力学习和达到学习目标的重要性。

52．鼓励高中学生适当参加城市、乡镇或学校董事会等会议，学会参与社会事务。

54．鼓励中学生担任选民登记的志愿者，如果达到投票年龄，鼓励他们参加投票。

55．教学生学会写便条表示感谢，比如向给予他们思想教育的人表示感谢。

56．在评价学生的工作时要给他们充分的反馈，阐明是如何获得成功的，还能如何改进等。

57．让年龄大的学生做一些力所能及的事，比如为他们的父母做一顿饭，整理房间等。

58．班上每月开展一次"才艺展示"活动或全校性的活动，如对门厅进行装饰。

59．全班或全校学生一起动手，在规定的时间内打扫教室或学校的场地。

60．尊重其他宗教和文化。和学生们探讨道德和公正处理事情的必要性。

61．当"受害的一方"受到不公平的对待时，要对他或她提供道义上的支持，并把这件事作为一个教学案例。

62．让孩子们在周末或放假时把小动物或植物带回家，学会照看它们，并谈谈关爱其他生物的必要性。

63．列出一项班级或全学校的资源再利用计划。讨论怎样有效利用你的东西，养成节约的良好习惯。

64．让学生们打扫社区，并将枯枝落叶收集起来，在园里种上花草，在墙壁上作画，或清理河滩。

65．在全校强调某些促进品格教育的计划，以此达成学校的发展目标。

66．重温校歌，给学生，特别是新生，讲解歌词的含义，要求学生们在每一次学校活动中都要唱校歌。

67．如果你的学校没有校歌，可以以竞赛方式让学生创作一首。作为一个社区学校，谈一谈在这首歌里应该包括什么样的教育理念和道德思想。

68．强调学校举行各种仪式的意义。

69．鼓励学生看望年老或生病的邻居。

70．让你的学生和另一个州或国家的学生结交笔友。分享学生了解到的笔友的生活信息。

71．日常课堂上进行品格教育。例如语言课上就某一种品格为题进行写作：假设"你踩了别人的脚了"，怎么办？

72．同学之间开展批评与自我批评，相互帮助。

73．强调道德的作用，并在体育运动、游戏以及与他人的日常互动中认真遵守道德守则。

74．要允许学生参与制定学校的规章制度。让他们研究不同的规章制度带来的各种结果，并把他们的研究结果提交给行政管理人员和教师作为参考。

75．搜集一些有趣的、引人思考的名言。例如，"假设我们每一个人都是宇宙的中心，那么，真理就绝不会是明确的。"（Thomas Merton）。要求学生做类似的事。

76．推荐一系列品格教育的读物。

77．提出学校的校训，要求全校师生员工都在行动中体现这条校训的精神。

78．张贴师生员工良好品格的光荣榜。

79．通过提供机会使学生获得真正的学术和社会挑战及成就，来促进学生自尊的发展。

80．举行教师／员工会议和学校"道德建设"的研讨会，提出学校道德生活的具体目标。

81．宣传学校的道德标语，并且在学校所有的活动中及建筑物的显要位置彰显该道德标语。

82．设置一个"交换网络"或"公告栏"，教师和行政人员可以通过它们来分享自己的"促进品格教育的 100 种方法"。

83．把值得赞颂的学生轶事写在学校给家长的校内简讯中。

84．制作一个剪贴簿，粘贴上反映学校历史和成就的照片、新闻故事、大事记。让所有的师生员工都参与收集和保存，展示给来学校参观的人。

85．要使学校中的每个人都认识到学校的那些"无名英雄"的工作和成就——传达员、修理工、秘书、食堂工人和志愿者——正是他们每天的劳动才使学校正常运转。

86．在讲授学习中的自律和坚忍不拔的重要意义时，布置合理数量的家庭作业，对学生进行激励。

87．设计一条校训，写进学校的文件里，以及给家长看的文件里，让学生每周背诵。

88．对于学生着装要有明确的规定，解释着装在改善教育环境中的作用。

89．利用学生在家的时间组织一些活动，增强凝聚力，以及培养对学校的感情。

90．创造机会为家长和学生共同完成一项学校活动。例如，跳舞、专题讨论会、宴会或郊游。

91．保持墙面清洁，让所有的学校成员共同承担清洁任务。

92．在学校生活中引入一些商业活动，比如聘请私人教师，或为学生小组聘请辅导员。

93．成立一个为新员工和新学生设立的俱乐部。

94．邀请当地成功的企业家向学生谈谈良好的道德品质在工作中的重要性。

95．让学校运动员与教练共同协商制定一套学校体育运动的规则。

96．在你的社区举办一次品格教育的公众论坛。

97．要求每个班级设计一条班训，代表本班的品格特点。

98．每两个月举行一次碰头会，教师们聚集在一起，学习文学、历史、哲学或其他包含伦理道德的作品。

99．为家长提供一套有益的阅读书目，使他们能和自己的孩子一起阅读，以激励家长与学生之间进行有关良好品格的谈话。

100．为学生创办一个课外阅读俱乐部，阅读那些与其年龄相适应的文学作品，重点是作品所阐释的道德意义。

第三节　高中英语促进品格教育的案例分析

一、课堂教学案例 1

很多单元的主题本身是品格，这些单元具有品格教育的内容优势，非常适合开展基于单元整合式学习的品格教育。Friendship 即是这样一个单元，其主题 friendship 本身就是高一新生最急需发展的品格之一。

表 5-1　*Friendship* 单元教学案例

教学内容	Friendship	
教学对象	高一学生	
单元目标	语言能力	能通过学习掌握友谊话题的相关词汇、语句结构等，并能用于解决自己面临的友谊问题；同时能理解所学文章的主旨大意，从所学文章中获取或处理相关信息，通过上下文理解所学文章中生词的基本语义。
	文化意识	能发展对友谊的认知、体验，形成正确的友谊观，解决高一新生进校后的友谊问题。
	思维品质	能通过概念澄清发展思维的准确性。
	学习能力	能将学习英语与自身生活需要建立密切联系。

表5-2 第一课时教学设计

运用任务	Task of Unit 1: Making new friends in your school. Task of Period 1: Find out for what purposes you would like to make new friends in our school; and make a list to tell the class: What do you hope your friend would be like?			
教学过程				
时间	教学步骤	教师活动	学生活动	教学目的
第1-2分钟	导入	教师告诉学生：经过学校调查，高一新生最大的疑惑是学习，第二大疑惑是友谊。询问学生：What is friendship in your opinion? 针对某一学生的回答询问全班学生：Do you all agree? Are there any different opinions? 寻求不同意见。	学生了解问题现状，思考、回答教师问题，听其他同学发言，思考并提出自己的观点。	通过播放视频，激发学生兴趣，激活学生已有的图式。
第3-5分钟	启动教学	教师展示一些自己的照片，对学生说：It's me and an old professor, Chen Lin. He is a very famous professor. We work together and we travel together. This is me and another friend. We work together and we have lunch together. You're new in this school. Do you want new friendship? Now, please think: What is friendship? Friendship is ... (e.g. Friendship is help in need.)	观看教师和其朋友的照片，思考并回答什么情境下的交往是友谊，什么不是，思考具有友谊的标准、条件等。	利用生活照片和亲身经历让学生感受友谊的含义。简单明了，贴近学生生活，学生更容易接受。
第6-10分钟	任务准备	教师通过提问导入第一页的调查问卷：Are you good to your friends? 并要求学生用事实证明，然后布置学生做调查问卷：Do the survey on Page 1. Work out your score, add up them and see how many points you get. ... Now please check how many points you get. After class, you can discuss with your friends about the points you get.	学生做调查问卷，检测自己是否对朋友友好。	通过调查问卷，可以让学生们了解自己是否对朋友友好，以及友好的程度。

第11-13分钟	词汇学习	教师就问卷中的重点词汇进行必要的讲解：When you cannot understand some words in the survey, what did you do just now? Whenever you have any difficulties while learning, tell me! If not, I'll check whether you have got the target language items or not. Here are my sentences about my friends and me. （例句略） What are your sentences about you and your friends?	学生学习重点词汇，并进行造句。	词汇能够帮助学生更好地理解文章内容，同时也为后续的活动扫除语言障碍。
第14-15分钟	任务导入	教师通过提问导入本单元的任务并指导学生回答问题：Now I have a question. Do you think friendship is important to you? Why or why not? Please briefly introduce one of your friends to the class. Who would like to try?	学生回答教师的问题，并简单介绍自己的朋友。	导入本课时任务
第16分钟	呈现任务	教师呈现本单元和本课时的任务：You're new here. Friendship can help you a lot now. While learning this unit, try to make new friends in our school. At the end of this period, you will: find out for what purposes you would like to make new friends in our school; make a list to tell the class: What do you hope your friend would be like? (kind, helpful, good at maths, makes me happy, brings me much pleasure,…)	学生了解本单元的任务和本课时的任务。	以真实的任务开展教学，让学生明确学习目的，提高学习自觉性，激发学生的学习兴趣。

（续表）

第 17 分钟	课文导入	教师提出问题，引导学生思考并回答问题：Does a friend always have to be a person? What else can be your friend?	学生思考并回答问题。	引导学生思考还可以和其他哪些东西做朋友，导入课文内容。
第 18-22 分钟	读前任务	教师呈现读前任务（Pre-reading task）并引导学生思考和回答问题： 1. Who is Anne's best friend? 2. What words/phrases may be used in the text to describe Anne's friend? 3. What words/phrases will you use when you describe your friend? 4. Write at least five words/phrases that come to your mind.	学生猜测 Anne 的好朋友是谁；并思考哪些词可以用来描述她的好朋友以及你的好朋友。	读前问题可激活学生相关背景知识，提高其阅读兴趣；读前的猜测活动有助于学生快速阅读并获取信息。
第 23-34 分钟	读中任务	教师通过下面活动指导学生完成读中任务 (While-reading task)： 1. Read the text and find what words/phrases to use to describe a friend. While you are reading, circle all the words/phrases used in the text to describe Anne's friend. A tip: While you're reading, try to guess the meaning of the words/phrases you don't know. 2. Check the words/phrases you wrote before reading. Were the words/phrases used in the text?	学生阅读课文找出描述朋友的词汇并思考这些词汇的使用目的。学生听课文录音，跟读课文。做练习题 1 和 2。	锻炼学生从阅读材料中获取信息和处理信息的能力。纠正学生的发音，并进一步熟悉课文内容。

（续表）

| 第35-39分钟 | 读后任务 | 3. Work in pairs. Discuss: What words/phrases were used in the text to describe Anne's friend. For what purposes they were used.
4. Follow the tape, read the text aloud and focus more on the sense groups which can help you understand the text better.
5. Then do Exx. 1 and 2 on Page 3.

教师通过下面的活动指导学生完成读后任务（Post-reading task）:
1. Work in pairs and find out words/phrases from the text that you can use to describe your friend. If you need, you can look for some words/phrases in the survey on Page 1. Pay attention to the purposes you use these words/phrases for.
2. Make a list of at least 5 words/phrases.
3. Share your list in group of 4 and choose 3 best words/phrases from all the lists. Then share with other groups. | 学生小组活动，从文章中找出可以描述你的朋友的词汇并与其他小组共享。 | 找出描述朋友的词汇，为任务完成作准备。 |
| 第40-44分钟 | 完成任务 | 教师通过下面活动指导学生完成本课时任务:
Task of Period 1: Find out for what purposes you would like to make new friends in our school; and make a list to tell the class: What do you hope your friend would be like?
1. Finish your list and try to share it with your group members. Try to use the words from the text.
2. Report to the class your list and your purposes. | 学生完成任务。 | 通过以上教学环节的任务准备，完成本课时的任务，从而为完成本单元的任务打下基础，作好准备。 |

（续表）

时间		教师活动		教学目的
第45分钟	布置作业	教师布置课后作业： 1. Search for more information about Anne's Diary from books or online if you want to know more about Anne. 2. Follow the tape to read the text until you can read it in correct sense groups. 3. Do READING TASK on Page 44. （Tips: Find any language items in the text difficult for you and try to solve them by, for example, reading Notes to the Text or Grammar at the end of your textbook. ）	学生记下课后作业。	培养学生主动学习和自觉解决问题的能力，培养学生的资源策略意识。

表5-3　第二课时教学设计

运用任务	Task of Period 2: At the end of this period, the students will: list what his/her new friend should be like, and talk about why he/she would like to make such a friend.			
教学过程				
时间	教学步骤	教师活动	学生活动	教学目的
第1-3分钟	复习导入启动教学	教师检查上一课时的任务完成情况，既达到复习作用，也激活学生所学的知识：Report to the class your list and your purposes.	学生回答教师的问题。	复习上一课时，任务导入，承上启下，激活学生所学的知识，为本课时任务的开展作准备。
第4-7分钟	词汇学习	教师指导学生学习词汇：Are there any language items in the text difficult for you? If yes, tell the class. Let's help each other.	学生学习重点词汇，并进行造句。	词汇能够帮助学生更好地理解文章内容，同时也为后续的活动扫除语言障碍。

（续表）

第8-15分钟	词汇巩固	教师指导学生完成第4页练习1、2，以达到巩固所学词汇的目的。	学生做练习，巩固所学的词汇。	练习巩固可以促进学生掌握这些词汇。
第16-18分钟	任务导入	教师通过提问帮助学生复习上一课时的内容并导入本课时的任务：Last period, we learnt the story of Anne. 1. Why did Anne long for making friends? 2. Who's Anne's best friend? 3. Why did she make such a best friend? 4. Why do you hope to make new friends in our school? 5. What should your new friend be like?	学生回答教师的问题。	复习上节课的内容，导入本课时任务。
第19分钟	呈现任务	教师呈现本课时的任务： At the end of this period, you will: list what your new friend should be like, and talk about why you would like to make such a friend.	学生理解和接受任务。	学生明确本课时学习任务，可以提高学习自觉性和主动性。
第20-22分钟	语法导入	教师引导学生讲述自己与朋友之间的故事：Who was your best friend in your junior high school? Tell us a story between you and your friend.	学生讲述自己和朋友之间的故事。	通过真实情景导入到语法的学习和运用。
第23-25分钟	语法呈现	教师指导学生写出刚才自己或同学谈论的句子：Try to write what you and your friend talked. Here are my sentences about my friend and me.（例句略） What are your sentences about you and your friend?	学生了解语法内容，明确语法的运用目的。	明确语法的运用目的，让学生学习更具有目的性。

（续表）

		Can you find out how I report to you what we talked? Now I will tell you how to report Something to somebody, so that you can report your school life to your parents.		
第26-32分钟	语法学习	教师指导学生通过下面的活动学习语法知识： 1. Study the examples in Ex. 1 on Page 5 and work out the rules to change direct speech into indirect speech. 2. Compare your rules with those in Grammar on Pages 87-90. 3. Tell the differences.	学生阅读例句，找出不同，总结语法规律。	在教师的引导下，总结语法规律，培养学生的自我探究能力。
第33-37分钟	语法巩固	教师指导学生做练习：Do Exx. 2 & 3 on Page 5.	学生做相关练习。	在练习中巩固所学的语法。
第38-39分钟	语言运用	教师要求学生在讲述自己和朋友之间的故事时运用间接引语：Retell your story about you and your friend and check if you used the indirect speech correctly.	学生讲述自己和朋友之间的故事，并在讲述过程中注意间接引语的使用。	通过真实情景培养学生的语言运用能力。
第40-44分钟	完成任务	教师指导学生完成本课时的任务：Revise your list of what your new friend should be like by using stories we just checked.	学生完成任务。	运用所学的知识，完成本课时任务，从而为完成本单元任务作准备。
第45分钟	布置作业	教师布置作业：Do Exx. 1 & 2 on Pages 41-42 in USING WORDS AND EXPRESSIONS.	学生听教师布置作业。	进一步巩固所学的知识。

表 5-4 第三课时教学设计

运用任务	**Task of Period 3:** Discuss with your group members about your list of what your friend should be like and what problems may appear between you and your friend, and then revise your list.

教学过程				
时间	教学步骤	教师活动	学生活动	教学目的
第1-3分钟	启动教学	教师提出问题，激活学生相关背景知识： 1. What should your new friend be like? 2. Why do you make such a new friend? 3. What problems do you think might appear if you have such a new friend?	学生回答教师问题,讨论并汇报朋友间的问题。	通过对朋友间友谊问题的问答，激活学生相关的背景知识，导入到任务呈现。
第4分钟	呈现任务	教师呈现本课时的任务并指导学生思考：At the end of this period, you will: discuss with your group members about your list of what your friend should be like and what problems may appear between you and your friend, then revise your list.	学生了解和接受任务。	以真实的任务开展教学，让学生的学习更有目的性，同时也增加了学习的趣味性。
第5-11分钟	听前任务	教师呈现听前任务（Pre-listening task）并引导学生思考：Many problems may appear between friends. The key is how to solve them. There's a letter that Lisa wrote to Miss Wang of *Radio for Teenagers*. Read the letter on Page 6 and find out what problem she has. Predict what Miss Wang will say to help Lisa.	学生阅读来信，找出问题，预测可能的解决方案。	通过学生来信这种较为真实的情景导入到朋友间的问题，并在此过程中锻炼学生对听力内容的预测能力，培养学生的听力策略。

177

（续表）

第12-22分钟	听中任务	教师呈现听中任务（While-listening task）并引导学生做练习：Do Exx. 2 & 3 on Page 6.	学生听听力材料，做练习。	锻炼学生从听力材料中获取和处理信息的能力。
第23-32分钟	听后任务	教师呈现听后任务(Post-listening task）并引导学生思考：Do you agree with Miss Wang's advice? Discuss it in group of 6. You may use the following expressions in your conversation. **AGREEING:** I agree.　　　　Yes, I think so. So do I.　　　　Me, too. Exactly.　　　　No problem. Sure.　　　　Certainly. Of course.　　　　All right. Good idea. I think that's a good idea. You're right/correct. **DISAGREEING:** I don't think so.　　Neither do I. That's not right.　　Yes, but … I'm afraid not.　　No way. Of course not.　　I disagree. I'm sorry, but I don't agree.	学生对Miss Wang的建议发表自己的观点。	锻炼学生的分析判断能力，同时提高了学生的口语表达能力。
第33-34分钟	词汇学习	Here are my sentences about my friend and me.（例句略） What are your sentences about your friends and you?	学生学习词汇，并进行造句。	为完成后面的任务扫除语言障碍。
第35-44分钟	完成任务	教师指引学生通过下面的小组活动完成本课时任务： 1. Work in groups and discuss with your group members about your list of what your new friend should be like.	学生修改完善自己的交友条件。	完成本课时任务，为单元任务作准备。

（续表）

第45分钟	布置作业	2. Find out if you agree or disagree with others and tell if your list is proper or not. 3. Give advice to your classmates, and then revise your list.		
第45分钟	布置作业	教师布置课后作业： 1. Listening Task on Page 43. 2. Find stories and proverbs about friends and friendship that you can share with your new friend.	学生听教师布置作业，记下作业。	进一步加强听力训练，提高学生的听力水平，丰富学生的背景知识。

表5-5　第四课时教学设计

运用任务	Task of Period 4: Try to make your decision on what friends you want to make and find out how to make friends with them.

教学过程				
时间	教学步骤	教师活动	学生活动	教学目的
第1-4分钟	启动教学	教师引导学生分享朋友间的故事：Share with class: What stories about friends and friendship have you found?	学生分享朋友间的故事。	激活学生已有的图式，激发学生兴趣。
第5分钟	呈现任务	教师呈现本课时的任务： After learning this period, you will try to make your decision on what friends you want to make and find out how to make friends with them.	学生了解和接受任务。	以真实的任务开展教学，让学生的学习更有目的性，同时也增加了趣味性。
第6-12分钟	导入	教师分享自己的交友经历，提出问题并引导学生思考：What's your experience of making friends? How do you solve the problems between you and your friend?	学生回答教师提出的问题，思考如何解决朋友间出现的问题。	通过思考，提高学生学习的积极性与主动性。

（续表）

第13-16分钟	写前任务	教师呈现写前任务：Read the letter on Page7 that Miss Wang received from Xiaodong, and find out what problem he has.	学生阅读信件，找出Xiaodong的问题。	培养学生的阅读能力，以及发现问题的能力。
第17-19分钟	词汇学习	教师帮助学生学习信内的重点词汇： Here are my sentences about my friends and me.（例句略） What are your sentences about your friends and you?	学习重点词汇，并进行造句。	为完成后面的任务扫除语言障碍。
第20-32分钟	写中任务	教师引导学生通过下面活动完成写作任务： 1. Brainstorm with a partner about ways to change the situation. 2. Make a list of your ideas and give your reasons. 3. Decide which are the best ideas and put them into an order. 4. Write down your advice and explain how it will help. The following expressions may help you write your advice. First, why not …? If you do this, … Secondly, you should/can … Then/That way, … Thirdly, it would be a good idea if … By doing this, …	学生头脑风暴列出解决问题的建议并进行回信。	在教师的引导下，逐步完成写作。培养学生的写作技巧和能力。
第33-36分钟	写后任务	教师通过下面活动帮助学生完成写后任务： 1. Swap your letter with your partner. 2. Look at his/her work and help to improve it.	学生同伴互相修改回信。	同伴互相修改，完善写作。

（续表）

第 37-44 分钟	完成 任务	3. Pick out any mistakes you see in spelling, verb forms, or punctuation. 4. Swap back. 5. Correct any mistakes and write it out.		
第 37-44 分钟	完成 任务	教师通过下面的活动帮助学生完成本课时的任务： 1. Work in group of 6 and discuss what friends you need and how to make friends with them. 2. Report your decision and your findings to the class.	学生完成任务。	运用语言完成本课时的任务，为单元任务作准备。
第 45 分钟	布置 作业	教师布置课后作业：Finalise the list of your requirements for new friends, using the suggestions you have found. **Friends wanted** I'm Kwesting from Class 104. I want some new friends who are kind and love nature, good at English, can give me advice about learning English and share feelings and thoughts with me.	学生听老师布置作业。	培养学生的资源策略意识，为下一课时的单元任务完成作准备。

表 5-6　第五课时教学设计

运用 任务	Task of Period 5: Finalise the list of requirements for new friends you want to make.
教学过程	

（续表）

时间	教学步骤	教师活动	学生活动	教学目的
第1-2分钟	任务呈现	教师呈现本课时的任务：In this period, you will finalise your list of requirements for new friends. After learning this unit, I hope you will make some friends with students or teachers in our school.	学生理解并接受任务。	呈现任务，让学生在任务的驱动下更有目的地学习。
第3-4分钟	任务准备	教师通过实例让学生了解任务：Here's the example. **Friends wanted** I'm Kwesting from Class 104. I want some new friends who are kind and love nature, good at English, can give me advice about learning English and share feelings thoughts with me.	学生学习教师给出的例子。	范例可以帮助学生更好地完成任务。
第5-16分钟	完成任务——小组讨论	教师布置小组讨论问题：Introduce your list to the group. Group check: 1. Is the friendship between them good to each other? 2. Did the reporter use some language items from what we learned in this unit? Are the language items correctly used?	学生小组内针对自己的列表进行讨论。	小组讨论，修正自己的列表。
第17-28分钟	完成任务——班级讨论	教师布置班级讨论问题：Try to introduce your final list to the class. Class check: 1. Is the friendship between them good to each other?	学生在班级内进行讨论。	班级讨论，修正自己的列表。

（续表）

		2. Could you give some advice to the reporter? 3. What language items from this unit did the reporter use in his/her list?		
第29-36分钟	总结	教师提出问题，指导学生在回答问题时总结并复习所学的词汇： 1. What did you do in learning this unit? 2. What did you learn from these things? 3. What problems have you solved after learning this unit? 4. What difficulties do you still have after learning this unit? My introduction to my new friend … Here is my introduction to my new friend. Please make your try.	总结本单元所学的内容，并复习所学的词汇。	总结反省自己的学习，同时复习所学的词汇。
第37-44分钟	欣赏歌曲	教师播放并教唱一首关于朋友及朋友间友谊的歌曲，增强学生对本单元内容的理解：Now, let's enjoy and learn to sing a song about friendship. Wish you make more friends in our school and enjoy the friendship!	学生欣赏关于朋友的歌曲，并跟唱。	增加学生的兴趣，增强对友谊的理解。
第45分钟	布置作业	教师布置课外作业：Do the writing task on Page 46.	听教师布置作业	进一步巩固所学的知识。

　　本单元第一课时突出介绍了人类的共性：孤独中对友谊的呼唤。这是很好的跨文化教育主题，因为我们不仅要看到人类不同文化的差异，更应看到人类文化的共性。在第二、三、四课时，通过学习，引导学生深度理解友谊，思考友谊的特性，学会给朋友提出建议，使自己成为可以帮助他人的人，从而成为他人学习、生活中的好朋友。到第五课时，教师希望学生能在一周内结识新的朋友，开始新的友谊，在学习理解、应用实践、迁移创新的学习过程中，发展学生对中外关于友谊的优秀文

183

化的认知和对友谊品格的认知，并在高中第一周尽可能开始新的友谊，从而实现品格的发展。

二、课堂教学案例 2

表 5-7 *Disabled People* 单元教学案例

教学内容	Disabled people	
教学对象	高二学生	
单元目标	语言能力	能通过学习掌握与残障话题有关的词汇的意义及用法；能通过图式建构来获取和处理篇章信息，理解语篇意义；能利用阅读技能获取文章主旨和作者意图；能写简单的建议。
	文化意识	能发展对残障人士的关爱。
	思维品质	能通过分析残障人信息来发展批判性思维。
	学习能力	能基于主题进行巩固性学习。

表 5-8 第一课时教学设计

	从以下任务中选定一项作为你学习本单元要完成的任务。 1. 阅读课文，理解课文的语用目的（介绍残障人士的生活、学习和工作情况，表达相互尊重、相互理解和相互关爱的生活态度），了解残障人生活中的困难，写出帮助残障朋友必做的五件事（Five must-dos）； 2. 阅读课文，学习如何运用委婉的语言提出建议，用委婉语写建议； 3. 听对话，学习如何向朋友表达祝愿和祝贺，编对话，表达对某人的祝愿与祝贺； 4. 阅读课文，把握不同阅读图式的建构，并利用图式分析篇章体裁和题材，提高阅读理解和完形填空的解题效率，提高学习成效。
任务	本课时由选择以下任务的小组完成任务：阅读课文，理解课文的语用目的（介绍残障人士的生活、学习和工作情况，表达相互尊重、相互理解和相互关爱的生活态度），了解残障人生活中的困难，写出帮助残障朋友必做的五件事。

（续表）

			教学过程		
预设时间	学习步骤	学习目的	教学方案	学习方案	学习资源
	预习	对残障人生活有大致了解。	1. 教师要求学生预习至少一篇介绍残障人生活、学习和工作情况的文章。 2. 教师要求小组完成必做的五件事初稿。	1. 学习如何分析自己的起始水平，如何确定适合自己的学习目标； 2. 学习如何根据自己的性格、兴趣选择任务； 3. 确定学习目标； 4. 确定任务； 5. 预习课文； 6. 选择 Five must-dos 任务的学生组成小组，完成自己设计的必做的五件事第一稿。	课前学习方案。
第1-3分钟	教学热身与启动	体验残障人生活困难。	教师告诉学生：Today, you'll get a chance to have some special experience.（教师请一位学生到自己身边，用一块很厚的布完全蒙住这位学生的眼睛，拉着转几圈，再让他找到自己的座位、文具等。2-3 位学生体验。）Now you can tell us how difficult it is for a blind person to find something. 今天我们开始学习关于残障人	学生听老师介绍，观察教师对游戏的演示。学生参与小组游戏。2-3 位学生体验蒙眼找物。	教师讲解。

185

（续表）

			的单元，希望大家学习后能够深入了解残障朋友们的困难，能给予他们更多的帮助。		
第4-5分钟	任务呈现	了解任务。	教师告诉学生：我们本单元共四项任务，每天由一项任务组担任学习主导工作。每项任务的小组都必须进行课前准备。Today's learning will mainly focus on Five must-dos groups. 教师请 Five must-dos group 到前台就座（学生分为前后两部分相对而坐，任务主导组在前，面向其他组，教师在中间）。	选择 Five—must-dos 任务的学生到指定位置就座。	课前学习成果。
第6-10分钟	运用能力学习	激活完成任务所需的知识与能力。	教师引导学生完成教材 Warming Up 部分的内容，引导学生关注不定式使用是否正确。	学生完成教材 Warming Up 部分的内容。Five must-dos group 汇报小组讨论结果。全班评价学习，设计 4 个动词不定式的语义理解题。	教材的 Warming Up 部分的内容。
第11-17分钟	读中活动	理解课文宏观问题。	教师设计 Five must-dos, 必须了解残障朋友的困难和感受。课文是一个案例。第一遍阅读：Who is Marty? What difficulties did Marty have in his life?	学生阅读课文，写出答案。Five must-dos group 回答问题，其他同学评价他们的回答，补充答案。	课文内容。

（续表）

第18-26分钟	读中回答	理解课文细节。	教师指导小组活动，非 Five must-dos group 的小组每组就课文一部分设计一个问题。教师检查 Five must-dos group 是否完全理解课文。引导学生关注不定式的含义。	学生再次阅读课文。非 Five must-dos group 的小组讨论设计问题。Five must-dos group 准备回答问题，其他同学评价他们的回答，补充答案。	同伴学习成果。
第27-35分钟	读后活动	理解课文的语用目的。	教师设计读后问题，引导学生讨论，并相互评价： 1. For what purposes did Marty write his story? 2. What help did he need? Find the supporting contents from the text.	Five must-dos group 回答并呈现他们的答案，其他同学评价他们的回答，并补充。	课文内容。
第36-44分钟	任务展示	对任务完成情况进行成果展示。	教师检查全班其他同学是否理解其语句。	Five must-dos group 陈述课前写的 Five must-dos。全班讨论 Five must-dos 的内容，并评价其不定式的用法。	同伴任务成果。
第45分钟	布置作业	巩固强化。	教师布置作业：完成第 48 页活动 1、2、3。	巩固所学的词语。	课后学习方案。

课后学习

1. Read and get to know more about the Family Village.

2. Read and discuss: Is it wise for Oscar to attend London Olympics?

3. Cloze test. (具体内容从略)

表5-9　第二课时教学设计

任务			本课时由选择以下任务的小组完成任务：阅读课文，学习如何运用委婉，用委婉语写建议。		
教学过程					
预设时间	学习步骤	学习目的	教学方案	学习方案	学习资源
第1分钟	导入	明确任务。	教师呈现任务：今天的主角是 Suggestions Group 了。请 Suggestions Group 台前就座。	学生了解任务。	教师话语。
第2-5分钟	热身	激活学生关于残障人生活困难的了解。	教师请学生呈现自己发现的残障人生活困难的情况，并加以说明。教师提出讨论话题：How can we make a cinema more accessible for people with walking difficulties? (Activity 1 on Page 7)	学生呈现自己发现的残障人生活困难的情况，并加以说明。Suggestions Group 必须呈现，其他组随意。	课前学习方案。
第6-10分钟	读前活动（预测）	激活已有知识结构，并据此进入本课时主题。	教师告诉学生："预测"是进入阅读的"钥匙"。合理、积极的预测能降低阅读难度，提高理解水平。"预测"的依据通常是标题、关键词、介绍等文字信息以及图片、图表等非文字信息。From the format of letter, what can you predict? From the coloured words, what can you predict? From the topic sentence of each paragraph, what can you predict?	学生听教师讲解，并根据教师的要求，进行预测。	课文。

（续表）

第11-35分钟	读中活动	浏览全文，获得大意。（5分钟）	教师告诉学生：文章的首尾段落和段落的首尾句通常是"主题段/句"，可以从中获取文章或段落的大意。	学生读主题句，了解文章的主旨大意。	课文。
		仔细阅读，寻找细节。（10分钟）	教师引导学生完成教材第8-9页的活动2、3、4。	学生完成教材第8-9页的活动2、3、4。	课文。
		讨论。（10分钟）	教师引导学生讨论论说文论点与论据的关系以及论据的形式。	学生陈述论说文论点与论据的关系，论据的形式。	课文。
第36-44分钟	任务展示与评价	检测学生的语言运用能力。	教师要求Suggestions Group陈述他们自己的建议，其他学生讨论。	Suggestions Group积极主动陈述自己的建议。	学生成果（对话和梗概）。
第45分钟	布置作业	扩展阅读，巩固阅读技能。	教师补充阅读内容。	学生完成课后学习方案。	课后学习方案。

课后阅读：（具体内容从略）

表 5-10　第三课时教学设计

任务	本课时由选择以下任务的小组完成任务：听对话，学习如何向朋友表达祝愿和祝贺，编对话，表达对某人的祝愿与祝贺。				
教学过程					
预设时间	学习步骤	学习目的	教学方案	学习方案	学习资源
第1分钟	导入	明确任务。	教师对学生说：今天的主角是 Best Wishes and Congratulations Group 了。请 Best Wishes and Congratulations Group 台前就座。	学生了解任务。	教师话语。
第2-7分钟	预测	通过学前活动建构图式。	教师呈现海明威照片，告诉学生：Tell me what you know about Hemingway.　教师出示乞力马扎罗山风景照片，问学生这与海明威有什么关系以及著名小说 The Snows of Kilimanjaro 与本单元学习有什么关系。教师请学生预测：盲人如何登上乞力马扎罗山?	目学生根据教师的引导，预测课文内容，激活已有图式，建构新图式。	海明威及乞力马扎罗山的风景照片。
第8-15分钟	听力训练	建构图式。	教师引导学生听教材中的对话，通过检测预测是否正确建构图式。	学生听对话，完成活动1、2、4、5。学生通过检测预测是否正确建构图式。	教材6-7页 Listening and speaking 部分。

（续表）

第16-20分钟	预测	通过预测建构图式。	教师指导学生进行预测：Hawking 的病症，肌无力病症；体验只用一根中指完成写作、吃饭、穿衣等动作。	学生进行预测，建构图式。	教师话语，Hawking 及张云成的照片。
第21-30分钟	阅读	建构图式。	教师指导学生阅读教材第51页文章，并基于信息建构图式。	学生阅读课文，建构图式。	课文。
第31-40分钟	语言运用	巩固阅读内容，加强阅读理解，平衡语言技能。	教师设计采访张云成时的提问、祝愿与祝贺，帮助学生构建图式。	学生将故事中的人物、事件等与自己的生活阅历联系起来，从而进行对比、反思、拓展阅读等活动。	课文及活动成果。
第41-44分钟	讨论	建构图式。	教师指导学生回读第8页课文，再次建构论点与论据的关系图式。	学生阅读课文，建构图式。	课文。
第45分钟	布置作业。	巩固阅读图式建构的能力。将图式建构与完形填空练习结合、融通。	教师布置学生课后分析完形填空篇章中蕴含的图式。教师要求学生自由组成小组讨论阅读图式建构与完形填空之间的关系。	学生分析完形填空篇章，分析其中包含的图示。	教师提供的完形填空材料。教师提供的学习资源网站。

课后阅读：（具体内容从略）

191

表 5-11　第四课时教学设计

任务	本课时由选择以下任务的小组完成任务：阅读课文，把握不同阅读图式的建构，并利用图式分析篇章体裁和题材，提高阅读理解和完形填空的解题效率，提高学习成效。				
教学过程					
预设时间	学习步骤	学习目的	教学方案	学习方案	学习资源
第1分钟	导入	明确任务。	教师告诉学生：今天的主角是 Reading and Cloze Group 了。请 Reading and Cloze Group 台前就座。	学生了解任务。	教师话语。
第2-5分钟	复习	了解信息词。	教师引导学生再次回读第 51 页文章，归纳文章主旨大意，圈出关键信息词。	学生回读第 51 页文章，归纳主旨大意，圈出关键信息词。	课文。
第6-15分钟	学习完形填空	体验阅读与完形填空练习的关系。	教师引导学生讨论：如果你得了大奖却不能亲自领奖是否会感到遗憾。教师帮助学生完成第 48 页活动 1。	学生讨论教师提出的问题，然后完成填空练习并分析每个词的信息含量。Reading and Cloze Group 陈述完成过程。	课文。
第16-20分钟	训练完成	进一步学习完形填空的练习。	教师引导学生进行完形填空训练。	学生两人一组，每人一篇互不相同的文章，尝试删去文章中有关主旨大意的 10 个词。	课中学习方案。
第21-30分钟	阅读与讨论	进一步学习完形填空的练习。	教师引导学生交换文章后阅读，再讨论并说明主旨大意，并猜测：删去的词是什么？(What words have been deleted?)	学生两人小组内交换文章后阅读，读后讨论并说明文章的主旨大意，并猜测：删去的词是什么？	课中学习方案。

第31-36分钟	讨论	明确阅读与完形填空的能力关联。	教师引导学生进行小组讨论：分析自己理解和猜测中存在的问题。教师要求 Reading and Cloze Group 呈现小组讨论结论。	学生小组讨论：分析自己理解和猜测中存在的问题。Reading and Cloze Group 呈现小组讨论结论。	课中学习方案。
第37-41分钟	进一步练习完形	进一步明确阅读与完形填空的能力关联。	教师引导学生完成练习，并就完成的顺利程度、自信程度等进行提问：When you chose the first answer, were you sure your choice was right?	学生再完成一篇10个词补全完形填空练习。Reading and Cloze Group 陈述完成过程。	课中学习方案。
第42-45分钟	总结及布置作业。	巩固本单元训练的阅读技能、阅读图式建构、完形阅读等能力。	教师引导学生总结：完形能力是阅读能力与词汇运用能力的结合。学会对阅读材料的关键词、信息词进行猜测对完形很有帮助。教师布置学生课后至少完成三篇完形阅读的设计练习并与同学分享、交流阅读理解的经验和收获，从而进一步巩固和强化语篇运用能力。	学生有意识地进行反思和自我评价。（有意识地反思和自我评价是学习者进步的基础和动力。对学习资源的整合和改编，特别是技能转换是优秀学习者的素质之一。）	课后学习方案。

三、课堂教学案例 3

表 5-12　*The Million Pound Bank Note* 单元教学案例

教学内容	《英语》（人教社）必修三，第 3 单元（*The Million Pound Bank Note*）
文化意识发展目标	让学生通过阅读、表演，理解相关人物心态，探讨金钱和人性的关系，批判拜金主义，促进学生发展正确的财富观、人生观和价值观，也通过讨论这个事件对 Henry 是否公平、是否会伤害他的生活，进而发展学生的思维能力。
主要教学过程	
导入	教师呈现一张百万英镑的钞票（a million pound bank note）并对学生说：What is it? How much RMB is one million pound equal to? If you are given such a large sum of money, how will you spend it? 如何使用一大笔财富反映了同学们的财富观和价值观，有的同学可能用于自身享受，有的同学可能用于提升自身学识素养，还有些同学可能用于孝敬父母或帮助他人。不管是哪种选择，要求学生给出充分的理由，让各种观点互相碰撞，让学生在倾听、对比同伴的答案中反思自己的价值观和财富观。然后对学生说：Do you believe that with a million pound bank note, you can survive 3 months without even spending it? Is it possible or impossible? Give your reasons. 一分不花可以过三个月，乍一听像是天方夜谭，不可能之事，但"一张百万英镑的钞票"能将不可能变为可能。那么 a million pound bank note 在现代社会可能带来什么样的魔力？为何有这样的魔力？通过这些问题，让学生初步思考金钱对人性、家庭和社会的影响。
了解戏剧结构	教师提出问题启发学生对戏剧结构进行思考并用图片对学生进行解释：What is the writing style? Is there anything special for a play? There are different parts in a play. What do we call them? NARRATOR: It is the summer of 1903. Two old and wealthy brothers, ... ⟹ the narrator's part RODERICK: Young man, would you step inside a moment, please? ⟹ Lines Henry: (*A servant opens a door*) Thanks. ⟹ Stage directions 这是高中课本第一次出现戏剧，有必要让学生了解戏剧的文本特点和结构要素，以及从旁白获取背景信息的阅读策略。

（续表）

听取 大意	学生边听录音边阅读课文，充分感受戏剧中人物对白所呈现出的思想感情，并回答几个简单的问题，了解这一幕戏剧的大意。 How many characters are there in Scene 3? Who are they? Where are they? Who is the main character? Where does he come from? When and where did the story happen? What happened in this scene? Use one sentence.

细读
课文

学生细读课文并填写表格。

Occasions	What Henry says or does	How Henry feels	What the two brothers do or say	How they appear to be
Before Henry enters the house			Watch Henry in their house	
After Henry enters the house			Ask questions to know about Henry's situation and decide if Henry is the right person for the bet	
After Henry explains his situation			Give Henry the letter	
After Henry gets the letter			Stop Henry from opening the letter	
After Henry knows there is money in the letter			Persuade Henry to keep the letter	

全班阅读后讨论出答案如下：

Occasions	What Henry says or does	How Henry feels	What the two brothers do or say	How they appear to be
Before Henry enters the house	Wanders around	Anxious, worried	Watch Henry in their house	Relaxed and maybe excited to have a target
After Henry enters the house	Explains his terrible situation	Hungry, hoping to be given a job	Ask questions to know about Henry's situation and decide if Henry is the right person for the bet	Happy and lucky to have found the right person

195

（续表）

After Henry explains his situation	Decides to leave	Felt Angry and disappointed at the brothers' response	Give Henry the letter	Happy, excited and satisfied
After Henry gets the letter	Wants to open it at once	Curious and maybe hopeful	Stop Henry from opening the letter	Mysterious and suspicious
After Henry knows there is money in the letter	Explains he wants a job not a charity	Unhappy to be given money rather than a job	Persuade Henry to keep the letter	Mysterious and suspicious

此环节旨在培养学生基于戏剧的语言和动作对角色的情感态度、心理活动作出有理据的判断和猜测的能力，尤其是对比 Henry 的感受和两兄弟的反应，体会由于阶层、身份、财富、处境、目的等的不同带来的不同的情感体验。在归纳出表格后教师提问：Roderick says: "Please don't go, Mr Adams, You mustn't think we don't care about you." Do you think the two brothers really care about Henry's situation? Do you think they mean to help Henry? Do you think the bet is fair for Henry? How do you think the bet will change Henry's life? 通过第一和第二个问题的讨论让学生认识到这个赌从头到尾只是有钱人的游戏，无关有钱人对落魄者的关心和帮助。同时也通过讨论这个事件对 Henry 是否公平、是否会影响他的生活，进而发展学生的思维能力。

人物分析	教师将学生分成四人小组，让一组学生观察剧中的一个角色，然后告诉其他同学他们认为他们所观察的角色的性格是什么，并充分表达他们的理由。例如：

Name	Personality	Evidence
Henry	1. Proud 2. Honest, direct and trustworthy 3. Hardworking …	1. He wants work but not charity. 2. He tells the truth to the brothers though they are strangers. 3. He works for his passage as an unpaid hand. …

（续表）

Oliver and Roderick	1. Mischievous 2. Polite and formal	1. Prepared to bet on so much money just for fun 2. "I wonder, Mr Adams, if you'd mind us asking a few questions." "May we ask…."

	此环节旨在让学生通过对剧本语言和内容的解读，理解戏剧如何运用语言和动作表现人物的性格特征，品味戏剧语言的魅力，同时学习 Henry 虽然穷困而依然自尊自强、诚信有礼、自食其力的优秀品质，从而发展学生的文化意识。
表演和改写	教师将学生分成四人小组，每个组选择一个角色并扮演这个角色，要求通过语言、动作、神态等传神地再现人物的性格特征、心理活动和情感态度。教师要求学生把戏剧改写为小说，力图在小说中体现戏剧所不能体现的人物心理、神态、情感、态度等，并与原著进行对比，以更好地理解原著精髓并提高自身写作能力。这一单元的教学让学生深度理解自强自立精神品格的价值表现，在学习理解、应用实践、迁移创新的学习过程中，发展学生的这一品格。

四、课堂教学案例 4

表 5-13　*Nelson Mandela* 单元教学案例

教学内容	*Nelson Mandela—A Modern Hero*; Elias' story
文化意识发展目标	让学生了解曼德拉的领袖魅力，突出其责任感（曼德拉愿意为了黑人利益牺牲个人的稳定生活），促进学生领导（leadership）品质的发展。同时让学生了解曼德拉还关注种族平等、人格平等的本质价值，展示其对白人监狱看守及其他白人的宽容。
主要教学过程	
导入	1. 师生共同观看曼德拉雨中追悼会（约 2 分钟），并呈现奥巴马、卡梅伦、李克强等国家领导人对曼德拉的评价，问学生：What do you know about Nelson Mandela? Why did the whole world mourn his death? Why was he so highly thought of by so many politicians? 要求学生结合视频内容和已有的背景知识进行讨论，初步感知曼德拉的伟大和影响力，激发学生了解曼德拉光辉一生的兴趣。

（续表）

2. 呈现 PPT

ELIAS' STORY

教师对学生说：Today we are going to read "Elias' story", and it is a true story. What do you think is the relationship between Elias and Nelson Mandela? What do you think the story is about? 学生根据图片、标题和对曼德拉已有的认识作出猜测：This is a story about how Nelson Mandela helped Elias.

整体阅读

学生整体阅读课文 (Elias' story & the rest of Elias' story)，找出 Elias' problems, What Nelson Mandela did to help Elias, How Elias' feelings changed。

Elias' problems	Elias' feelings	Nelson Mandela's help	Elias' feelings
1. He was a poor black worker. 2. He had little education. 3. He didn't have a passbook.	sad, worried, hopeless	He offered him guidance and helped him get the correct papers.	grateful, more hopeful, happy
4. He had a hard life in prison.	painful, sad, hopeless	He taught him and encouraged him to get a degree.	feel good, more confident
5. He couldn't get a job.	painful, sad, hopeless, worried	He gave him a job.	grateful, lucky, proud

学生通过完成表格，梳理了文章的细节，更重要的是感受到 Elias 在曼德拉的帮助下生活和情感的变化，从而理解曼德拉事业对黑人的积极影响。

（续表）

细读	教师提问，然后布置阅读任务：Why did Nelson Mandela help Elias? Was it because he was particularly poor? Why did Nelson Mandela say "The last thirty years have seen the greatest number of laws stopping our rights and progress, until today we have reached a stage where we have almost no rights at all."? Now please read and find out the black's situation at that time. 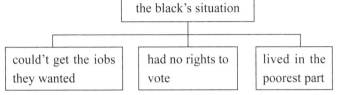 曼德拉帮助 Elias 并不是出于同情或私人关系，而是因为 Elias 是曼德拉众多受到不平等待遇的黑人同胞中的一员。通过这些问题的追问，让学生了解曼德拉牺牲个人安稳生活（律师职业），为争取黑人平等权利而战斗终身，为他人自由而放弃自己自由的伟大贡献和意义。
归纳 判断	教师提出需要学生归纳的问题，并指导学生讨论：The title of this unit is *Nelson Mandela—A Modern Hero*. What qualities do you think made Nelson Mandela a great hero? Find evidence from the passage to support your answers. 学生通过讨论，归纳出曼德拉的高贵品格和作为领袖的非凡魅力。 1. He was a black lawyer who could live a comfortable life. 2. He offered guidance to the poor black people. 3. He helped Elias to improve his life. 4. He fought for the rights of black people. 5. He taught the prison guards. 6. He encouraged Elias to get a degree. 7. Elias joined the ANC Youth League and helped him blow up some government buildings.　⟹　generous, kind, helpful, willing to sacrifice for a great cause, brave, responsible, respectful, inspiring, influential, forgiving, tolerant, charming, considerate, intelligent, activating, persistent, optimistic …

199

（续表）

	教师通过指导学生回答问题，培养学生乐观、关怀、平等、宽容、成就自己也成就他人的价值观和情操：Not everyone can be as great as Nelson Mandela, but there is something we can learn from him as a common person. What do you think it is?
课后拓展	这一课时（本单元的课文阅读理解课时）引导学生在学习理解、应用实践、迁移创新的学习过程中，深度感知、体验、理解曼德拉的宽容品格，促进学生宽容品格的发展。教师告诉学生：There are many books about Nelson Mandela, such as his auto biography *Long walk to freedom* and many videos on the internet about him. I would like you to know more and learn more about him after school. Next class please share with us some of his stories or famous sayings and tell us how it influences you. When I walked out of the prison cell towards the door leading to freedom, I have made it clear his own pain and resentment if not able to stay behind, so in fact I still in prison. <div align="right">—Nelson Mandela</div>

五、课堂教学案例 5

表 5-14 *Satisfaction Guaranteed* 单元教学设计

教学内容	*Satisfaction Guaranteed*
品格教育目标	让学生体验虚荣导致的巨大打击，发展学生克制虚荣心的品质，引导学生建构机器人伦理观念。
教学内容分析	品格教育是英语课程的组成部分，但不是唯一目标，不应脱离英语课程的其他内容进行品格教育，而应整合融入英语课程的其他内容，在具体教学中应利用课文教学优势进行。本单元教学材料优势分析： 1. 教材设定的本单元语法教学内容是进一步巩固 to be done 结构，这一结构本班学生已经完全掌握，理解没有任何困难，极少学生略微存在运用困难。故而对于语法内容，本单元无需在课文教学中进行专项教学，只需进行一课时专项巩固即可。为便于在巩固时关联课文语境，在课文教学中涉及这一语法结构时，老师应给予必要的显性提示，为随后的巩固进行铺垫。

2．本单元课文文化主题是人类与机器人的关系，这是当代人类文化中普遍存在的话题，不是英语国家文化独特的话题。在今天，中国家用机器人比英语国家乃至全世界更为广泛。但是，本单元课文在话题层面文化教育的优势不够显著，所以教师在教学过程中应尽可能向学生渗透。

3．本单元课文故事的核心是主人公 Claire 爱上了机器人 Tony，因为 Tony 比 Claire 的丈夫 Larry 更加善解人意，更加关心爱护 Claire，而且能帮助 Claire 解决生活中的各种难题，为 Claire 赢得商店店员对她的尊重，甚至让 Claire 的邻居与朋友们嫉妒她有这个英俊能干的男朋友。本质上是 Tony 满足了 Claire 的虚荣心。Gladys 等人嫉妒 Claire 有如此英俊能干的男朋友，本质上也是其虚荣心所致。虚荣心是人类普遍存在的品格弱点，也是高中学生可能存在的、需要不断努力克服的品格弱点。这使得本单元课文具有显著的品格教育优势。

当然，本单元也可以很好地发展学生的其他品格，比如 Tony 为什么比 Larry 更受 Claire 喜爱，因为 Tony 做什么都只为 Claire 着想，而 Larry 无论是要求 Claire 承担公司的机器人实验，还是在 Tony 进入家庭后马上出差三周，都没有征得 Claire 的同意，即使 Claire 不想承担机器人实验，Larry 还是要求她承担。但 Claire 也应理解 Larry 出差是工作需要，接受实验是为了工作。这可以发展学生为他人着想的品格。

经过课前对学生的分析，教师发现，克制虚荣心是一个更加急迫需要发展的品格。

发展克制虚荣心的品格，属于英语课程所规定的品格教育内容，也属于人类品格教育目标，更属于中国文化与西方文化，乃至世界文化的共同成分。2017 高中英语课标明确要求高中英语课程发展学生"正确的价值观""积极的道德情感"，克制虚荣心则是其中的重要内涵。而且，无论是孔子，还是亚里士多德都将克制虚荣心作为基本品格，人类各民族都有大量嘲讽虚荣的故事、小说、戏剧、影视，甚至网络文学作品。

虚荣的致命之处是虚，若是"实"荣，则是一种光荣感、自豪感、荣耀感。所以，单纯反对虚荣，并不能有效发展克制虚荣心的品格。荣，若控制在一定程度上，则是一种光荣感、自豪感，过度了，才成为虚荣心。对于本班（奥赛班）学生，参加国际奥赛为国争光，甚至考上哈佛大学、清华大学，以后成为国际一流科学家，为中国乃至人类作出巨大科学贡献，并不是虚荣，而是

（续表）

	"实"荣，但若以此而炫耀，甚至自我膨胀、顶撞教师、不遵守学校与课堂纪律、不尊重其他同学，则是过度的"荣"，也就成了虚荣。这是发展本班学生克制虚荣心品格的关键。 4．本单元故事需要深度理解，这个故事的行为过程与情感过程变化，是理解故事的基础，而这一变化过程，尤其是二者相互印证的关系，使得本课文故事在发展学生理解过程及其推进的逻辑合理性的思维能力方面具有显著优势。 5．本单元是高二选修课程的内容，本班学生经过教师一年多的系统与深度训练，已经形成较为有效的自主与合作相辅相成的英语语言学习能力，学生英语成绩不仅全年级第一，而且基本稳定在较高水平。所以，无论本单元是否具有语言学习能力发展优势，建构新的语言学习能力都不是本班的教学重点，本班只需要较稳定地运用已有学习能力即可。
教育 教学 重点	基于以上分析，本单元教育教学重点确定为： 1．基于人物情感分析，引导学生了解虚荣心的可能影响，根据需要有度地发展克制虚荣心的品格，适度涉及为他人着想的品格教育。 2．基于故事情节与人物情感变化过程及其逻辑关联，发展学生把握与分析因果关系逻辑性、行为与情感或现象与本质逻辑关系的思维品质。
	教学过程（实录）
导入	在课文教学之前，教师用一课时的时间指导学生阅读本单元第二篇课文，以便让学生先了解该故事的作家以及其作品特征，尤其是机器人三原则，以作为本故事阅读的铺垫。在本故事阅读之前，教师让学生先看教材中的作者像，并以回答基本信息问题的方式回忆上一节课所阅读的内容，尤其是最为重要的机器人三原则。教师首先提出预设的基本信息问题：Who is he? 学生齐声给出正确答案 Isaac Asimov。这只是一个回忆信息层面的问题，作为第一个问题，难度不大，适合学生进入学习状态。教师随即提出预设的第二个作者背景问题：What did he write? 学生给出多种答案，有的说 science fiction，有的说 books，有的说 robots。教师根据不同学生的回答进行追问，如：What book? Did he write robots or stories about robots?

（续表）

<table>
<tr><td></td><td colspan="2">学生继续给出答案。这一追问要求学生给出具体信息，而不是不具体的信息。这种对信息的具体内涵的追问，有助于发展学生思维的准确性，不仅有助于学生准确理解，也有助于学生准确表达，也可以基于此发展学生的科学精神等积极品格。教师接着进一步追问：Did he put up some theories? 教师发现学生有些摸不着头脑，于是进一步提问：Did he put up some laws about robots? 以此对前一问题进行解释说明，帮助学生建立 theory 与 law 之间的范畴意识，然后再问学生：What are the three laws for robots? 落实到思维的准确性，从而形成思维发展的问题链，继续发展学生的科学精神。</td></tr>
<tr><td>整体感知故事</td><td>人物性格特征感知</td><td>随后教师引导学生进入故事学习。教师首先导入故事标题 Satisfaction Guaranteed，询问学生二词词义之后，追问：Whose satisfaction? How guaranteed? 学生给出自己的理解与猜测。教师此时不予追问，以激发学生的发散性思维，并在随后讨论中进一步验证，以发展学生基于证据合理推测的能力。二词均与情感有直接关系，教师引导学生关注二词的情感特色，建议学生在随后的阅读中基于 satisfaction 与 guaranteed 二词，尤其是 satisfaction 的个人情感特色，关注故事的情感内涵、主人公的情感变化，以及相关情感的合理性，从而为随后的道德品格教育活动，起到非常有效的铺垫作用。

课文后半部分插图
教师选择课文后半部分的一张插图，让学生描述图片内容。然后教师提问：Based on the title, the picture and what we have learned about Isaac Asimov, what do you think the story is about? 因为学生已知单元情境，基本都能预测出：It's a story about robots and human. 有学生说：I think it</td></tr>
</table>

（续表）

		is about a robot falling in love with a woman. 教师追问：Why do you think so? 学生回答：I have read many stories like this. 教师追问：Are you fond of such stories? 学生回答：Yes, because they are very imaginative. 显然正是教师的一系列追问，学生需要系统、深度、准确地表达，从而发展思维的准确性、系统性和逻辑性。教师问学生：Who are the people out of the window? Why are they watching this? Is it good? Is it polite? 这一活动更是让学生关注窗外人物，猜测各种可能以及原因，促进学生对此道德品格的判断。 在看图预测故事之后，教师问学生：How many paragraphs are there in the story? 有学生不去数，而是直接回答：Many. 教师追问：How many? 认真数过段落的学生集体回答：Twelve. 这一问题看似简单，学生只需数一数就能得出答案，但首先这一问题可以帮助学生对故事形成整体感知，尤其是发现其段落长短特性，从而对随后的阅读分析起到一定感知性的作用；其次这一追问要求学生给予准确数据，有助于发展思维准确性。感知插图、感知段落数量与长短，是对于感性的唤醒，这对于学生在文学理解中形成移情，尤其是基于感性理解故事中 Claire 的情感变化，具有非常重要的基础性作用，尤其是对于这一各学科奥赛学生组成的班级，若不唤醒感性，其随后的故事理解可能会延迟。所以，对于基于感觉的思维这种本能性思维能力，在需要其发挥作用时，需要提前并及时唤醒。基于感性的理解不仅对这些学生理解随后的课文很重要，也有助于发展学生的积极情感，以及对于积极情感的理解。
故事情节与人物情感变化感知		教师让学生整体阅读故事，找出故事中的主要人物，弄清楚他们的身份及特征，完成以下表格。 **Who are they?** | **Characters in the story**	**Who are they?** | |---|---| | Larry Belmont | | | Claire | | | Tony | | | Gladys Claffern | | 在学生阅读填表之后，教师与学生就这些问题展开问答。对于这些人物信息、性格特性，学生基本能很快答出，但对于 Gladys Claffern，教师要进行追问。教师首先问：What information can we get about Gladys Claffern from the passage?

学生根据课文答出：She was rich and powerful. 教师接着问：Did Claire have a close relationship with her? 学生找出答案：No. Claire envied her. 教师追问：Why did Claire envy her? 学生答：I think she was richer and more powerful than Claire. 教师再问：From Claire's perspective, why? 学生再答：She was poorer and less powerful than Gladys. 如此追问不仅有助于理解人物，而且可以通过引导学生从不同视角看同一问题而发展学生思维的丰富性。尤其是引导从不同人物的视角进行思考、分析、判断，促进学生形成理解他人的积极道德品格。在引导学生对故事人物特性进行分析之后，教师让学生再次就主要情节与主人公 Claire 的情感变化对应性完成阅读课文，这有助于学生形成对故事的整体把握，更有助于学生从情感变化这一线索理解故事，而不只是基于故事情节把握情感变化。

Events and Claire's feeling

Time	Events	Claire's feelings
Before Tony was tested out	Tony was going to _____ by Claire.	
While Tony was being tested out	1. She saw Tony was _____ _____ and _____ with _____ hair and a _____ voice, making him more like a _____.	
	2. Tony asked Claire whether she needed _____.	
	3. Tony offered _____ to Claire when she mentioned her sense of _____.	
	4. Tony helped Claire make herself _____.	
	5. Claire felt Tony's skin was _____ and _____.	
	6. Tony made the clerk _____ _____ to Claire.	

（续表）

		7. Tony _____ when she fell off the ladder.	
		8. Tony _____ his arms around her, _____ his face close to her and _____ he didn't want to leave her.	
		9. Claire was _____ by the women.	
		10. Claire remembered Tony was just a machine.	
	After Tony was tested out	11. Tony had to _____ because he had women _____ with a machine.	

教师在这一过程中引导学生讨论 Claire 情感变化的因素，引导学生对其情感变化的内在、外在多种因素进行思考、分析，促进学生对情感变化的理性思考和价值判断。

学生通读整个故事之后，教师并不急于与学生马上就每一情节与情感的答案进行核对，而是让学生形成一个较为模糊的整体理解，然后逐段讨论，以此发展学生思维的系统性、准确性，以及通过行为与情感变化关系的分析，发展学生思维的逻辑性。同时，这一表格将行为与情感变化的关系明确呈现出来，有助于学生关注行为与情感变化的逻辑联系，以及行为与情感变化发展的整个过程，从而发展学生思维的逻辑性、系统性，并基于此深化情感体验，加深对道德品格的认知和判断。

细节理解

在故事理解中，教师也不断通过有深度地提问发展学生的思维能力和情感理解。在理解第二段后，教师问：Why didn't Claire want the robot in her house when her husband was away? 有学生回答：She might be afraid that the robot would attack her. 教师询问是否有其他推测，另一学生回答：She might be afraid that she might lose control of the robot. 教师继续询问学生是否有不同推测，有学生回答：She might be afraid that the robot might know her secret. 教师追问：What kind of secret? 学生不愿详细描述：Beyond description. 教师让其他同学说说这位同学不肯明确说出的 description 会是 What kind of description，同学们开始基于这个

学生的心理特征以及对这位同学的了解而进行推测。这一组问题显然先基于故事内容推测，然后基于同学特性进行推测，从而可以发展学生基于理据进行合理推测的思维能力。这一过程也有助于深度强化学生对 Claire 情感表现背后的价值取向的理解，从而为发展对 Claire 情感变化的积极的道德品格判断打下非常重要的基础。

教师通过推进学生对故事语言的深度理解而发展学生的思维能力和情感理解。在第二段理解中教师就其中一个语句进行了提问：In the sentence "... the robot wouldn't harm her or allow her to be harmed", does "allow her to be harmed" mean the same as "allow others to harm her"? 一位学生回答：No. It includes Clair harming herself. 教师追问：What kind of behaviour is harming oneself? 这位学生继续回答：Eating junk food even though I know it is harmful to my health. 教师进行评价：Yes. So please stop eating junk food. 然后问学生是否还有其他案例，另一位学生回答：When we don't do well in exams, we don't sleep or eat well. 教师指出：Yes. It doesn't help at all. So just figure out the reasons and try harder and believe next time you will do better. 还有一位学生说：Committing suicide. 教师马上指出：Life is too precious to be so foolish. 这一组观点追问不仅有助于发展学生思维的丰富性，而且教师坚持不断提出积极的人生态度，也有助于发展学生思维的正当性，将思维品质与文化发展深度融合，这恰恰是很多思维能力培养和文化意识发展严重忽略的。

在学生出现困顿时，改变提问方式，有助于不同层次的学生发展思维能力和情感理解。教师提问：What does "bonus" mean here? 学生似乎无法回答，教师追问：Is it about money here? 一位学生回答：No. 教师进一步追问：If something is a bonus, is it something expected beforehand? 然后教师引导该学生回答出完整的答案：Bonus here means that the machine might bring Claire a big surprise. 显然，这一降低难度的追问，可以帮助这位学生发展思维能力。我们经常听到很多抱怨，认为学生语言能力太弱，不能发展学生思维能力。人的思维能力是从婴儿即已开始发展的，并不受语言能力限制，这一案例更说明当学生语言能力遇到困难时，恰恰可以用发展思维能力来帮助学生发展语言能力，基于语言能力再加深对情感及其相关品格的准确理解。在基于感性体验发展思维能力层面，教师抓住教材中 deep voice 一词，

（续表）

先问：What does "a deep voice" mean? 学生无法描述，教师马上换一个问题：What is a "deep voice" like? Who has a deep voice in our class? 多位学生齐声答出：Wang Xiaolin. 教师于是说：Wang Xiaolin, would you please read something to let us appreciate your deep voice? 王小林同学于是朗读了一段课文，全班报以热烈掌声。这说明学生完全理解 deep voice 的语义，只是无法用英语解释其语义，而完全可以换一种形式表达其理解，不是换一种语言形式，是换一种表达方式，这对于发展学生思维的丰富性非常有帮助。

在英语课堂，发展学生思维的丰富性的最常见方式就是语言本身的丰富性，基于这种丰富性发展情感体验具有显著成效。教师就第二段提问：What can we learn about Claire here? 一位学生说：Claire is not confident. And she is easy to be persuaded. 教师追问 What do you mean by "not confident"? 学生回答：She was not sure about what she believes. 教师问是否有更多观点，另一位学生回答：Claire is not adventurous. 教师追问：What do you mean by "adventurous"? 学生回答：She is afraid of taking risks. 教师再问是否有不同观点，另一位学生回答：Claire is conservative. 教师追问：What do you mean by "conservative"? 学生回答：It means she refused to try new things. 这三组问答首先从不同观点有助于发展学生思维的丰富性，然后从语义追问与解释，再次发展学生思维的丰富性，从而也加深了学生的情感体验。

随后教师就 Tony 要帮 Claire 穿衣服而问学生：Do you think it is appropriate for a man to offer to help a lady with her dressing? 学生回答 No 之后，教师追问：Then why did Tony do this? 学生回答：Tony didn't have feelings like human beings. 这一追问有助于学生理解 Tony 随后的行为。

在随后的阅读中，遇到生词 sympathy，教师询问：What is sympathy? 一位学生答 It is a feeling of being sorry for sb. 教师追问 For sb's what?，该学生回答 For sb's sad situation. 教师用 For sb's misfortune. 给予肯定和解释后继续问：Sometimes when we say "I am sorry for you. We don't really mean it. We are just being polite. So how can we really feel sympathy for someone's misfortune? 另一学生回答 When we understand their situation. 教师肯定并给予引导 Yes. Only when we put ourselves in others' shoes can we really have sympathy for others. 显然，这里从词义理解到情感认知发

（续表）

展，发展学生思维的逻辑性。而对于 sympathy 本身的讨论、举例，更是显著发展了学生理解他人的相关品格。

教师引导学生跟读本段阅读，再次分析 Claire，以此逐步发展学生思维的准确性，让学生可以体验到思维准确性的发展过程。教师问学生 What can we learn about Claire from this part? 一位男学生回答 I think she was a vain woman. 教师追问 What do you mean by "vain"? 学生无力解释，教师换一种方式追问 Will you like a vain girl? 该男生明确说 No. 教师追问 Why not? 该男生回答 Because she cares too much about herself. She is self-centreed. 教师继续追问 What does a vain girl care about? 该男生回答 Being rich, being beautiful and being famous. 然后教师给予肯定。这一组五问四答的连环提问，不仅有助于发展学生思维的准确性、逻辑性，而且可以发展学生的品格。随后第二位学生指出 I think she was very sensitive. 教师追问 What is a sensitive person like? 学生回答 She is easily affected by others' opinions. She cares a lot about others' judgment. 教师肯定两位学生的回答，并说出自己的观点：I agree with you both. In my opinion, she was quite superficial. A superficial person cares about something like being beautiful, having a beautiful house and fails to see or understand what really matters. She was also not proactive enough because a proactive person takes action to make things change rather than sitting around feeling sorry for the sad situation. Besides, she had a sense of inferiority. That means she was not confident. Finally she was emotional. 这一过程可以深度发展学生思维的准确性，教师的总结归纳可以发展学生思维的批判性、系统性，因为这一总结不仅合理地表达了不同观点，而且对每一观点都有具体的解释，同时非常全面地分析了主人公的性格特征。学生的表述经常只是看到主人公的一面，而在教师的引导下，学生形成了更加合理全面的对于品格的价值判断。这一讨论中，最为关键的 vain 一词并非教师直接说出来，而是通过教师引导，由学生自己说出来这个词，发现其品格。随后教师让学生讨论起 vanity 的特性，引导学生自己进行设身处地的情感体验和情感分析，促进学生发展克制虚荣心的积极道德品格。这一本节课事先确定的教学目标，讨论时间较长，案例较多，内容较丰富，也更有深度，尤其是不同学生的不同看法，都使得预设的教学目标在非刻意中实现。正是这样的不经意，才能真正实现有效的品格教育。

在第五段的理解中，遇到生词 absurd，教师提问：What does

（续表）

"absurd" mean here? 学生回答：Ridiculous. 教师追问：Then what does "ridiculous" mean here? 学生找不到合理解释，教师换一个视角追问：What do you think of a robot having soft and warm skin? 学生说：Unbelievable. 教师引导学生：So here, what does "absurd" mean? 学生回答：Unbelievable and unreasonable. 这一过程非常清晰地展示了追问、换一个视角追问对于发展学生思维能力的有效性。而其中的内容讨论，让学生开始关注到 Claire 对于 Tony 外在特征的关注，而不是对其内在品格的关注，引发学生进一步思考其品格。

故事中有一个情节，是 Claire 购物遇到不礼貌、不认真服务的店员，Claire 给 Tony 打电话，Tony 在电话里对店员说了几句话，店员马上改变了态度。对此，教师提问：What do you think Tony said on the phone to make the clerk change the attitude? 一个学生回答：Tony told the clerk that Claire was powerful and rich. 教师解读学生的回答：So you mean the clerk gave in to Tony. 另一学生回答：Tony had lots of knowledge about selling things and had a good talk with the clerk and they became friends. 教师解读这位学生的回答：You mean Tony earned the clerk's respect and friendship with his knowledge. 还有一位学生回答：I think Tony told the clerk something about the law. 教师解读这位学生的回答：You mean Tony defended Claire by law. That is quite reasonable. 这一环节不仅通过多种不同回答，而且通过教师对学生话语的解读，发展学生思维的丰富性。学生对此进行扮演，有助于学生进行设身处地的情感推演，从而加深情感理解与合理性的判断。

在故事中 Claire 发现自己可能爱上 Tony 之后，一把推开 Tony，回到自己房间大哭起来。对此教师问学生：Why did Claire scream and push Tony away? What was she thinking about in her room? 学生回答：I don't know. 教师让学生从自己视角回答并且追问：Then what would be your reaction if you were Claire? 学生马上有了观点，而回答：I would just thank Tony. 教师于是追问：Well. You are quite sensible. What did Claire forget at that moment? 另一学生回答：Claire forgot Tony was a robot and fell in love with Tony. Then she remembered Tony was a machine and spent the rest of the day feeling sorry and ashamed. 教师给予肯定性鼓励。这一追问是当学生无法回答时教师让学生从自己视角设身处地地进行思考与回答，从而引导学生发展思维。

（续表）

	在 Claire 发现自己爱上 Tony 之后，教师换一个视角提问：Do you think Tony fell in love with Claire? 学生回答：No. 教师追问：Why? 学生回答：Tony was a machine. He was just programmed to behave in this way. He didn't have feelings. 教师进一步追问：Then why did Tony say he didn't want to leave Claire and opened the curtain? 学生回答：To improve Claire's confidence. 教师进一步追问：In what way does it help to improve Claire's confidence? 学生回答：Claire might think that she was attractive. 教师引导学生得出结论：So it helped Claire to feel good about herself. 这一组提问不仅把视角从 Claire 转到 Tony，而且就内容进一步追问。这种从不同人物视角提问、理解、分析的方式，有助于发展学生的批判性思维能力。 对于故事中 Claire 情感高潮的一幕"邀请 Gladys 等邻居来家聚会"之后的情感，教师提问：How do you understand the word "victory" here? 学生无法回答，教师换一方式提问：When will we say we win a victory? 学生回答：When we win a battle, a war, a competition, a race … 教师追问：So is there a war in the story? Who is on the other side? 学生回答：There was no real war in the story. Claire was always comparing herself with other women. It was like a war. 教师追问：Do you think it is good to compare yourself with others all the time? 学生回答：No. 教师再追问：Why not? 学生回答：Losing ourselves. 教师引导学生：So don't compare your life to others. You have no idea what their journey is all about. Just try to be your personal best. 教师继续就此提问：Why does the writer describe the victory as "sweet"? Why not just say "It is a victory"? 学生回答：Usually sweet is used to describe candies, but here it is used to show that Claire felt very good. 教师追问：Felt good about … 学生回答：About being envied by other women. 教师继续追问：Is the victory really sweet for Claire? 学生回答：She felt sweet. 教师再追问：What victory do you think it is? 有学生回答：I don't think it a real victory. It's a vain victory. 显然，这一组问题的回答过程不仅发展学生思维的准确性，而且发展学生思维的深刻性，帮助学生从 a sweet victory 的表面语义一路追问，让学生经过思维的过程，发现本质意义，从而发展思维的深刻性。这里对于 sweet 的真实性的讨论，更是让学生关注到 Claire 虚荣的内心世界。

（续表）

	随着故事发展，本质性问题越来越突出。到理解第11段时，教师问：What do you think Claire cried about? 一个学生回答：She cried because Tony was not a real man but a machine. 教师追问：But Claire was a married woman. How could it help if Tony was a real man? 学生回答：Because Claire realised Tony was good to her because he was programmed to be like this, not because she was attractive or Tony loved her. 教师追问：Do you think Claire was hurt by the experiment? 多名学生回答：Yes. 教师追问：In what way was she hurt? 一位学生回答：She thought she was fooled. 这依然是通过多层追问，引导学生发现现象背后的问题本质，从而发展学生思维的深刻性。通过对 Claire 为什么伤心的讨论和深度探究，发现其因为虚荣带来的痛苦，从而将其痛苦的主要原因归于其自身的虚荣心，加深学生对克制虚荣心的认同。
整体 讨论	在完整理解故事过程之后，教师再回到故事标题，让学生展开讨论，并比较一开始的猜测，以此发展思维的准确性。教师问：How can we understand the title "satisfaction guaranteed" after reading this story? 教师进一步解读问题：The title is "satisfaction guaranteed"? Who is satisfied? Why is it guaranteed? 学生回答：The company is satisfied. 教师追问：Then why is it "guaranteed"? 另一学生回答：It means in the future robots will satisfy all our needs. It is sure to happen. 教师再追问：Then why did Tony have to be rebuilt if the company was so satisfied? 学生给出支离破碎的答案，教师提出自己的观点。 教师引导学生继续讨论：Do you think it acceptable for human being to fall in love with a robot? 多名学生提出不同观点，教师对每位学生观点进行归纳提炼，赞同的观点主要有：1) If I think a machine is human, then it is human. 2) It should not be forbidden because we have the right to make a choice. 3. Human beings can have children by technology even if we marry a robot. 反对的观点主要有：1) A robot has no feelings. 2) Being perfect is not perfect. 3) I won't fall in love with a robot because it is wired but I respect others' choice. 这一过程有助于学生发展思维聚焦的能力，有助于发展思维的深刻性。教师引导学生对于学生提出的 Being perfect is not perfect 的观点进行讨论，从而促进学生发展克制虚荣心的道德品格。 在学生系统阅读、深度理解故事之后，教师让学生尝试简要复

（续表）

述故事，而为帮助学生准备复述故事，教师对故事每一环节提出以下两个问题：What did Claire do? How did she feel? 并制作完成故事的情节曲线，形成以下结果：

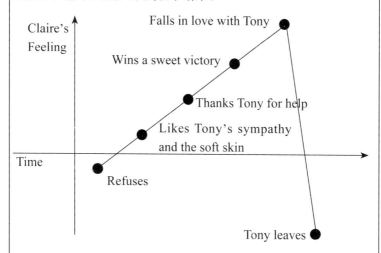

这一曲线图不仅呈现了故事中 Claire 的行为过程与情感变化，而且用曲线突出显示了情感的转折，这一形态对于该奥赛学生组成的班级，具有显著作用，可以帮助学生发展对于理科思维的形象表达。学生也就可以基于此复述故事，形成对故事过程的形象理解与记忆。这一过程也通过情感失落展示虚荣心带给 Claire 的巨大情感痛苦，引导学生发展克制虚荣心的积极道德品格。

　　这是一次真实的课堂教学，教师用三节课完成了整个故事教学。从学生课堂反应观察出，学生通过较长时间，较广泛、较有深度的讨论，深度体验了克制虚荣心、为他人着想的品格培养，在随后的课堂活动中也较好地表现出这些品格教育的行为。

　　如教师在引导学生讨论的过程中，提到一个月之前刚出版的具有世界影响的思想性著作时，看到班里一位学生课桌上恰好有这本书，教师赞扬这位学生阅读的前瞻性，然后请该学生分享他阅读这本书的感想。该学生非常谦虚地说还在理解之中，和同学们讨论后再分享，而其实教师发现该学生在阅读该书过程中已经在空白处进行多处批注，显然这位学生没有刻意炫耀他的阅读的前瞻性、思想的深刻性。

又如，在随后关于教室与宿舍清洁的讨论中，很多学生反应教室与宿舍清洁存在很多问题，教师问学生该如何解决这些问题时，有个别学生提出请更多的清洁工，但大部分学生都提出应该由他们自己打扫、清洁，包括利用旧物装饰教室、清洗窗帘、打扫厕所以及将垃圾送到楼下大垃圾桶去等等。再如，学生在随后一节课反复强调要把教室里灯笼上的蜻蜓摘走，原因之一是因为有一次吓着地理教师了，让他以后经过那个灯笼时总是感到害怕。这两个例子都说明学生更加关注于为他人着想。

当然，这只是部分同学的部分行为表现，但品格教育从来不是一蹴而就的，而是需要经过长期的学习和培养，尤其是克制虚荣心这种几千年来人类一直在不断强化的品格，更不可能是三节45分钟的课堂上经过几十分钟的讨论可以实现的。不过，也正是我们一节课一节课的努力，才可能真正促进学生品格教育的发展。

同时，这不仅是三节促进学生道德品格教育的课，而是三节常规的英语课。在英语课堂中，教师引导学生学习理解相关品格，通过应用实践、迁移创新，非常恰当、自然地渗透促进学生道德品格教育的活动，让学生在学习英语的过程中，发展道德品格，从而实现道德品格的有效发展。

这三节课的思维品质的发展也独具特色。

在这一课例中，教师通过提问，尤其是追问等深度提问技术，有效地发展学生的思维能力，总结一下主要具有以下显著特性：

1. 问题的全面性：这一课例自始至终采用问答方式引导学生理解故事，而不是常见的"四选一"选择题的方式。这种全面提问方式，非常有助于学生在日常学习中发展思维能力。

2. 问题的深刻性：教师在引导学生理解故事时，对故事情节、原因、结果、语言进行具有深度的追问，有时追问四轮、五轮，而且常常在同一问题上对多名学生进行追问，从而非常有效地发展学生思维的深刻性。

3. 回答的多样性：教师在提问中，总是尽可能让更多的学生回答问题，让学生在自己回答中、在听不同学生的回答中、在分析与评价不同答案中，发展思维的丰富性、准确性、逻辑性。

4.归纳的道德性：教师在一些关键问题上，对学生的回答中出现的、涉及可以提升学生思维的道德性的问题，及时给予引导，从而使思维品质发展本身不至于成为纯粹的思维能力、思维技术发展，而强调思维本身的道德性。

5.发展的过程性：思维品质、思维能力发展不是一蹴而就的，本课例多次就同一问题展开讨论，而且在不同活动中发展同一思维能力，以此在一个较长时间发展学生的思维品质。

这更说明，在一节不以文化意识为重点目标的英语课堂上，只要我们恰当地开展文化意识教育，我们就可以实现文化意识教育的目标。

本章小结

高中英语促进学生文化意识发展的核心在于品格教育，中外文化理解、传播中外优秀文化是品格教育的基础。

品格教育的基本方法是：首先把握学生品格教育内力呈现形态与时机，然后通过语言材料学习活动，创造品格教育外在环境与条件，形成对内力的促生作用，再引导学生在语言学习活动中，理解品格内涵、体验品格教育情境，最后实现学生品格教育。

情境在促进品格教育中作用显著，苏格拉底式提问可以帮助学生尽可能准确地理解情境。发展品格有很多具体技巧，值得尝试。

推荐阅读材料

冯德正 . 2015. 英语教学中的人文道德教育：正面价值观的多模态语篇建构 [J]. 外语界 . 2015(1).

杨韶刚 . 2013. 美国中小学品格教育实施策略 [J]. 中小学教育 . 2013(7).

第六章 高中英语文化意识发展评价

第一节 2017 高中英语课标对品格教育评价的要求

2017 高中英语课标对高中学生的英语学业水平发展有着清晰的评价标准，这些标准是我们评价学生文化意识发展的基础。

英语学科的学业质量是学生完成英语学科课程学习后的学业成就表现，英语学科的学业质量标准是以英语学科的核心素养及其表现水平为主要维度，综合课程内容，对学生英语学业成就表现的总体描述。2017 高中英语课标对高中英语学业水平进行了相应描述，其中有部分内容是对文化意识发展的学业成就表现的描述，主要内容有以下方面：

水平一学业水平标准中与文化意识相关内容（此处只介绍学业水平标准中与文化意识相关的主要内容，学业水平标准的其他内容与其他素养的标准见 2017 高中英语课标）：

表 6-1 水平一学业水平标准中与文化意识相关内容

序号	质量描述
1-1	在听的过程中，能抓住日常生活语篇的大意，获取主要事实、观点和文化背景。
1-5	能口头介绍中外主要节日等中外文化传统和文化背景。
1-12	能识别语篇直接陈述的情感态度、价值观和社会文化现象。
1-13	能介绍中外主要节日和中华优秀传统文化。

表 6-2 水平二学业水平标准中与文化意识相关内容：

序号	质量描述
2-1	在听的过程中，能抓住熟悉话题语篇的大意，获取其中的主要信息、观点和文化背景。

216

（续表）

2-5	根据交际场合的正式程度和行事程序，选择正式或非正式、直接或委婉的语言形式表达道歉、请求、祝愿、建议、拒绝、接受等，体现文化理解，达到预期交际效果。
2-7	能在表达中借助语言建构交际角色，体现跨文化意识和情感态度。
2-8	能识别语篇中的主要事实与观点之间的逻辑关系，理解语篇反映的文化背景。
2-12	能识别语篇间接反映或隐含的社会文化现象。

表 6-3　水平三学业水平标准中与文化意识相关内容:

序号	质量描述
3-1	能通过听，抓住较为复杂的口语语篇的大意，理解其中的主要信息、观点和文化背景。
3-6	根据社会交往场合的正式程度、行事程序以及与交际对象的情感距离，选择正式或非正式、直接或委婉的语言形式恰当地交流和表达态度、情感和观点，体现文化理解，达到预期交际效果。
3-9	能阐释和评价语篇所反映的情感、态度和价值观。

2017 高中英语课标要求高中英语学业水平考试和高考全面考查英语学科核心素养。英语学业水平考试和高考命题要着重考查学生在具体社会情境中运用英语理解和表达意义的能力，特别是听、说、读、看、写的能力。同时，要通过语言材料的选择、考查重点的设置、考试项目和考试形式的设计等，直接或间接地考查考生的思维品质、文化意识和学习能力。比如，在阅读理解部分，可以适当选择涉及文化背景和文化差异、情感态度和价值观的语篇，试题的设计可以引导学生对其中的文化差异进行理解和判断，对语篇反映的情感态度和价值观进行分析和阐释；写作试题可以引导学生对现象、观点、情感态度进行比较和分析，并在此基础上发表自己的观点、态度和价值判断，以考查学生的思维能力。

高中英语评价由形成性评价与终结性评价两类，高中英语两类评价皆应评价学生的文化意识发展。

第二节 高中英语文化意识发展形成性评价

评价文化意识中的品格教育可以采用量表形式进行。量表策略可以在学习前、学习过程中、学习后使用，通过纵向对比，发现学生品格的发展，或者通过横向比较进行评价。

一、量表评价

1. 自信心量表

以下是著名的罗森伯格自信心量表，在评价学生自信心发展时，可以参考。

表6-4 自信心量表

指示：以下是一组有关自我感觉的句子，请按你的情况作答。

1 = 很不同意　2 = 不同意　3 = 同意　4 = 很同意

1. 我认为自己是个有价值的人，至少基本上是与别人相等的。 1 2 3 4
2. 我觉得我有很多优点。 1 2 3 4
3. 总的来说，我觉得我是一个失败者。® 1 2 3 4
4. 我做事的能力和大部分人一样好。 1 2 3 4
5. 我觉得自己没有什么值得骄傲。® 1 2 3 4
6. 我对于自己是抱着肯定的态度。 1 2 3 4
7. 总体而言，我对自己感到满意。 1 2 3 4
8. 我希望我能够更尊重自己。® 1 2 3 4
9. 有时候我确实觉得自己很无用。® 1 2 3 4
10. 有时候我认为自己一无是处。® 1 2 3 4

总分：
注："®"表示该测题要反过来计分。

《自信心量表》使用说明

一、量表简介

《自信心量表》（Rosenberg Self-Esteem Scale）由美国心理学家罗

（续表）

森伯格（M. Rosenberg）制定，它是世界上最常用的测量个人自信心的量表，共有 10 道题，用以测量个人对自我感觉的好坏程度。该量表具有简单易懂、操作方便、可信度高等特点。

二、计分方法

受测者在 3 点评尺上对测题作答：1= 非常同意 (strongly agree)，2= 同 意 (agree)，3= 不 同 意 (disagree)，4= 非常不同意 (strongly disagree)。因此，其最低得分为 10 分，最高得分为 40 分。在 10 个条目中，第 3, 5, 8, 9, 10 五个条目的算分是反向的（即 1 分算作 4 分，4 分算作 1 分；2 分算作 3 分，3 分算作 2 分）。

三、得分解释

10—15 分：自卑者

你对自己缺乏信心，尤其是在陌生人和上级面前，你总是感到自己事事都不如别人，你时常感到自卑。你需要大大提高你的自信心。

16—25 分：自我感觉平常者

你对自己感觉既不是太好，也不是太不好。你在某些场合下对自己感到相当自信，但在其他场合却感到相当自卑，你需要稳定你的自信心。

26—35 分：自信者

你对自己感觉十分良好。在大多数场合下，你都充满了自信，你不会在陌生人或上级面前感到紧张，也不会因为没有经验就不敢尝试。你需要在不同场合下调整你的自信心。

36—40 分：超级自信者

你对自己感觉太好了。在几乎所有场合下，你都充满了自信，你甚至不知道什么叫自卑。你需要学会控制你的自信心，变得自谦一些。

2．自尊量表

以下是我国心理学家开发的自尊量表，可在评价学生自尊品格教育时参考。

表 6-5　自尊量表

自尊量表

一、**题目指导语**：这个量表是用来了解您是怎样看待自己的。请仔细阅读下面的句子，选择最符合您情况的选项。请注意，这里要回答的是您实际上认为您自己怎样，而不是回答您认为您应该怎样。答案无正确与错误或好与坏之分，请按照您的真实情况来描述您自己。您的回答绝对不会向外泄漏，因此您完全不必要有这方面的顾虑。请您注意要保证每个问题都作了回答，且只选一个答案。谢谢您的合作！

选项：A. 非常符合 B. 符合 C. 不符合 D. 很不符合

	非常符合	符合	不符合	很不符合
1. 我感到我是一个有价值的人，至少与其他人在同一水平上。	4	3	2	1
2. 我感到我有许多好的品质。	4	3	2	1
3. 归根结底，我倾向于觉得自己是一个失败者。	1	2	3	4
4. 我能像大多数人一样把事情做好。	4	3	2	1
5. 我感到自己值得自豪的地方不多。	1	2	3	4
6. 我对自己持肯定态度。	4	3	2	1
7. 总的来说，我对自己是满意的。	4	3	2	1
8. 我希望我能为自己赢得更多尊重。	1	2	3	4
9. 我确实时常感到自己毫无用处。	1	2	3	4
10. 我时常认为自己一无是处。	1	2	3	4

二、简介和评分

自尊量表（SES）是设计用以评定个体关于自我价值和自我评价的总体感受。该量表由 10 个条目组成，设计中充分考虑了测定的便利。受试者直接报告这些描述是否符合他们自己。分四级评分，1 表示非常符合，2 表示符合，3 表示不符合，4 表示很不符合。总分范围是10—40 分，分值越高，自尊程度越高。

本量表已被广泛应用，它简明、易于评分，是对自己的积极或消极感受的直接评估。

（续表）

> 评分的建议：
> 1. 对于 1、2、4、6、7 题（正向记分题），"很不符合"记 1 分，"不符合"记 2 分，"符合"记 3 分，"非常符合"记 4 分；对于 3、5、8、9、10 题（反向记分题），"很不符合"记 4 分，"不符合"记 3 分，"符合"记 2 分，"非常符合"记 1 分。分值越高，自尊程度越高。
> 2. 考虑到中西方文化差异，将第 8 题改为正向记分。
> ——来源于"自尊量表使用过程中的问题及建议"，韩向前、江波、汤家彦、王益荣。

三、解释和常模

根据常模，给出总分数的情况评定，例如：

本测验您的得分为：_____ 分；说明您的自尊程度（较高、中等、较低）。

二、文化意识发展过程性评价

我们可以对学生在文化意识发展过程中的行为表现、作品进行评价，这类评价既可以是形成性的，也可以是终结性的。

以下是对学生参加 Global Understanding 主题营学习孔子仁政思想、向美国学生介绍孔子仁政思想成果的 2 个案例进行的形成性评价，用以介绍如何开展此类形成性评价。

这类评价要先建立评价标准，然后逐项进行评价。

案例 1：孔子专题作业 1（A 级学习成果）

The fact that Confucius still has followers centuries after his time stands as a testament of his wisdom（文化态度明确，有自我判断）. His teachings in virtue and social relationships（文化知识准确）are applicable to many real world situations to this day（文化态度明确，有自我判断）. He emphasized the idea of improving society rather than self-improvement（文化知识略有偏差）. Despite his belief that one should seek individual wisdom, this wisdom was only a means to the end of societal progression（文化知识略有偏差）.

Confucius believed that virtue is closely tied to knowledge and introspective (文化知识准确). To become virtuous, a man must complete a system of steps, beginning with investigation of objects around him (文化知识准确). Along with worldly knowledge, a virtuous man knows his place in the social hierarchy (文化态度略有偏差，hierarchy 不够中性) and accepts his role with grace. For example, a son must serve his father, a father must serve his family, the family must serve its state, and the state must serve (文化态度合理，用词有价值判断) its people.

All this goes to prove that Confucius believed in the idea that power is a responsibility and not a privilege (文化知识准确，符合作者态度). He believed that if a ruler does not respect his people and keep them happy, he is not fit to rule them (文化知识准确，符合作者态度). While not as dramatic, the same principle applies on a smaller scale within families. Fathers must provide for their families and, in return, families would dutifully serve their fathers. (文化表达有不足，此段两观点之间的关系应基于孔子思想进行清楚地转接说明。)

孔子专题作业 1 较为准确地阐述了孔子的相关思想，基于文化知识的理解较为准确，基于文化态度的判断大多合理，部分略有偏差，文化表达总体清晰得体，关联性略有不足。

这一作业说明该课程发展该学生的文化能力有效。

该作业得分：A。

案例 2：孔子专题作业 2（B 级学习成果）

Confucius was a great ancient Chinese philosopher. He has withstood the test of time (文化态度明确) and is still relevant and well known even today. The Chinese people still celebrate Confucius's birthday (文化知识准确), even though he has been dead for hundreds of years(文化知识略有偏差，应较为准确地表述为 more than two thousand years). Confucius taught the Chinese people many things about how to run their daily life (文化知识准确). For example, he taught that everyone had relationships that they must follow (文化表达合理). These relationships were ruler and subject, father and son, elder brother and younger brother, husband and wife, and friend and friend (文化知识准确). To Confucius, each of these relationships was very important part of society. Confucius was also a very powerful writer (文化态度明确). To get his teachings to spread across China, he had to write them down in powerful, persuasive ways (文化知识不够准确,孔子主要不是写下他的思想,而是说出他的意思). His ability to do this allowed Confucius' ideas to spread across China and over its borders. (文化知识不够准确,孔子思想传播不是因为语言,而是因为价值)

孔子专题作业 2 较为准确地阐述了孔子的相关思想,但对孔子思想在今天的影响判断有误,从其作业内容看,主要是其学习伙伴对其观点的影响。这也说明该作业的文化态度有待改进,判断能力有待加强。该作业文化表达总体清晰得体,语句错落有致,形成有效表达。

这一作业说明该课程发展该学生的文化能力比较有效。

该作业得分:B。

显然,在这一主题活动中,学生的文化自信、自尊、家国情怀、国家认同等品格,均有明确发展。这一案例显示,在学生学习过程中,对学生的文化意识进行过程性评价,不仅完全可行,而且十分必要,并能激励学生更好地发展相应的文化意识。

第三节　高中英语文化意识发展与高考

高考各项试题均可评价中外文化理解能力,写作等试题可评价中外优秀文化传播能力。

一、阅读理解中的文化意识评价

高考阅读理解部分几乎每一篇文章皆评价了学生的中外文化理解能力。以下是四篇高考阅读理解短文。

短文一

You probably know who Marie Curie was, but you may not have heard of Rachel Carson. Of the outstanding ladies listed below, who do you think was the most important woman of the past 100 years?

Jane Addams (1860-1935)

Anyone who has ever been helped by a social worker has Jane Addams to thank. Addams helped the poor and worked for peace. She encouraged a sense of community (社区) by creating shelters and promoting education and services for people in need. In 1931, Addams became the first American woman to win the Nobel Peace Prize.

Rachel Carson (1907-1964)

If it weren't for Rachel Carson, the environmental movement might not exist today. Her popular 1962 book *Silent Spring* raised awareness of the dangers of pollution and the harmful effects of chemicals on humans and on the world's lakes and oceans.

Sandra Day O'Connor (1930-present)

When Sandra Day O'Connor finished third in her class at Stanford Law School, in 1952, she could not find work at a law firm because she was a woman. She became an Arizona state senator (参议员) and, in 1981, the first woman to join the U.S. Supreme Court. O'Connor gave the deciding vote in many important cases during her 24 years on the top court.

Rosa Parks (1913-2005)

On December 1, 1955, in Montgomery, Alabama, Rosa Parks would not give up her seat on a bus to a white passenger. Her simple act landed Parks in prison. But it also set off the Montgomery bus boycott. It lasted for more than a year, and kicked off the civil-rights movement. "The only tired I was, was tired of giving in," said Parks.

这篇短文考查的是对一些名人的生平事迹的阅读理解能力，与2017 高中英语课标对理解名人事迹的要求一致。

短文二

Grandparents Answer a Call

As a third-generation native of Brownsville, Texas, Mildred Garza never planned to move away. Even when her daughter and son asked her to move to San Antonio to help with their children, she politely refused. Only after a year of friendly discussion did Ms Garza finally say yes. That was four years ago. Today all three generations regard the move as a success, giving them a closer relationship than they would have had in separate cities.

No statistics show the number of grandparents like Garza who are moving closer to adult children and grandchildren. Yet there is evidence suggesting that the trend is growing. Even President Obama's mother-in-law, Marian Robinson, has agreed to leave Chicago and move into the White House to help care for her granddaughters. According to a study by *grandparents.com,* 83 percent of the people said Mrs. Robinson's decision will influence grandparents in the American family. Two-thirds believe more families will follow the example of Obama's family.

"In the 1960s we were all a little wild and couldn't get away from home far enough or fast enough to prove we could do it on our own," says Christine Crosby, publisher of *Grand*, a magazine for grandparents. We now realize how important family is and how important it is to be near them, especially when you're raising children."

Moving is not for everyone. Almost every grandparent wants to be with his or her grandchildren and is willing to make sacrifices, but sometimes it is wiser to say no and visit frequently instead. Having your grandchildren far away is hard, especially knowing your adult child is struggling, but giving up the life you know may be harder.

这篇短文考查的是对美国社会文化现象——代际关系、老人生活态度——的阅读理解能力，与 2017 高中英语课标对理解主要英语国家社会文化现象的要求一致。

短文三

I am Peter Hodes, a volunteer stem cell courier. Since March 2012, I've done 89 trips—of those, 51 have been abroad. I have 42 hours to carry stem cells（干细胞）in my little box because I've got two ice packs and that's how long they last. In all, from the time the stem cells are harvested from a donor（捐献者）to the time they can be implanted in the patient, we've got 72 hours at most. So I am always conscious of time.

I had one trip last year where I was caught by a hurricane in America. I picked up the stem cells in Providence, Rhode Island, and was meant to fly to Washington then back to London. But when I arrived at the check-in desk at Providence, the lady on the desk said: "Well, I'm really sorry, I've got some bad news for you—there are no flights from Washington." So I took my box and put it on the desk and I said: "In this box are some stem cells that are urgently needed for a patient—please, please, you've got to get me back to the United Kingdom." She just dropped everything. She arranged for a flight on a small plane to be held for me, re-routed（改道）me through Newark and got me back to the UK even earlier than originally scheduled.

For this courier job, you're consciously aware that in that box you've got something that is potentially going to save somebody's life.

这篇短文考查的是对美国志愿者工作的阅读理解能力，与 2017 高中英语课标对理解主要英语国家社会现象的要求一致。

短文四

The meaning of silence varies among cultural groups. Silences may be thoughtful, or they may be empty when a person has nothing to say. A silence in a conversation may also show stubbornness, uneasiness, or worry. Silence may be viewed by some cultural groups as extremely uncomfortable;

therefore attempts may be made to fill every gap (间隙) with conversation. Persons in other cultural groups value silence and view it as necessary for understanding a person's needs.

Many Native Americans value silence and feel it is a basic part of communicating among people, just as some traditional Chinese and Thai persons do. Therefore, when a person from one of these cultures is speaking and suddenly stops, what may be implied (暗示) is that the person wants the listener to consider what has been said before continuing. In these cultures, silence is a call for reflection.

Other cultures may use silence in other ways, particularly when dealing with conflicts among people or in relationships of people with different amounts of power. For example, Russian, French, and Spanish persons may use silence to show agreement between parties about the topic under discussion. However, Mexicans may use silence when instructions are given by a person in authority rather than be rude to that person by arguing with him or her. In still another use, persons in Asian cultures may view silence as a sign of respect, particularly to an elder or a person in authority.

Nurses and other care-givers need to be aware of the possible meanings of silence when they come across the personal anxiety their patients may be experiencing. Nurses should recognize their own personal and cultural construction of silence so that a patient's silence is not interrupted too early or allowed to go on unnecessarily. A nurse who understands the healing (治愈) value of silence can use this understanding to assist in the care of patients from their own and from other cultures.

这篇文章更是直接考查了对文化异同的阅读理解能力，与 2017 高中英语课标对人类文化异同的理解的要求一致。

显然，四篇阅读短文从不同领域呈现了中外文化，其试题评价了学生对于中外文化的理解能力，只是阅读材料中中国文化内容偏少，而且试题主要评价学生的语言理解能力，而对其他文化要素理解能力的评价较少。尽管语言能力也是中外文化理解能力的组成部分，但只评价语言能力显然不足以说明其评价了学生的中外文化理解能力。

我们知道，现在还有很多阅读理解短文直接考查学生对介绍中国文化的语篇的阅读理解能力，如下面这篇文章直接考查学生对介绍中国的著名苗寨上郎德寨的语篇的阅读理解能力。

When visiting Miao villages becomes a topic, Miao villages in Southern China's Hunan and South-Western China's Yunnan are probably first introduced.

As a visitor to over 30 Miao villages in China, I would like to take Shanglangde (Upper Langde) in Guizhou located between Hunan and Yunnan to you. Shanglangde is also named as Langde Shangzhai which means the Upper Village of Langde, twinning with Lower Village of Langde, which is one of the earliest Miao villages open to tourism since 1985. The pressure to turn it into a theme park was great but it was lucky to get the rare protection status from declaring the whole village as provincial level cultural relics. Tourism development and facilities were kept to the minimum—absolutely no serious pollution from the tourism industry like kara-ok shops and bars. The flow of mass tourism was diverted to the nearby mega-scale theme park Xijiang after its opening. It was able to make Shanglangde less crowded and became a much better cultural destination for heritage lovers during non-holidays. Some families in the village provide basic accommodation for tourists where food was amazingly great. Local people were kind-hearted and very friendly so that there was no worry of any tourism traps. There was no ticketing gate or a big entrance fee. It was not a popular theme park.

The touristy shows required a ticket and it was similar to other theme parks but the village neighborhood feeling was very nice. The performing site was small and looked more like a part of the village's daily life space. It was on the ground and did not have distinctive separation from the performer stage area to the audience section. There were many children and none of them did ask for money. Photo taking was welcome and no asking for money afterwards. Actors were more like local villagers than strangers from professional troupes. Costumes were largely the original authentic Miao textile instead of the cheap stage inventions in theme parks. Quite some young ladies were carrying their babies. Many ladies were doing traditional embroidery while waiting for their turn. Old ladies were chatting ... There was something relatively close to true ethnic life of the past. This was the event I took most of time to enjoy in the village.

Although I visited the village twice last year, it is still my tour destination.

二、写作中的文化意识评价

2017高中英语课标对于文化意识要求的一个非常重要的维度是传播中华优秀文化，这一要求可以在写作中进行较为充分的考查，如以下写作试题考查了学生介绍中国文学瑰宝唐诗与唐代文化的能力。

> 假定你是李华，正在教你的英国朋友 Leslie 学习汉语。请你写封邮件告知下次上课的计划。内容包括：
> （1）时间和地点；
> （2）内容：学习唐诗；
> （3）课前准备：简要了解唐朝的历史。
> 注意：
> 1. 词数 100 左右；
> 2. 可以适当增加细节，以使行文连贯。

再如以下试题则考查了学生对中国文化中在全世界最受欢迎的饮食文化及其所体现的生日文化的传播能力。

> 假如你是李华，你的外国朋友 Billy 发来邮件告诉你他在网上看到中国制作长寿面的视频节目后对中国生日文化很感兴趣，请你写封邮件向他介绍中国生日文化。
> 注意：
> 1. 词数 100 左右；
> 2. 可以适当发挥，以使行文连贯；
> 3. 开头和结尾已为你写好，不计入总词数。

我们知道，高考是评价能力的考试。品格，则不是高考评价的任务。所以高考试题不直接评价学生的品格教育，而是通过多种形式，间接评价学生品格的发展。

本章小结

高中英语在促进学生文化意识发展方面需要有好的方法，也需要，甚至更需要有好的评价。对于中外文化理解能力、传播中外优秀文化的能力，我们可以通过高考等各类考试进行评价，但对于品格的发展，我们则需要采用问卷，或者课堂观察分析的方式进行评价。

推荐阅读材料

Thomas, Ronald S.. Assessing Character Education: Paradigms, Problems, and Potentials [J]. The Clearing House. 1991. 65(1): 51-53.

参考书目

Gert, B. 1995. Moral Impartiality [J]. Midwest Studies in Philosophy, 20 (1):102-128

Park, N., Peterson, C., Seligman, M. 2006. Character Strengths in Fifty-four Nations and the Fifty US States [J]. *The Journal of Positive Psychology*, 1(3): 15, 118~129

Peterson, C. & M.E.P. Seligman. 2004. Character strengths and virtues: A handbook and classification. New York: Oxford University Press and Washington, DC: American Psychological Association.

UNESCO. 1982. The Final Report of World Culture Policy Conference[R]. Paris: UNSECO. 1, 46

UNESCO. 1989. Introduction to intercultural studies [M]. Paris: UNESCO. 14

蔡春 . 2010. 德性与品格教育 [D]. 上海：复旦大学 . 14, 60~80

冯德正 . 2015. 英语教学中的人文道德教育：正面价值观的多模态语篇建构 [J]. 外语界，(01): 181~182

鲁子问 . 2006. 中小学英语跨文化教育理论与实践 [M]. 北京：中国电力出版社 . 73

鲁子问等 . 2010. 英语教学论 [M]. 上海：华东师范大学出版社 . 9, 11

马克思，恩格斯 . 1957. 马克思、恩格斯选集（第一卷）[2] . 北京：人民出版社 . 48, 74

苏蓉 . 2012. 我国中学生品格教育的现代性审视 [D]. 苏州：苏州大学 . 7, 14

钟启泉等 . 2001. 为了中华民族的复兴　为了每位学生的发展〈基础教育课程改革纲要（试行）〉解读 . 上海：华东师范大学出版社 . 73, 90, 94~98